ALSO BY CHRISTOPHER DICKEY

The Sleeper: A Novel
Summer of Deliverance: A Memoir of Father and Son
Innocent Blood: A Novel
Expats: Travels in Arabia, from Tripoli to Teheran
With the Contras: A Reporter in the Wilds of Nicaragua

SECURING

THE CITY

INSIDE AMERICA'S BEST COUNTERTERROR FORCE— THE NYPD

Christopher Dickey

SIMON & SCHUSTER
New York   London   Toronto   Sydney

SIMON & SCHUSTER
1230 Avenue of the Americas
New York, NY 10020

First Simon & Schuster hardcover edition February 2009

SIMON & SCHUSTER and colophon are registered trademarks
of Simon & Schuster, Inc.

For information about special discounts for bulk purchases,
please contact Simon & Schuster Special Sales at
1-800-456-6798 or business@simonandschuster.com.

Designed by Suet Y. Chong

Manufactured in the United States of America

10 9 8 7 6 5 4 3 2 1

Library of Congress Cataloging-in-Publication Data
Dickey, Christopher.
   Securing the city : inside America's best counterterror force : the NYPD /
Christopher Dickey.
      p. cm.
   1. New York (N.Y.). Police Dept.   2. Police—New York (State)—New York.
3. Law enforcement—New York (State)—New York.   3. Terrorism—New
York (State)—New York—Prevention.   4. Terrorism—Prevention.   I. Title.
HV8148.N52 D53   2009
363.325/1609747—dc22   2008043085

ISBN-13: 978-1-4165-5240-6
ISBN-10:   1-4165-5240-5

For twenty-three fallen heroes

CONTENTS

SECTION III:
THE PRECARIOUS BALANCE

When you catch a terrorist and look at the map in his or her pocket, it is always a map of New York; it's not a map of some other place.

—Mayor Michael Bloomberg, July 2006

Fidelis ad mortem

—Official motto of the New York City Police Department

SECURING
THE CITY

PROLOGUE

The winter air is cold and the light hard-edged as the unmarked New York City Police Department helicopter meanders through the winds above the five boroughs. The morning is clear in a way—in that way—that is always a little heartbreaking if you were here on September 11, 2001. There were police choppers in the New York sky then, too, but not like this one, which can see so much from so far. It is a state-of-the-art crime-fighting, terror-busting, order-keeping techno toy, with its enormous lens that can magnify any scene on the streets almost one thousand times, then double that digitally; that can watch a crime in progress from miles away, can look in windows, can sense the body heat of people on rooftops or running along sidewalks, can track beepers slipped under cars, can do so very many things that the man in the helmet watching the screens and moving the images with the joystick in his lap, NYPD Detective David Zschau, is often a little bit at a loss for words. "It really is an amazing tool," he keeps saying. On the left-hand screen is a map of Manhattan. He punches in an address on the Upper East Side, my address. The camera on the belly of the machine swivels instantaneously, focuses, and there on the second screen is my building seen from more than a mile way now, but also up close and personal from this surprising astral angle. The cameras and sensors are locked on to it, staying with it as the chopper turns and homes in.

I am glad that I am up here looking, and not down there looked at unknowingly. There is always an uneasy tension between the right to security and the right to privacy and this morning I can feel it, can see it in bold relief as we fly only a few hundred feet above the city's highways and avenues, parks and alleys, museums, monuments, skyscrapers, train stations, hotels, stores, stadiums, stock markets, churches, synagogues, mosques, schools, and homes—all those homes. A city is not an abstraction like "homeland," it is home, full stop, to millions of people. And if you live here, and are part of it, what would you be willing to do to defend it? What *wouldn't* you be willing to do? New York City is the most target-rich environment for terrorists imaginable, a dense metropolis waiting to be ground zero. Yet from this height it seems so peaceful. And this morning in January 2007 it is, and for the rest of this year it will be.

How is that possible? What does it take to make a city safe in the twenty-first century? And what, in particular, does it take to secure *this* city, which was for so many generations a maelstrom of crime and always an inviting target for mass destruction? Thirty years ago, the placid cityscape beneath us was written off as an urban wasteland, bankrupt financially and morally. A blackout on a single summer night in 1977 brought on riots and led to three thousand arrests. By the 1980s, the homicide toll had soared and paranoia with it. People were killing one another at the rate of six a day; babies were taking stray bullets; all strangers were suspect. The city seemed out of control, a cloaca pulsing with chaos and danger—and it was.

The rest of the country turned its back on Gotham, writing it off in a long series of grim caricatures. In 1970, country singer Buck Owens thrummed a nationwide hit with the refrain, "I wouldn't live in New York City if they gave me the whole dang town." A steady stream of police films showed the sleazy underside of the urban world—*The French Connection, Serpico, Dog Day Afternoon, Fort Apache: The Bronx*—until by 1981, Hollywood director John Carpenter was imagining Manhattan as one vast prison island in *Escape from New York*. When

President Gerald Ford said he wouldn't cough up the federal funds to ease its deepening financial crisis in October 1975, the *Daily News* ran the iconic headline: "Ford to City: Drop Dead."

But more than thirty years later, there the city was beneath the lenses and sensors of the police chopper, which showed it very much alive: a city of survivors, and then some. Above Ground Zero the lacuna left by the World Trade Center loomed, an aching emptiness that anyone could see. But only those who had been immersed for years in the annals of terror would notice the other places on the grid where saboteurs and mass murderers had struck the city. In July 1916, on a spit of New Jersey land that juts into New York Harbor, German saboteurs blew up a munitions dump and created a blast so powerful it sent shrapnel into the Statue of Liberty, shattered windows throughout Manhattan, and rumbled like distant thunder hundreds of miles away. In September 1920, a huge bomb in a horse-drawn cart exploded in front of the J.P. Morgan building at 23 Wall Street, killing thirty-three people and injuring hundreds. The scars it left in the stone are still visible. In the 1940s and early 1950s, "Mad Bomber" George Metesky, a disabled and disgruntled electrical worker, planted explosives at dozens of vulnerable, high-profile targets, including Radio City Music Hall, the New York Public Library, Penn Station, Grand Central, and several movie theaters.

In the three decades I've been reporting on guerrilla wars and terrorist conspiracies, the fanatical hatred of countless groups has focused on New York City like a compass needle quivering toward magnetic north. Puerto Ricans and Palestinians, the Japanese Red Army, crazed Islamists and radical Jews, all have schemed to bring terror to the city's streets, and the shock of September 11 did not stop the threat for a second. "There's a plot taking shape on New York City every day of every week since 9/11," NYPD Intelligence chief David Cohen told me when I started the reporting that led to this book. "What that plot consists of, who's doing it, and where it's percolating from can change, but there's someone out there every day of the week thinking about that."

The job of securing any big city seems at first glance almost impossible; the results obtained in New York almost a miracle. What's required is an incredibly sensitive equilibrium among disparate and contradictory forces: coercion and finesse, political expediency and public interest; basic cop-on-the-beat police work and sophisticated intelligence gathering; respect for the law but a willingness to bend rules; ostentatious spectacle and secret surveillance; lots of police on the street, but maybe a few outside the country; cooperation with federal agencies, but also competition. And, then, there's the matter of personalities like Cohen's or that of his boss, Commissioner Raymond Kelly.

As I came back to New York from years in the Middle East and Europe, what fascinated me about the NYPD was that it offered an alternative to the dangerously ill-conceived, mismanaged, and highly militarized "global war on terror" that had taken the United States into the gruesome occupation of Iraq and helped inspire a violent loathing for Americans around the world. (When Commissioner Kelly says the acronym as a single word, "the GWOT," it's with a twinge of irony that makes it sound almost obscene.)

Invading faraway lands is the worst and should be the last option when fighting to make ourselves safe at home in this twenty-first century. Having blasted our way into Baghdad to stop a terrorist threat that was largely hypothetical, Americans found themselves trapped, trying to hold together a failed state where real terrorists proliferated locally to fight globally. As the menace from organized enemies operating behind definable borders declines, the threat grows from what French criminologist Alain Bauer calls "world chaos," the symbiotic cooperation of crime and terror mutating opportunistically and metastasizing wherever there is a weakness. The most pragmatic responses are effective diplomacy and espionage abroad, including covert action; reliable real-time intelligence on every front; and a strong police presence with solid public and, indeed, neighborhood support. "Cops are it," the Rand counterterrorism expert Brian Jenkins wrote in 2006. "We are going to win this at the local level."

Ray Kelly had known that for a long time. A Marine reserve colonel and night-school lawyer, he held every rank in the NYPD before serving his first tour as commissioner in 1992 and 1993. It was on his watch that the murder rate first started falling. It was also on his watch that the group later known as Al Qaeda first attacked the World Trade Center, and then tried again to hit tunnels and monuments all over the city.

After Kelly left the NYPD at the end of 1993, he served with the United Nations in Haiti, the Treasury Department in Washington, which is where I met him, and eventually became security chief for the Wall Street firm Bear Stearns. In November 2001, weeks after Al Qaeda's devastating assault on New York and Washington, and days after he learned he'd be brought back as police commissioner by newly elected Mayor Michael Bloomberg, Kelly sketched out a plan on a piece of butcher-block paper that would begin transforming the way cops everywhere fight their own war on terrorists. There would never be time to just wait for the slow-moving Feds. "In policing, you've got to act quickly every day," says Kelly. "It's the 911 culture, the nine-one-one call-for-help culture." But now you had to do much more, and much faster.

"What's the difference between a soldier and a cop?" I asked Kelly one morning in his office at One Police Plaza.

"When you talk about a military person," said the Vietnam veteran, "particularly at the entry-level position, we teach them, and teach them well, to fight and to kill. That's their job." But "a policing job," said Kelly, "is more complex. We expect a lot more of them. They have to be diplomats, they have to be social workers, they have to be in physical condition to stop violence, and they have to know about other parts of government so they can direct people to the right services. We ask modern-day, big-city police officers to be aware of the possibility of a terrorist attack all the time and in everything that they do: normal traffic stops, normal interaction with people. We say, 'Look at your world through the prism of September 11. Everybody's life changed. Your life changed. Look at the conditions that you encounter; the situations that you encounter. Is there anything of a suspicious nature?' So the life of a cop has become a lot more complex."

A lot of the job is about real-time information, some of which is held by a federal government reluctant to share it. That's why Kelly pushed up the number of NYPD detectives working with the Federal Bureau of Investigation at the Joint Terrorism Task Force. There were only seventeen when he took over as commissioner in January 2002. There are about one hundred and thirty now. That's why Cohen created a seat-of-the-pants intelligence organization in a hidden Chelsea loft and pushed to station his men in more than ten countries overseas. That's also why Cohen maintained a direct channel to his old employer, the Central Intelligence Agency, so he could be read into anything that might touch on New York City, including whatever information captured members of Al Qaeda spilled as they gagged and choked on the CIA interrogators' waterboards at "black sites" on the far side of the world.

Would all this preparation and awareness and intelligence have stopped the attack on New York that clear-skied Tuesday in September? Probably not. But, then, that was the last war. The NYPD under Kelly and Cohen focused on stopping the *next* attack, and, so far, the strategy has worked. So people get used to peace in the streets of the city, there beneath the long lenses of the police helicopters. But always the questions come back: What would you do to make your home safe? What *wouldn't* you do?

THE SCRAMBLE
FOR SAFETY

THE COP

The Rise of Ray Kelly

He had seen war, Ray Kelly. In 1966, when the United States began to make Vietnam's front lines its own, he was a twenty-four-year-old first lieutenant serving with the Second Battalion, First Marines. Up until about the time Kelly arrived, the Americans had been leery of pitched battles against the Vietcong, leaving that job to South Vietnam's army as much as possible. But now the escalation had begun. Washington was pouring in troops, pushing them out into the rice paddies, ferrying them by helicopter from the bases at Da Nang and Phu Bai. Then Kelly was moved up to Khe Sanh as the enemy began closing in on that highland outpost near the Laotian border. In 1968, Khe Sanh would make headlines around the world as a symbol of American troops under siege. But Kelly was there and gone before that, "before the big Khe Sanh," as he puts it. No need to embellish. He saw plenty of combat as a forward artillery observer, calling in barrages of high-powered munitions on real and suspected enemy positions. He took plenty of risks at Khe Sanh just flying in and out of the base, where planes running down the short airstrip seemed to drop off the mountain before gaining speed and peeling away toward safety. The war was what it was. He did his duty.

Even then, Kelly's career was running on two tracks, the military and the police force. Three of his older brothers were Marines, and it had seemed natural to him to earn his commission while working his way through Manhattan College studying business administration. But Kelly also joined a police cadet program for students and got a job manning the switchboard at police headquarters. There were no cops in his family; his father had been a milkman and then worked for the Internal Revenue Service, his mother worked at Macy's (and so did he, from time to time, to earn his tuition). His high school sweetheart, Veronica Clarke, was the daughter of a cop, but she insists that fact played no role in Ray's career choice. Her father left the force after twenty years. Ray wanted to make it his life. When he graduated from Manhattan College, in short order he married Veronica, served five days on duty with the NYPD, then went away for three and a half years on active duty with the Marines.

When Kelly returned to New York City in 1968, it had become a kind of war zone, too. The Bronx was burning. Police recruits who had only fired fifty rounds at a pistol range put on blue uniforms and went into the streets alongside more experienced cops to face riots in the crumbling city. "I felt equipped for it coming from Vietnam," Kelly remembers. "You know it was just funny, I felt relatively comfortable having paint cans and bricks coming down off the roof. It was like . . . it didn't faze me. It was exciting!" He thought back as he sat in the commissioner's office almost forty years later. "It was exciting," he repeated. Even now, Kelly has the powerful frame and the battered face of a fighter. Seen on TV talking crime, his expression is grim, almost threatening. But one-on-one he smiles often and easily, with a kind of Popeye twist to his grin. "There were shootings. But I just remember a lot of airmail coming down. Yes . . ." He sort of chewed the idea. "I had to keep looking up."

Kelly was multitasking before anybody ever used the word, working on a law degree and serving in the Marine reserves. (He was at Camp Lejeune, North Carolina, during the 1977 blackout and riots.) He went on to spend a year at Harvard's Kennedy School and get a master's in public administration. But he was hooked on the adrenaline rush of policing. "I fell in love with running over the rooftops." At the age of twenty-seven, he was already a police sergeant. He had studied for the test and passed it even before he entered the academy.

Kelly did a lot of his early crime fighting in East Harlem. One night, many years later when he was working in the private sector for Bear Stearns, we drove through some of his old haunts and he pointed out the street corners he used to stake out. At the time, early 2001, he thought he'd never be a cop again, and the nostalgia for those rooftops and those mean streets was running strong. "I had a lot of patrol experience. I was a CO, commanding officer, for four precincts," said Kelly. "I was in twenty-five different commands in the department, so, you know, I was all over the organization."

But the organization was falling apart during Kelly's first years as a cop. Corruption scandals in the early 1970s already had done much to destroy the NYPD's reputation. Then in 1975, with the city bankrupt, Mayor Abe Beame laid off five thousand members of the police force. One of the things cops had counted on was job security. Kelly, by then a lieutenant in the Tenth Precinct, was solid, but he had to let go a lot of his guys. The force was demoralized, and so was he. "After that, it always seemed like we didn't have enough cops to do anything," said Kelly. One night he was on duty on West Twentieth Street in the Tenth when someone came into the station, saying a woman was being stabbed a few blocks away. There was no one but Kelly and a clerk in the station, so he started running. It was maybe two a.m. He found the scene between Eighth and Ninth avenues. "Blood was all over the place." The woman was on the floor, unconscious, a gash in her cheek. The perp was still there, rifling through her bag. "He was drunk. He was easy enough to arrest." But there was no one to pick him up. An ambulance came for the woman, and left. Still, Kelly was left waiting for a radio car as if alone in a sea of crime.

What was bad for the force in those days wasn't always bad for Kelly. He was the senior officer who kept getting called on to fix things. The breaks that led to his first turn as commissioner, by his own account, began when an ugly scandal—a torture scandal—shook the department in 1985. Officers from the 106th Precinct, Ozone Park in Queens, had used a stun gun to work over a suspected drug dealer. These were lawless times, even for lawmen. Crack cocaine ruled the streets, the murder rate was soaring, police corruption was rampant. And this was a neighborhood where the rule of law was a loose concept to begin with. It was famous as the home turf of big-time Mafia bosses like John Gotti. But there was nothing big-time about this case. It was just sadistic, ugly, stupid, and seemed emblematic not only of a bunch of cops and a precinct, but a department and a city out of control.

A thirty-seven-year-old physical education instructor named Mark Davidson had been grabbed by a car full of narcotics cops, who said one of them had bought a bag of marijuana from him with a ten-dollar bill. Maybe that was true, maybe not, but they couldn't prove it because they couldn't find the bill that they wanted for evidence. The cops started working Davidson over with a stun gun, searing the flesh up and down his torso with fifty-thousand-volt shocks. They never did get the ten, but Davidson got a lawyer, who eventually forced the city to pay the victim $700,000. Two of the cops went to jail.

Ben Ward, the police commissioner at the time, "stormed into the 106th," as columnist Jimmy Breslin wrote afterward. "Everybody from sergeant up to the Queens chief of patrol was knocked off the job."[1] Then Kelly was assigned to clean up the mess. He was a deputy inspector of police and a lieutenant colonel in the Marine reserves, and his mission was "to take charge of this precinct," he said. By his own reckoning, Kelly drew a lot of attention in the process, and Ward soon promoted him and assigned him to a succession of administrative posts, including special operations, which in those days included everything from horses to helicopters. "Then Ward took me back here"—to headquarters—"because he missed me," Commissioner Kelly said with that lopsided smile.

In the 1980s the New York of *Fort Apache: The Bronx* had given way to Tom Wolfe's *Bonfire of the Vanities*. On Wall Street, greed was good; masters of the universe and social X-rays partied in the penthouses of Park Avenue. But out on the pavement everybody was still afraid. Gangs all over the city were fighting for control of the crack cocaine trade. In 1985, 1,384 people were murdered and each year that figure kept rising until, in 1990, New York City counted 2,245 homicides.

The force had never fully recovered from the firings in the 1970s, although Mayor Ed Koch had slowly tried to build up the numbers. (He won the first of his three terms in office in 1977 after saying he would have called out the National Guard to restore order during the blackout riots.) But the problem was always money. Mayor David Dinkins, who took office in 1990 after beating the hard-charging, law-and-order candidate Rudy Giuliani, couldn't find the tax dollars to pay for the cops that were needed, and many politicians questioned whether more cops could do the job anyway.

Dinkins brought in Lee Patrick Brown, famous in law enforcement circles as "the father of community policing" in Houston and Atlanta, to be the new commissioner. But neither Brown nor his approach were a good fit for New York. With his wife sick and dying and his roots in Houston (where later he was elected mayor), the new commissioner became known as "Out-of-Town Brown." Kelly, the quintessential New York cop, was named Brown's "number two guy: first deputy commissioner," a job that Kelly understood "takes care of administrative things" but isn't in the direct chain of command.

Random gunfire killed more than forty children in New York City during the first six months that Dinkins was in office. "Dave, Do Something!" screamed the front-page headline of the *New York Post*.[2] " 'Another five thousand cops!' became the mantra," says Jeremy Travis, now president of John Jay College of Criminal Justice, and a deputy police commissioner in the early 1990s. "But Lee Brown couldn't say how many he needed." Instead, Brown asked Kelly to pull together a study for what would be called the "Safe Streets, Safe City" program. With a team of about seventy people, Kelly set about rethinking manpower for a police department held in such low esteem that some critics charged it was actually too big and bloated. Kelly begged to differ. If the report's conclusions were couched in the language of community policing, there was nothing theoretical about its bottom line: "You need the bodies," said Kelly.

But none of this was in place on the night of Monday, August 19, 1991, when a three-car motorcade for Lubavitcher Rebbe Menachem Mendel Schneerson raced through an intersection in Crown Heights, Brooklyn. The last car didn't make it, crashing into another vehicle, then careering out of control onto the sidewalk, where it pinned two young black children. The mostly Caribbean-American and African-American neighborhood erupted. Shouts of "kill the Jews" rang through the streets. The violence lasted through that night, then into the next, and the police seemed almost helpless.

Brown had organized his administration so that Kelly had no direct command over cops on the street. But Kelly knew Crown Heights. He had been commander of the Seventy-Seventh Precinct there, or "the Seven-Seven" in cop speak. That week in August 1991, "I had no operations role," said Kelly, "but I had seen some things that had gone wrong." Finally on Wednesday afternoon Brown asked Kelly to take charge. Among the forces he quickly brought to bear were fifty mounted police. By the end of the night, the riots were over.

"These things were kind of on my résumé," said Kelly. Then Lee Brown resigned to take care of his dying wife, and in October 1992, Dinkins appointed Kelly commissioner. Over the next several months, he would start to reestablish order in the city. The crest of the crack wave was passing. The homicide rate began to stabilize. But a whole new threat was just beginning to take shape.

There had been some sort of explosion at the World Trade Center, maybe a transformer; nobody was sure, but something big. Kelly was in his office at One Police Plaza four months after taking charge and only a few hundred yards away from the scene of the blast. He decided to go look at the damage for himself. "I saw this sea of flashing lights. Smoke was coming out of the building." People were pouring out of the doors of the towers. Helicopters hovered high above, evacuating terrified office workers who had fled to the roof.

At first no one realized the extent of the damage. The police set up a command center at the Vista Hotel, right next to the Twin Towers, but it had only been in operation a few minutes when an engineer from the Port Authority warned Kelly the building where he was standing might collapse. The blast had opened up an enormous cavern reaching down through five levels of the subterranean parking garage.

Neither Kelly nor anyone with him really understood what they were looking at that day. As the investigation unfolded, it *might* have alerted the police to the growing threat of what were then called "the Arab Afghans." These were fanatical veterans of the war against Soviet troops in Afghanistan in the 1980s who, in the early 1990s, looked to turn their skill as guerrillas and terrorists against new targets—first, their own dictatorial governments in countries like Egypt and Algeria, then the United States, "the far enemy," which supported so many of the forces they hated in their midst, whether Arab tyrants or Zionist occupiers.

But back in 1993 as the FBI and the NYPD detectives on the World Trade Center case began to connect the dots, the picture that emerged of ragtag groups with no state sponsors and little clear-cut organization came to seem at once improbable and ineffectual as a threat to the city.

Two days after the blast, a New York cop searching the rubble found the van's differential with a serial number on it and the FBI traced that quickly to a Ryder truck rental agency in New Jersey. Amazingly, the man who had rented it, a Jordanian named Mohammed Salameh, was fool enough to go back to the agency, claiming the van was stolen and asking for his deposit back. Instead, the FBI arrested him and quickly tracked down the rest of the conspirators. It turned out several of them were linked to the murderer of radical Jewish activist Meir Kahane, gunned down in New York's Marriott Hotel one night in 1990. Some also had ties to a blind sheikh from Egypt who preached at mosques in Brooklyn and Jersey City and raised money for the fight in Afghanistan. But the mastermind of the bombing was a recent arrival, a strangely flamboyant figure known as Ramzi Yousef, born in Kuwait to parents from Pakistani Baluchistan and educated in England.

Yousef was attracted to terrorism, not least, by his love of spectacle. In 1993 he wanted to bring one of the World Trade Center towers crashing down onto the other. He laced the bomb with cyanide, hoping that toxic fumes would kill people who managed to survive the initial blast. But the towers had remained standing, and, unlike the Vista Hotel, never appeared likely to collapse. "This building could never come down," the Port Authority's engineer told Kelly at the time. The cyanide burned up when the bomb went off, and poisoned no one. The blast did kill six people and injured almost a thousand, but somehow that small death toll heightened the sense of disconnect between the plotters' ambitions and what they achieved. Even the discovery a few months later of a related conspiracy targeting the city's tunnels, several landmarks, and the United Nations building did not seem to be the kind of threat that—well, that it turned out to be.

"There was the assumption that the federal government was taking care of business, and, you know, that was true in '93," said Kelly. The investigations moved quickly, with a clear focus. "That gave us, I think, a false sense of security that we really had this threat under control."

The hunt for Yousef lasted almost two years. The Feds tracked him to the Philippines, where he plotted to murder Pope John Paul II and to blow up airliners flying across the Pacific to the United States. An accidental fire in the makeshift lab where he concocted explosives thwarted his plans and he managed to flee again, but left behind a laptop computer that revealed some of his plans. (Other files were encrypted, and never have been opened.) U.S. officials put a price of two million dollars on Yousef's head. Finally, they tracked him to Pakistan, where an informer fingered him for the reward in early 1995.

A few days later Yousef was flown back to New York City in shackles. One of the FBI agents with him pulled up the prisoner's blindfold and nudged him as they flew in a helicopter over Manhattan. The lights of the World Trade Center's Twin Towers still glowed in the clear night. "Look down there," the agent told Yousef. "They're still standing."

"They wouldn't be," said Yousef, "if I had enough money and explosives."[3]

It seemed the bravado of a man facing execution or a lifetime in jail. But, in fact, there were other members of Yousef's family who shared his taste for spectacular terror. Soon they were building ties to a veteran of the Afghan war occasionally mentioned in the press as "renegade Saudi billionaire Osama bin Laden." Money would no longer be a problem.

A little more than six-and-a-half years after Kelly left his job as police commissioner—after his tours with United Nations peacekeepers and in Washington—he had landed his lucrative job overseeing security for the international banking firm Bear Stearns. He was happy to be back in New York, and happy that it was a much safer city than the one he had left in 1994, even if it rankled that the credit had gone mainly to his successor, Commissioner William Bratton, and to the headline-grabbing mayor, Rudy Giuliani.

Ray and Veronica Kelly had turned the page. Their two sons were grown. One of them was a television correspondent for the local cable news station NY1. They had a comfortable apartment at the lower end of Manhattan in Battery Park. They traveled when they could, especially to France. On this particular day, in fact, Veronica was in Paris, and Ray had gone early to the Bear Stearns headquarters in midtown to have breakfast in the executive dining room. When he got up to his office a little before nine in the morning, the first airliner had blasted into one of the World Trade Center towers. Then Kelly and his colleagues watched on television as the second plane hit at 9:03.

Bear Stearns had just built a new glass-and-steel tower of its own near Grand Central Terminal, a block away from the old headquarters. It was tall enough to have a view of the burning Trade Center buildings at the far end of the island, and in the few offices that were occupied, people were panicked by what they saw, not on television, but with their own eyes. There was something at once more immediate and more surreal when you could watch the apocalypse for yourself. There was no question now that New York was under attack, and no one had any idea how many more planes were on their way, how many other explosions were about to erupt.

"I calmed people down," said Kelly, "and then I went up to the thirty-sixth floor." Kelly was talking to workers there at 9:59 when one of them shouted, "Look! It's falling!" The first tower cascaded in on itself as they stared. An enormous column of smoke and dust rose into the sky. "I remembered the conversation that I had with that engineer," said Kelly, thinking of the bombing in 1993. "It came right back to me. He said, 'This building can never fall.' And I was shocked, amazed that the building fell. It was something that was just totally . . ." Even years later, describing that morning, Kelly was at a loss for words. "When I saw it, I was just dumbfounded. First one building, then the other, I saw looking out the window with my own eyes. And I just kept thinking: Jesus! How many people have died in this thing!"

I was in New York City that Tuesday, watching as the columns of ash and dust soared into the sky and trying to write for *Newsweek* everything I had ever learned about Osama bin Laden, his people, and his ideas. I'd been reporting on him and his networks for almost ten years at that point. I thought one of his aides named Abu Zubaydah, who masqueraded as a honey merchant and acted as a gatekeeper to Bin Laden's organization, could be especially important to tracking down the plotters. I pored over my notes from the 1993 attack on the Trade Center, and from the trials of other conspirators arrested afterward, including a terrorist who had planned to bomb Los Angeles International Airport. When I could get the phones to work, I called Jordan and Egypt, following up possible leads on the conspiracy. And that afternoon when I glanced at the television, I saw Ray Kelly. When the segment was over, I dialed his cell phone, and to my surprise got through.

"Nice suit," I said to ease the tension. Kelly was always as dapper as Jimmy Cagney playing George M. Cohan.

"You like this suit?" he said. "Good, because it's the only one I've got." The whole area around the Trade Center, including Kelly's apartment in Battery Park, was cut off by the police lines. The former commissioner had no credentials to cross them anymore. In fact, he had no place to stay until CNN offered to put him up in a fleabag hotel near Penn Station. When he went on TV that night, he felt like he was singing for his supper.

"It was really such a lonely feeling, you know," Kelly remembered. "I stayed there for a couple of nights. I went to work the next day—I felt that I had to somehow take care of the universe of people in Bear Stearns. Very few people showed up."

When Kelly was at the Treasury Department running the Customs Service in 2000, businessman Michael Bloomberg went down to Washington to have lunch with him. They'd known each other in passing over the years, but now Bloomberg was thinking of running for mayor of New York, and Kelly had the feeling he was being sized up either as a potential rival, or as a backer.

The terror attacks of September 11 had interrupted the 2001 race for mayor in its closing weeks. When the campaigning resumed, Bloomberg had Kelly's endorsement, but Kelly had few expectations. "People were calling me: 'What? Are you out of your mind?' Conventional wisdom was 'this guy can never win.' "

The mood among Bloomberg's people was pessimistic on election night. He told campaign staffers he hoped they all had jobs they could go back to. "Then the returns started coming in, and things started to look very good," said Kelly.

To celebrate late that night, Kelly went to the cigar bar Club Macanudo, a favorite hangout for Giuliani's crowd. They were all there. Everyone was pleasant and polite, as Kelly recalls the evening. Everybody knew Ray Kelly would be headed to his old office on the fourteenth floor of One Police Plaza. And now, as Kelly's former deputy Jeremy Travis put it, "He came back with a vengeance."

THE SPY

The Unusual Career of David Cohen

David Cohen may not have been the perfect spy, but by the time he retired from the Central Intelligence Agency in 2000 he was one of the most well rounded. His career path was never quite the same as anyone else's. He eventually became the head of all the Agency's overseas operations, but never once did a tour in a foreign country. He served as the acting head of all analysis, but in a shop full of country specialists—Sovietologists, Sinologists, and so on—Cohen never had a country he could call his own. He was always, in a sense, the outsider on the inside. "I rose fairly rapidly in the Agency," he likes to say with good-humored false modesty. "No one could ever figure out why."

When Cohen joined the CIA in 1965, he still had the rough edges of a street-smart Jewish kid from Boston, and he never did lose the dropped-*r* accent. He had gone to Northeastern University and gotten a master's degree in international relations from Boston University, but those weren't the kind of credentials that commanded a lot of respect among the Ivy League elites at the CIA. In those days, aging spies who had served with William "Wild Bill" Donovan in the Office of Strategic Services during World War II still worked at Langley and in the field.

Donovan had recruited academics and labor organizers, socialites and Socialists to "the most brilliant yet motley group of peacocks ever assembled in a Washington agency," as one of his biographers put it.[1] But the Central Intelligence Agency created in 1947 also assumed a particular Waspish allure. (Cohen noted in passing many years later that Donovan, a Catholic, could not find a place in the new organization and "ended up being the ambassador in Thailand" instead of director of Central Intelligence as he'd wanted.)

When Cohen joined the CIA, only eighteen years had passed since its founding, only nine since it incited a disastrous uprising in Hungary, and only four since the debacle at the Bay of Pigs. In Cuba, not only had the rebel army trained by the old-boy network failed to overthrow Fidel Castro and been shot up badly from the moment it landed on the beach, the Agency had deceived itself, arrogantly and utterly, about the support the invasion might have among the Cuban people. The failure was analytical as well as operational, the humiliation absolute. As Cohen began his rise, the organization, by some estimates, already had begun a long period of decline. In fact, his whole thirty-five-year career was spent navigating among the multiple disasters, many of them self-inflicted, that are the modern history of the CIA.

"In the fifties, an intelligence agency was an exciting place to go if you were interested in the outside world," says Admiral Bobby Ray Inman Jr., who served throughout the U.S. intelligence network, including as deputy director of the CIA. But when Cohen settled in behind his first desk at Langley in 1965 the Agency's field of vision was narrowing. President Lyndon Johnson wanted to focus resources on Vietnam (this was the same year Ray Kelly's contingent of Marines deployed to Phu Bai) while cutting back information gathering elsewhere. According to Inman, the CIA curtailed in-depth coverage of Latin America in 1966, of Africa in 1967, and of Western Europe in 1968.

And then came the scandals of the 1970s: the CIA-sponsored military coup in Chile, revelations of hare-brained assassination plots against Castro, the Senate investigations, the reorganizations. The rot ran deep. The Agency's ultimate patrician, the intellectual, inscrutable, and unstable counterintelligence chief James Jesus Angleton, who was master of and mastered by the mind-rattling process of double-think and triple-think, had become obsessed with the presence of a Soviet mole that he could not admit he could not find—if indeed the mole existed at all. As Cohen entered his second decade in the CIA, the old gods were overthrown; the old focus on human intelligence sources and covert action—the old romance of coups and countercoups—was fading to black. The new emphasis was on big-ticket big birds, satellites and planes taking pictures and sucking up signals intelligence. They could accumulate vast quantities of information that was often as much about the volume of communications as the content, and some of it was an analyst's dream.

Cohen thrived in the new environment. Although assigned for a while to work on Japan and what was then called "the Far East," he had never gone native, never developed clientitis, never "fallen in love," as they say at the Agency, with any particular part of the world. "Most of the people in the CIA's analytical arm were regional experts or country experts," he would remember. "You knew Latin America and that's what you spent most of your career on. You might have moved around in it. You might have gone out. But you came back to Latin America." Not Cohen. "I worked on world commodity markets; I worked on international oil issues." And while he learned about what in the world interested, or ought to interest, his bosses, Cohen also learned about the world that was Washington.

Much later, I met Cohen one morning in the office of the Intelligence division at Police Headquarters in New York City. He apologized for the lack of china in which to offer me a coffee, pouring mine in a Styrofoam cup, and his, black with no sugar, into a mug that bore the eagle and the compass rose that are the great seal of the CIA. "By the mid-1970s," he said, "I had risen to a high enough level to know that on any given day you were going to see the Agency in a political vortex."

In 1980, Americans elected the former Hollywood actor and California governor Ronald Reagan to be president, not least because the CIA under President Jimmy Carter had failed to foresee the fall of the Shah of Iran and, even worse, was unprepared for the 1979 seizure of the U.S. embassy in Tehran. Its diplomats and its CIA operatives were held for

444 days. Diligent student revolutionaries pieced together their shredded files. To this day the embassy building in the Iranian capital is called "the Den of Spies."

Reagan appointed William J. Casey as director of Central Intelligence. The old men were back, or at least one old man was. Casey had run the London operations of the Secret Intelligence Bureau of the OSS in World War II, mounting an operation recruiting German prisoners of war and sending them back to the Fatherland to spy for the Allies. He'd gone on to build an influential New York law practice and become chairman of the Securities and Exchange Commission, but never lost his passion for espionage. Historian Arthur Schlesinger, who knew Casey in the OSS and maintained a cordial if wary friendship with him, wrote in his journal in 1984 that "Bill loves power, and covert action has apparently become his baby . . . Should one dislike people who do evil? Probably."[2]

Before Casey's death in 1987, he helped drag the Agency into yet another and still more devastating scandal, the Iran-Contra fiasco in which arms were sold to the Islamic revolutionaries and hostage takers in Tehran to win the freedom of Americans seized in Lebanon while the proceeds were sent to anti-Sandinista rebels in Nicaragua to circumvent a ban on funding for them imposed by Congress. Casey must have felt like the master of a magnificent game, until it all went wrong.

Yet there was a time early on in his tenure when Casey did focus on analysis. "There was a major restructuring of the Directorate of Intelligence," Cohen remembers. "And out of that they created an Office of Global Issues. It was the odds and ends of the analytical arm of the CIA. It was the things that didn't fall into Latin America or the Soviet area or Africa or things like that. And I became the deputy director of that for four years, and then I headed it for two."

Terrorism, which had been one of those odds-and-ends kinds of issues, suddenly loomed front and center in the 1980s. Public paranoia was fueled by fiction, like the bestselling thriller *The Fifth Horseman* in which Libyan dictator Muammar Qadhafi[3] plants a nuclear bomb in New York City, and also by semi-fact: journalist Claire Sterling argued in her book *The Terror Network* that Moscow aided, abetted, and incited just about all the terrorism in the world. Casey loved that idea, and he did everything he could to squeeze a National Intelligence Estimate out of the CIA that confirmed Sterling's conspiracy theory. The effort met with so much internal resistance that he had to commission an outside academic to write it.

The real world of terrorism that Cohen had been watching was much more subtle and complex than the one Sterling portrayed or Bill Casey wanted to believe in. And among the pros in the Agency in the early 1980s, Beirut became the crucible where their thinking about terrorism was tested and refined. In the midst of Lebanon's long-running civil war, Israel launched a full-scale invasion of its northern neighbor in hopes it could wipe out the forces of the Palestine Liberation Organization who operated there. As Israel laid siege to Beirut in the summer of 1982, its Christian-Lebanese militia allies massacred Palestinian refugees. The United States, France, and Italy sent soldiers to stabilize the situation but Lebanon's blood-drenched kaleidoscope of cynical alliances and savage betrayals quickly drew the peacekeepers into the war.

In April 1983, a suicide bomber blew up the U.S. embassy on the Beirut seafront, murdering more than sixty people, including seventeen Americans. Almost all the CIA operatives in the country were killed by that blast, along with Robert Ames, the national intelligence officer for the Near East, who was visiting from Washington. Ames was a legendary figure who had recruited agents from within the terrorist ranks of the Palestine Liberation Organization itself. A Catholic convert and college basketball star whose father was a factory worker in Philadelphia, Ames had nonetheless outclassed the Ivy Leaguers in the Agency. "He was a real hero to many of us," says Cohen. "He came out of the Directorate of Operations, and in those days for someone to go from the Directorate of Operations to become a national intelligence officer, which is really the senior community analyst in many respects, was very unique. And Bob did it and he did it with brilliance. It was a tremendous loss to all of us that very fateful day. I remember like it was yesterday."

Six months after the attack on the embassy, another suicide bomber blew up the U.S. Marine barracks near Beirut airport, killing 241. And four months after that, the American military pulled out of Lebanon for good. But the CIA stayed, and became increasingly vulnerable. In March 1984, the same Iranian-backed faction in Lebanon responsible for the earlier bombings—which called itself Islamic Jihad but was in fact part of the Shiite militia Hizbullah—kidnapped veteran operative William Buckley. He had replaced the station chief killed by the embassy bombing, and now it was his turn to die, but not so quickly. His captors tortured Buckley for more than a year before he succumbed. His remains were not found until 1991, in a plastic bag by the side of a road near the airport, which is near the Hizbullah-dominated southern suburbs of Beirut.[4]

"There was a burning element inside of us at that time—at least me, I can't speak for anybody else," says Cohen. "We lost a lot of people in Beirut to terrorism," and Cohen's Office of Global Issues was "just swept forward," he recalls. Cohen created a "terrorist analysis program" and a "counterinsurgency analytical element." These were the seeds of what would become the federal government's Counterterrorist Center (CTC) later in the decade, which pulled together analysts and operatives from all over the Agency. Its first director, Duane "Dewey" Clarridge, was a self-styled man of action. He had been one of the architects of the covert "Contra" program, where one little war against Communists in Nicaragua was played off against another one waged by Communists in El Salvador. Clarridge liked to play spy vs. spy, terror vs. terror. But Cohen in those early days saw his own main interest as "how to think about these things." His Office of Global Issues would be "a thinking person's organization."

Cohen's reputation as a capable analyst and competent manager kept growing. "He made decisions," says one of his Agency colleagues. "There wasn't a lot of second-guessing." In the late 1980s, Robert Gates, the deputy director of Central Intelligence at the time, tapped Cohen to head up the national collection program inside the United States. That is, he took Cohen the analyst from DI and put him on the other side of the towering bureaucratic wall to work in the DO, the Directorate for Operations. Cohen was going from his ivory tower to some very mean bureaucratic streets, where even a job well done can have fearsome consequences. "Bob Gates called the DO the heart and soul of the agency," as one longtime operative explained, "but Gates would also say it's the one part that can put you in jail."

Until Cohen took over, CIA activities inside the United States had two faces: a public one that was fairly straightforward, debriefing college professors or businessmen who might have traveled in countries that interested the Agency; and a more secretive side that aimed to recruit foreigners who were in the United States to work as American spies in their homelands or help recruit others who would. Cohen's task was to fold the two operations into one, and in the process try to ease the inevitable frictions with other federal agencies, notably the FBI, which saw any CIA presence in-country as out of bounds. "The FBI, very irrationally, hates anything the Agency does inside the United States," says one of Cohen's admirers in the CIA. "He was recognized in the Agency as having done a *great* job, but for two or three years he was eyeball-to-eyeball with the FBI at the level just below director, and he had constant problems, constant turf battles."

Abroad, the CIA kept getting blindsided by enormous events. It failed to predict the fall of the Berlin Wall in November 1989 and failed to anticipate Saddam Hussein's invasion of Kuwait in August 1990, but Cohen's unique career trajectory left him largely untainted by these world-shaking lapses, which tended to accrue to the regional specialists. As others faltered, he moved up another couple of rungs in the Agency hierarchy, assuming the title assistant deputy director for Intelligence. For all practical purposes, he wound up running the show while his boss, Doug MacEachin, focused on efforts to vindicate the Agency's reporting on the by-now-defunct Soviet Union.

But the bad times at the CIA just kept getting worse. In early 1994 the FBI arrested the first known mole in the Agency's history: Aldrich Hazen Ames (the son of another operative, but no relation to Robert Ames, who was killed in Beirut). Aldrich Ames had been selling secrets to Moscow for almost nine years. From the beginning of his treachery, the Agency's networks were exposed, its agents captured and executed, yet it would not or could not discover the reason; this, even though the binge-drinking Ames lived way beyond his declared means, driving a Jaguar and buying a half-million-dollar house with cash.

The mole's treachery had also cost the FBI at least two of the double agents it was running in the United States. Both were called back to Moscow and executed, so from 1991 onward, the two agencies had formed an uneasy and deeply suspicious partnership to look for the man who was causing all their problems. Ames became a prime suspect, but still nobody could nail him. Finally a former navy lawyer turned FBI agent, Leslie G. Wiser Jr., decided to have his counterintelligence team search Ames's garbage one dark night in September 1993. A torn-up Post-it with scrawled notes about a meeting in Bogotá sealed the mole's fate.

During the cleanup at the Agency in the Ames aftermath, Director James Woolsey, under pressure from Congress, "turned the CIA over to its worst enemy in Washington—the FBI," as one former field operative put it.

"The executioner the FBI picked for the task was Ed Curran, a serving FBI agent," recalled Robert Baer, one of the Agency's swashbuckling field operatives with a reputation that was part spy and part pirate.[5] In fact, a few salty stories were attached to Curran, too, a lanky father of four who reportedly had run a counterintelligence squad in New York City during the cold war that tried all sorts of tricks to turn Soviet agents and diplomats, even using call girls.[6] But Baer saw Curran as the enemy, pure and simple, and the feeling may well have been mutual. "From the day he took over the counterespionage group, Curran made it clear that he intended to run the place like a behind-enemy-lines commando unit," Baer wrote. "His first act was to fire anyone who knew anything, especially the little old ladies in tennis shoes—the CIA's institutional memory on Soviet espionage." By late 1995 more than three hundred people were under suspicion.[7] According to Curran, that many had failed their lie-detector tests. Today, Curran says he was ruthless because he knew there were other moles still at work in the CIA and the FBI. And indeed there were.

In a sense it was thanks to Special Agent Wiser and Special Agent Curran that CIA analyst David Cohen was about to get an extraordinary promotion, although he certainly wouldn't have seen it that way at the time.

* * *

Since Casey's death in 1987, directors of Central Intelligence—William Webster, Robert Gates, James Woolsey—had come and gone amid such turmoil and recrimination inside and outside the agency that it got hard to find anyone in Washington willing to take the job. For any shark who could scent a bleeding institution, and there are plenty of those inside the Beltway, the CIA smelled like it might be in its last throes. Former Senator Daniel Patrick Moynihan argued it ought to be put out of its misery altogether. But such a bureaucracy doesn't really die; like an old soldier, it just starts to fade away. Other, stronger bureaucracies start to whittle down its functions and prerogatives until at last they've been amputated.

The Pentagon created its own agency for human intelligence collection. The CIA had been master of the skies in the cold war days of the U2 spy plane in the 1960s and the Big Birds of the 1970s and '80s, but that function and the attendant enormous budget was shifted to Pentagon bureaucracies, too. And then to add insult to injury, the Feds began stationing agents, or "legal attachés" in embassies "from Moscow to Tallinn, Estonia, to Riyadh and Islamabad and Almaty in Kazakhstan," as FBI Director Louis J. Freeh put it. The former altar boy Freeh liked to say his agents would have nothing to do with recruiting spies in the places where they served overseas. Recruiting was somehow deemed dirty business, and might make the FBI look too much like the discredited CIA in those countries: "We were actually trying to help their law enforcement agencies, not penetrate them" and "to build a global network of trust."[8] The CIA's veterans, those that were left, figured this was all so much smarmy subterfuge. Those offices in embassies around the world "one day will displace the CIA," warned Bob Baer.[9]

In the spring of 1995, President Clinton finally leaned on Deputy Secretary of Defense John Deutch, a former provost at the Massachusetts Institute of Technology whose academic background was in chemistry, to assume the poisonous mantle of DCI. Deutch brought in Nora Slatkin, a former House staffer once described by *BusinessWeek* as a "data-devouring, Diet Coke-swilling workaholic," to be the executive director with the Augean task of reorganizing the Agency.[10] Deutch named as his number two another former staffer from the Hill and from the National Security Council, George Tenet. And as deputy director for Operations—the head of all the clandestine services—he picked David Cohen in August 1995.

Among the embittered elite who had made their careers recruiting agents in the field, those who had in some cases made their reputations risking their lives in hostile corners of forgotten countries, to name an analyst to run their lives was an insult and an injury. Bob Baer, in his score-settling memoir *See No Evil: The True Story of a Ground Soldier in the CIA's War on Terrorism*, rails against Cohen as someone "who had never met or recruited an agent," and who appointed inexperienced if not incompetent officers to run the vital CIA stations in Riyadh, Tel Aviv, and Nairobi.[11]

"At the DO, his first name wasn't David, it was 'Fucking Cohen,' " recalls another operative. "I remember the first time I saw him was in the men's room. He was standing there at the urinal, holding up a classified document, a cigarette dangling from his lip. He used to smoke four packs a day. He was in this cloud of smoke, peeing and reading, and I thought, *This* is the guy?" "A lot of people hated him in the DO—*hated* him—I mean despised him," says another former operative, even as he now praises Cohen for creating "the best counterterrorism center in the world" at the New York Police Department.

"People forget that in 1991, the Agency's personnel budget was reduced by twenty-five percent over eight years," said Cohen as we talked over this old history one afternoon. "That's an astounding change, because the Agency was not large to begin with. You know, it had a pattern of building itself up through contract employees during Vietnam, then coming down. The Casey years were very heavy in covert action, but much of that was staffed by contract personnel. So in 1991, when the budget comes out and it's a twenty-five percent reduction . . . how do you manage that? It's short of taking a knife and sticking it in your heart, but it's pretty darn close. When I became the DDO, there were seven people in clandestine service training. Seven! That's in effect saying, 'You guys are going out of business.' And that's what we were contending with. Try to run a restaurant when you tell the maitre d' that you're cutting his staff by twenty-five percent."

THE DARK SIDE

Cohen Among the Clandestines

In August 1996, when David Cohen had been DDO for just a year, Osama bin Laden issued his first "declaration of war" against Americans and Jews or, as he put it, against "the Zionist-Crusader alliance."

What to make of such a man? In those days, most Americans had never heard of him. But he was part of a history the CIA knew well. After the holy war against the Soviets that the United States had backed in Afghanistan in the 1980s, many Arab veterans of the fight went looking for new jihads. They turned against American allies, trying to overthrow the regimes in Algiers and Cairo, and this guy Bin Laden was funding them and coordinating some of their movements. He didn't command them so much as encourage them in much the same way the high-tech entrepreneurs of Silicon Valley ran incubators for Internet start-ups: people came with ideas and dedication; Bin Laden helped turn those into reality.

The 9/11 Commission Report gives Cohen credit for focusing on Bin Laden's methods and his madness when very few others in the government were paying attention: "In 1996, the CIA set up a special unit of a dozen officers to analyze intelligence on and plan operations against Bin

Laden. David Cohen, the head of the CIA's Directorate of Operations, wanted to test the idea of having a 'virtual station'—a station based at headquarters but collecting and operating against a subject much as stations in the field focus on a country." (This was classic Cohen, of course.) "Taking his cue from National Security Advisor Anthony Lake, who expressed special interest in terrorist finance, Cohen formed his virtual station as a terrorist financial links unit. He had trouble getting any Directorate of Operations officer to run it; he finally recruited a former analyst who was then running the Islamic Extremist Branch of the Counterterrorist Center." (That was Michael Scheuer, subsequently the anonymous author of *Imperial Hubris: Why the West Is Losing the War on Terror*.) "This officer, who was especially knowledgeable about Afghanistan, had noticed a recent stream of reports about Bin Laden and something called al Qaeda, and suggested to Cohen that the station focus on this one individual. Cohen agreed. Thus was born the Bin Laden unit."[1]

And yet—this gaunt, ascetic son of a billionaire who styled himself a knight of Islam still seemed more than a little quixotic. The Saudis had stripped him of his citizenship. The terrorists he'd supported in Algeria and Egypt were defeated by ruthless government repression. The Sudanese had forced Bin Laden out of their country and he wound up seeking shelter in Afghanistan among the radical Taliban, who were just then sweeping to power with the help of money, guns, training, and air support from Pakistan's intelligence service, which had very close ties to the CIA. So even there, Bin Laden's welcome was uncertain. He was on the run, not the offensive. He had no forces of his own to speak of, and he was struggling to forge alliances with other exiled radicals like the Egyptian Islamic Jihad leader Ayman al-Zawahiri. When Bin Laden issued his "declaration of war" in 1996, it was from the remoteness of Khurasan in the Hindu Kush mountains.

Scheuer saw all this as an opportunity. Other plots to snatch Bin Laden had been bungled before, most often at the bureaucratic level. But the CIA already was working with other Afghan "tribals" to hunt for another fugitive in the same area. The tribesmen might help track down Bin Laden, as well. Again, nobody in charge in the Clinton administration wanted to green-light the operation.

It was easy to imagine, as Ray Kelly and many others believed at the time, that the Feds had everything under control. There were other priorities. And if there was one individual in the Middle East who needed to be eliminated through covert action, Bin Laden wasn't at the top of the chart. Politics in Washington, as well as facts on the ground, still gave that distinction to Saddam Hussein.

Cohen's clandestine services were tasked to take out the Butcher of Baghdad.

The analyst-turned-operations-chief Cohen was not the architect of this covert action. One of his predecessors as DDO, Thomas Twetten, had started the ball rolling. But by the time Cohen took charge of the directorate in August 1995, there was no way he could stay aloof from the plotting. The Iraqi regime seemed to be cracking under the pressure of draconian economic sanctions. And then, suddenly, the dictator's son-in-law, Hussein Kamel, defected to Jordan and claimed he was the man who could overthrow the tyrant. Days later, the newly appointed Cohen led the CIA team that flew in to meet Kamel face-to-face.

"I spent about three hours with him," Cohen recalled. "Two hours and forty-five minutes of it he was talking to me, telling me what he was going to be doing and how the troops would rally to his cause with the blow of a whistle. And then I had to explain to him what we were willing to do and not willing to do," which was mostly nothing, since nobody really trusted this guy. "And then I got a phone call about four in the morning: 'He's thinking about going back.' I said that would be a mistake."

In fact, while the Agency doubted Kamel's ability to overthrow his father-in-law, it wanted to keep him around for a while. He had been the man who oversaw all of Saddam's programs to develop weapons of mass destruction: nuclear, chemical, and biological. Was there still a threat? Kamel insisted that all of the programs had been terminated and the weapons destroyed; either they were discovered by the United Nations inspectors who swarmed over the country after Saddam's defeat in the 1991 gulf war, or the Iraqis destroyed them on their own. But how could you be sure as long as Saddam was in power?

On that first critical trip as DDO, Cohen also spent a long time talking one-on-one with Jordan's King Hussein, who was making a dangerous transition from Saddam ally to Saddam enemy. The king committed himself to working closely with the CIA to help overthrow the dictator.

A few months later, Kamel followed up on his threat to return to Iraq, trusting to the tender mercies of Saddam and his cronies. As Cohen predicted, that was a fatal mistake: "They just slaughtered him." But the plotting continued.

When Cohen talks now about those years in the Directorate of Operations, it's in mostly utilitarian terms. "I think the most important work I did as the DDO was fix the way you pay people, the way you assign people, what you promote people for," Cohen told me one afternoon at One Police Plaza. "Those to me were things that someone with an analytical background could look at and say, 'This isn't right. It's dysfunctional doing it this way.' And so, I was able to fix it." But Cohen also talked about two particular bits of spying and counterspying that made him proud.

One was the discovery of yet another mole in Agency ranks: Harold J. Nicholson, a former chief of station in Romania assigned to "the Farm," the CIA's school for spies near Williamsburg, Virginia. Nicholson had decided to sell the trainees' identities to the Russians. According to Cohen, his shop identified the fact that there was a new mole, quickly discovered who it was, and nailed him. But when it came to counterintelligence at that point, the FBI in the person of Ed Curran apparently still had a role to play. In one telling of the story, in a book for which Curran was interviewed at length, FBI agents "slipped into CIA headquarters," where they bugged Nicholson's office phone, "installed a TV camera in the ceiling, and searched his car."[2]

At Nicholson's trial, the CIA would argue it could never calculate the damage Nicholson had done to its operations worldwide, but as Cohen saw it, the case actually was a morale booster. "In the wake of Ames, hardly any single operation was more important to the CIA's health and vitality than that specific event, and I'll tell you why: it was a public expression of CIA competence. And that meant a lot to me in running the DO."

The other moment Cohen likes to remember is the capture of Mir Amal Kasi, also known as Mir Amal Kansi. In 1994 the young Pakistani had fired an AK-47 assault rifle at drivers waiting to turn off Route 123 into CIA headquarters at Langley, Virginia. He managed to kill two employees and wound three others, then made his escape back to Pakistan and the border region of Afghanistan. In 1997 the CIA lured Kasi back into Pakistan and captured him. "That," said Cohen, "was a big, big deal . . . one of the high points of my professional life in the Agency."

The CIA and FBI never established any link between Kasi, who was executed by lethal injection in 2002, and any known terrorist organization. But by the time he was caught, the Agency was all too aware of the anger in the Muslim world directed at the United States. As Cohen recalled, "The Agency really was focused on it in a way that no one else quite understood." At least in Washington.

Those of us reporting in the field saw rage against Americans everywhere we looked, and we also saw that the amazing obliviousness at home only fueled the fury more. It was as if the United States was in the middle of a hurricane. All around it there was death and destruction, but Americans looked up and all they saw were blue skies.

In the early 1990s it didn't take only Bin Laden to convince Muslims that insults to their faith and threats to their identity were building up like a storm surge behind a seawall. A mosque was destroyed in India and the police just stood by and watched while it crumbled under the picks and shovels of Hindus. Hundreds of Palestinians were rounded up by the Israelis and sent up to a frozen mountain in Lebanon. There was talk about "the peace of the brave" after the Oslo Accords between Israel and the Palestine Liberation Organization in 1993, but the implementation quickly led to humiliation and mistrust.

Afghanistan had been allowed to slip into chaos. In Egypt, thousands of believers were arrested and beaten. Some of them were radicals and revolutionaries, many were not—until their experience in prison turned them toward violent jihad. American fighter planes swarmed the skies over Iraq, and Saddam claimed hundreds of thousands of children were going without food. In Somalia, 300,000 Muslims died of starvation before, slowly, the United States started to send aid, then troops. With Bosnia, at last, Washington recognized the need to stop the slaughter, but only after hundreds of thousands of Muslims were dead there, too, and after the brutal and systematic rape of countless thousands of women. None of the deeply felt anger, the reservoir of incandescent hatred in the world of Islam, was Bin Laden's creation—but he could stoke it, stir it, and exploit it. And so, still, could Saddam Hussein.

Cohen remembered he was busy chairing a meeting at Langley one morning in 1996, it would have been June: "I was trying to bring more rigor to what we were doing on the collection and operational side." It was one of those administrative demarches in which Cohen took such pride, trying to build coherence inside the clandestine services and support for them from outside. "Important questions were being asked about our activities in a particular part of the world, identifying the gaps, the things we weren't doing well and where we could improve, when I got a phone call." It was about the effort to overthrow Saddam in Iraq. "They told me that the team that was going across the border had been captured and possibly killed."

So began the final clandestine disaster that would undermine almost everything else Cohen had tried to do. "That was really a devastating moment," he said. "It was a very, very"—Cohen searched for the phrase—"watershed event."

By the end of that month, Saddam had arrested and killed more than one hundred officers and security men plotting against him. He also cut a deal with one of the Kurdish warlords who had been getting U.S. protection. It allowed Saddam to sweep through the bastions in northern Iraq from which the CIA had mounted its operations. Operatives, aid workers, and hundreds of the Iraqis who had worked for them and trusted them had to be evacuated in a debacle reminiscent of the Bay of Pigs or the last days of Saigon—except that few pictures were taken, and no memorable images lingered. The American public had known little about the operations when they began, and knew less when they ended.

Inside the Agency, however, Deutch's unhappy tenure as director came to an end. His deputy, George Tenet, wound up with the top job. And DDO David Cohen became a favorite target for anyone opining on how the Agency's reputation and operations could be salvaged. In May 1997 *The New York Times* ran an editorial titled "The Warrior Spies," suggesting Tenet "needs a deputy director for operations able to make change stick. David Cohen, the incumbent, is wobbly and should be replaced."[3] Tenet moved Cohen to New York City as the CIA's "senior representative" (read: "New York station chief") to serve there until he retired.[4] In 2000, at age fifty-seven and after thirty-five years in the CIA, Cohen took a job in political risk underwriting with the global insurance firm American International Group.

Ray Kelly didn't really know David Cohen well, but when he called him in November 2001 he knew just how to play him. They'd met in passing after Kelly left the police force, when Cohen was "the CIA guy in New York." Kelly thought that background made him just the kind of guy to transform the intelligence division of the NYPD into an operation with enough global vision to protect the city from global threats.

"It wasn't too hard," Kelly told me. "I know from people who leave government that, particularly when there is a crisis, they want to get back. And, in fact, I had the same feeling myself from sitting on the sidelines on September 11. And, you know, what do you do? You feel helpless. You know you think you have something to contribute but there is no vehicle to do that. So I knew that. I gave it a shot." Cohen listened to Kelly's proposition and told him he'd give him a response in two days. In fact, he called back an hour later and said yes.

On January 24, 2002, presenting Cohen to the press, Kelly described Cohen as the man who had been "the point of the spear directing the CIA's clandestine services against terrorists, as well as against traffickers in narcotics and weapons of mass destruction." Mayor Bloomberg reminded reporters that "the world no longer stops at the oceans, our world goes every place, and we have to make sure that we get the best information as quickly as we possibly can." Cohen himself, speaking in his still-strong Boston accent, delivered a simple message: "The city is my adopted home and has been for nearly five years and there isn't anything I wouldn't do for it."

As Cohen visited the division he was about to take over, one of the sergeants there remembers him just looking around, quiet, unassuming, so gray in appearance he could fade into the walls. But when he talked the sergeant noticed that "he had this little-boy gleam in his eye," curious about what he saw, enthusiastic about what could be done.

Now, when Cohen talks about the early days of the Kelly regime at the NYPD, those first fraught and frightening weeks and months in 2002 and 2003, it's with a hint of what the French call *nostalgie de la guerre,* yearning for a time when everything was so intense and anything seemed possible. "It was like putting tires on a speeding car," he says. Kelly had told Cohen "the Intelligence division is responsible for the ground-up work of terrorism." But what did that mean? "That was the broad mission," said Cohen. "But there was no playbook: you know—'Open to chapter two and do the following things.' That didn't exist."

How was a local police department supposed to build a division that could compete on an international scale? The NYPD might have fifty thousand employees and a budget of some $3.8 billion, but it was going where no local government agency had gone before, "totally new territory in which others had a monopoly—a monopoly!" as Cohen put it. He and Kelly were going to have to try build something different from the federal agencies if they wanted to make New York City secure: an organization with minimal bureaucracy and maximum freedom of movement, able to anticipate threats and able to act on that information. It would be the kind of intelligence operation that Cohen, and for that matter the Bob Baers of this world, really wanted to work for: focused, effective, and respected. But that was still a ways off in 2002. There were times in those first months when the whole NYPD intelligence operation felt like "a gaggle of guys chasing things around," Cohen recalls.

The think tank in which all these plans developed was the morning meeting that Kelly held with the heads of the Intelligence division and the Counter Terrorism division every weekday at eight o'clock sharp.

"Kelly never missed a morning," said Cohen, "and because of that, *I* never missed a morning . . . and this isn't bullshit, it's as real as real can get—from that meeting we created the playbook.

"The commissioner did *not* call a consultant to come in and advise us. If he had, we'd still be having focus group meetings." Cohen laughed into his CIA coffee mug, warming to the subject. "I had never been involved in anything like that in my professional history," he said. "It's just a remarkable story. It's an epic story, I got to tell you."

Cohen formally started his job on February 2, 2002, just as New York City was in the middle of hosting the World Economic Forum's annual meeting of global business and political leaders. Normally it took place in the remote and protected town of Davos, high in the Swiss Alps, and even there the forum was a target for violent "antiglobalization" anarchists. Now, not quite five months after 9/11, with most of that atrocity's jihadist planners still at large, many of their most-hated human targets had come from around the world to gather in the city they never stopped trying to attack. "I thought," Cohen said, smiling and shaking his head as he reminisced, "what the *fuck* am I into here?"

THE CITY

Anatomy of a Target

Cohen had been used to taking on the world, but from a certain distance. Now the world had come to him as this vastly complex but amazingly compact social organism with a sentience all its own. Pulsing, breathing, absorbing, secreting—New York City is a place of permanent transience, built and sustained by immigrants, generation after generation of them coming from, well, just about everywhere. More than a third of the city's current population, by some estimates almost 40 percent, was born outside the United States of America. But statistics don't convey the feel of streets where so many cultures are ambling around and through one another, the in-your-face rush of living in the middle of millions of human interactions happening at once, many of them incomprehensibly alien from one another, some of them potentially dangerous. At the Agency "the thought process was more macro," Cohen said in one of our talks. "You dealt with lots of facts, but they weren't as discrete, as *granular* as the material that you have to contend with as you work the issue of protecting New York City from another terrorist event."

Cohen loves that word "granular." He uses it especially when he talks about the change in perspective those first weeks and months on the job running the Intelligence division, as if he'd gone from looking at the beach to looking at the individual crystals of sand. "You're worried about Bosnia and you're with CIA, you want to understand the political dynamics in Bosnia, the key players, the order of battle of the military, stuff like that, but you're not going to worry about what goes on at the corner of X Street and Y Avenue," Cohen said. "At the investigative level, for the traditional NYPD detective, that granularity is grist for the mill. That's what they grow up on. But it's the context for that granularity that they're missing." And in February 2002, when Cohen took over, the context for the devastating attacks of five months before was absent entirely. "We had an intelligence division that did literally no work on terrorism. It was a six-hundred-fifty-person program that did other stuff. It didn't do that."[1]

Over the course of the previous eighty years the idea had settled in on the city's law enforcement agencies that stopping terror attacks was beyond their competence; basically a job for "the three-letter guys," as cops called them, which might mean the CIA or ATF or even the DEA, but mostly meant the FBI. The police could joke about the Feds being "Famous But Incompetent," but only Washington seemed to have the resources and the direction to take on foreign threats to domestic tranquility, and the agencies in D.C. were brutally jealous of their prerogatives. Cooperation with the NYPD, if it existed, was essentially a one-way street. Thus, there were hundreds of personnel from various branches of the government assigned to the FBI-run Joint Terrorism Task Force in Manhattan, set up "way back in 1980" as the FBI website tells us, to coordinate federal and local efforts.[2] But as of September 11, 2001, fewer than twenty of them were New York City police officers. Then Kelly put more than a hundred additional cops on the task force. "We muscled our way in," as he put it. "And of course, this is a city that has been attacked successfully twice," he said. "We had a certain standing to do that."

*　*　*

Kelly's vision of the NYPD as a unique force facing unique threats had deep roots in department lore and traditions, even if much of the specific history had been forgotten by the public and press. He knew perfectly well that in the course of a hundred years New York City had come under attack not twice but scores of times, but you just couldn't rely on anybody else in the country to remember that. Complacency sets in too easily, whether about petty crime or outrageous atrocities. "You've got to remind people every day," he said. Kelly also knew that in the past the NYPD had found truly extraordinary officers willing to use extraordinary means to meet the threat, especially in the early years during the stunning waves of terror that came in the days of ragtime and World War I, when the federal government was weaker and the NYPD was without question the most powerful police force in the country.

Even now you'll sometimes hear cops talking about Giuseppe "Joe" Petrosino, who was the first high-ranking Italian officer on the force at the end of the nineteenth century. Petrosino and his Italian Squad fought the Mafia, the Black Hand extortionists, and bomb-throwing anarchists determined to bring their arcane revolutionary movement to American soil. When Teddy Roosevelt was police commissioner in the 1890s he made Petrosino a sergeant detective, and in that great age of police-blotter sensationalism, the press made Petrosino a hero. He was short, swarthy, spoke with a thick Neapolitan accent, and gave no quarter to the bad guys. "He knocked out more teeth than a dentist," as one alderman said. Sometimes Petrosino presented himself as a sharply dressed detective complete with bowler hat, but he often moved through the streets in the rags of a day laborer, easily blending in with other recent arrivals in this city of immigrants.

Today, Petrosino is best remembered as the first NYPD cop assigned to work overseas. He was also the first and only one to be killed abroad in the line of duty. A century later, when Kelly and Cohen started rethinking and remaking the NYPD, and took the controversial step of assigning officers to London, Paris, Amman, Montréal, Santo Domingo, Singapore, and other foreign cities, the Petrosino precedent seemed as much a warning as an inspiration. His mission had been, like that of his modern-day counterparts, to share intelligence. There had been so many known Mafiosi coming to the United States in the first decade of the 1900s that Congress passed a law declaring that anyone found to have concealed a criminal record in his home country could be deported forthwith. Who better to check the Italian files than Petrosino? But in the United States Petrosino was a hero. In Italy he was just a peasant from Salerno who had emigrated thirty-five years before. Petrosino got little cooperation from Italian authorities, and no protection. The month after he arrived on Italian soil in 1909, a gunman shot Petrosino dead on a street corner in downtown Palermo.[3]

The cops the NYPD started deploying overseas in 2002 were told to keep very, very low profiles.

The first modern Age of Terror, in the sense that we understand it today, came during and just after the Great War that erupted in Europe in the summer of 1914, and many of the tactics used by the NYPD to fight the threat then would be repeated in various guises after 2001. The United States claimed neutrality but at the same time served as "the arsenal of democracy," shipping vital munitions to the Allies. The Germans responded with sabotage and terrorism. Berlin's military and naval intelligence services organized, funded, facilitated, and supplied explosives for the attacks, which were mainly in and around New York City, the transit point for almost all the weaponry bound for the Allies in Europe.

The NYPD had been on alert since the very beginning of the fighting in Europe. In August 1914 it set up a special thirty-four-man unit that came to be called the "Bomb and Neutrality Squad." It was run by Thomas Tunney, a big, burly, Irish cop who had joined the force when Teddy Roosevelt had run the New York police and already had plenty of experience fighting violent anarchists and extortionists.

With little regard for jurisdictional borders (a common criticism leveled at today's NYPD), Tunney sent German-speaking police officers to New Jersey to hang out in the beer gardens of Hoboken. The cops intercepted a letter from a retired sea captain who had been delivering materials to the house of a bomb maker and then carrying the finished explosives to agents on the docks. One of Tunney's men pretended to be a German secret agent who could help the old captain get reimbursed for his expenses, and the unsuspecting codger exposed the network as he whined about payments. Even after he was arrested, he trusted a German workman in the police station to get in touch with a list of contacts he wanted to warn. The workman was a cop. Tunney rolled up that whole operation.[4] But there were more and bigger attacks to come.

Liberty State Park on the New Jersey side of New York Harbor is now a way station for tourists headed to Ellis Island or the Statue of Liberty. But in July 1916 it was called Black Tom Island and served as a storage yard for munitions waiting for shipment to a war in Europe that still seemed very distant to most New Yorkers. Then, just a couple of hours after midnight—2:08 a.m. on the morning of July 30, 1916, to be precise—"with terrifying, ear-splitting explosiveness the Great War of Europe suddenly came to America."[5]

Shock waves thudded against skyscraper windows, shattering them by the thousands and showering glass onto the streets below, according to Jules Witcover's painstaking reconstruction of the attack and its aftermath, *Sabotage at Black Tom*. Shrapnel ripped through the metal skin of the Statue of Liberty and blasted gaping holes in the buildings of Ellis Island, where terrified immigrants, who thought they'd escaped the conflagration across the Atlantic, now huddled in terror. The blast knocked late-night revelers in Brooklyn to their knees and threw sleepers out of their beds. It killed a ten-week-old boy hurled out of his crib in New Jersey. People were rattled awake as far south as Philadelphia, many thinking they'd been hit by an earthquake. Even police in Maryland got calls asking them what was going on.[6]

The spectacle of destruction weirdly prefigured 9/11. "Terror struck motorists crossing the Brooklyn Bridge as the giant edifice swayed at the impact of the shock waves, and windshields in their autos shattered," Witcover writes. "The blast jolted the Hudson Tubes under the river connecting lower Manhattan with Hoboken and Jersey City, panicking the underground passengers who were still making a Saturday night of it. . . . Even the dead were disturbed; in the Bay View and New York Bay cemeteries, monuments and tombstones toppled and some vaults were jolted askew."⁷ All telephone lines between New York and Jersey City went dead and terrifying rumors filled the void. Panic swept the wards of hospitals and the cell blocks at prisons. And yet, unlike 9/11, as casualties were counted the known death toll was small: perhaps fifteen people killed. Tunney's vaunted Bomb and Neutrality Squad, having failed to prevent the attack, tried to call it an accident. The true story took years to come out, and by then most New Yorkers had forgotten Black Tom.

One thing federal authorities learned during and after the Great War was that the threat of foreign terrorists could be a great unifier and mobilizer of the American public. President Woodrow Wilson, the man who would win reelection in 1916 by claiming he "kept us out of war," and then plunged us into it, saw clearly how ruthless Americans could be, even craved to be, when they joined the battle. "Once lead this people into war," he said, "and they'll forget there ever was such a thing as tolerance."⁸

Yet tolerance, whether willing or grudging, whether in peace or war, is what New York City requires to function at all. Cops in the early 1900s might have yearned for a time when, in the words of one detective, "there were not so many different races up against you."⁹ But as Jacob Riis wrote in his hugely influential book of text and photographs, *How the Other Half Lives,* wherever there was an alley or courtyard in lower Manhattan you could find "an Italian, a German, a French, African, Spanish, Bohemian, Russian, Scandinavian, Jewish, and Chinese colony. Even the Arab, who peddles 'holy earth' from the Battery as a direct importation from Jerusalem, has his exclusive preserves at the lower end of Washington Street. The one thing you shall vainly ask for in the chief city of America is a distinctively American community. There is none; certainly not among the tenements."¹⁰

After the Great War ended in November 1918, Woodrow Wilson's Justice Department under Attorney General A. Mitchell Palmer replaced the threatening specter of barbaric Huns with the looming menace of Reds and the godless Bolshevik revolution in Russia. Communists, Socialists, and anarchists had to be rooted out before they could spread their revolutionary ideas through the land. But they were not about to go peacefully.

As often happens, the most extreme radicals and their most ruthless government oppressors fed off one another's violence. The anarchists sent parcel bombs through the mails. They rioted in New York City. They targeted Attorney General Palmer with a bomb in front of his Washington house that killed the would-be assassin and two passersby. (Palmer's neighbor, Assistant Secretary of the Navy Franklin Delano Roosevelt, only narrowly escaped injury as he got out of his car next door.)

Palmer appointed a viciously ambitious young man only a couple of years out of law school, J. Edgar Hoover, as head of the General Intelligence division of the Justice Department's Bureau of Investigation. Hoover would head up the hunt for Reds in America. The mass arrests began. In December 1919 the Feds loaded two hundred and forty-nine people of Russian origin, including the famous activists Emma Goldman and Alexander Berkman, on an old U.S. troop transport called the *Buford*. Bound for the Soviet Union, it sailed from Ellis Island. The symbolism of shipping people out from the place where so many had entered the country was unmistakable. Americans didn't want "those kind" in their country. On a single night in January 1920 Hoover and Palmer arrested four thousand people, to general public approval. The Red Scare had become a national hysteria encouraged at every turn by the powers that be in Washington.

In the fall of 2007, while working on a story for *Newsweek* about the way the administration of President George W. Bush tried to reconcile torture with the Constitution, I had a coffee at a sidewalk café in Chelsea with my friend Karen J. Greenberg, who runs the Center on Law and Security at New York University. Cruel and unusual punishments had become usual in the treatment of suspected terrorists, I suggested. Greenberg, a woman of elegant intelligence, said "come back to my office." She pulled a copy of *The Torture Debate in America* off a shelf and started flipping through the papers she had edited: a panel discussion on "Abu Ghraib and Beyond"; essays on "Liberalism, Torture, and the Ticking Bomb," "Magical Thinking in the War on Terror," and much more. "But this is the best part," Greenberg said with a spark of conspiratorial excitement, turning to the very end of the book. She had republished an open letter by twelve distinguished jurists, including Felix Frankfurter, that was written in May 1920, more than six months into the Red Scare:

> *Under the guise of a campaign for the suppression of radical activities, the office of the Attorney General, acting by its local agents throughout the country, and giving express instructions from Washington, has committed continual illegal acts. Wholesale arrests both of aliens and citizens have been made without warrant or any process of law; men and women have been jailed and held incommunicado without access of friends or counsel; homes have been entered without search-warrant and property seized and removed; other property has been wantonly destroyed; workingmen and working-women suspected of radical views have been shamefully abused and maltreated. Agents of the Department of Justice have been introduced into radical organizations for the purpose of informing upon their members or inciting them to activities; these agents have even been instructed from Washington to arrange meetings upon certain dates for the express object of facilitating wholesale raids and arrests.*[11]

It all sounded only too familiar, and too current.

Not long after my chat with Greenberg I went down to Wall Street to see another reminder of the Red Scare. Along the side of the building known as "the Corner," which houses the J.P. Morgan headquarters at 23 Wall Street, the stone is pocked by the impact of high-velocity shrapnel. It is the kind of icon left by horrific violence that you sometimes see in European cities where battles have raged through the streets. But it's not something you expect, or at least that you used to expect, in lower Manhattan.

Much of what happened here on September 16, 1920, is well documented. A cart pulled by an old bay horse was reined to a stop in front of J.P. Morgan & Co., which is near the New York Stock Exchange and the statue of George Washington that stands in front of Federal Hall.

The bells of old Trinity Church started tolling twelve o'clock. Office workers poured onto the street to take their lunch breaks. It was just at that moment that the driver of the horse cart dropped the reins and ran away. Or maybe he just walked. Was he an Italian, as one witness remembered? Or "an East Side peddler" as another testified? Or was he someone of an entirely different background? Casual prejudices make for sloppy observations. Nobody was looking that closely. And then the entire picture changed.

A blindingly bright light gave way to a terrible stillness where the only sound was the tinkling of shattered glass falling through a fog of acrid smoke, falling from shattered windows like sharp-edged rain into the street, falling on the bodies and pieces of bodies of the dead and the horribly wounded. Only those at a distance would actually have heard the blast, low and rumbling like thunder, and as some of them rushed to the scene, elbowing their way through the crowds now fleeing for their lives, they saw the cobblestones of Wall Street slick with gore. "Almost in front of the steps leading up to the Morgan bank was the mutilated body of a man," wrote an Associated Press reporter who witnessed the explosion. "Other bodies, most of them silent in death, lay nearby. As I gazed horrorstruck at the sight, one of these forms, half-naked and seared with burns, started to rise. It struggled, then toppled and fell lifeless to the gutter." The leg of a horse lay across the steps of one building, a woman's head, still wearing a hat, was stuck to the wall of another. A fatally wounded messenger pleaded for someone to deliver the securities he clutched in his fist. At least thirty people died on the spot. Thomas Joyce, Morgan's chief clerk, died at his desk. *The New York Times* eventually reported the death toll as forty, with some three hundred people injured. Many had been wounded by lead fragments: bits of the weights normally used to hold down the hems of Victorian draperies, which the bomb maker had packed around the explosives to serve as shrapnel.

At ten that night, Michael J. Flynn of the Justice Department's Bureau of Investigation arrived from Washington and let it be known that he had everything under control. And in fact there were several arrests over the months and years that followed, but no one ever was convicted of the Wall Street bombing. Little more is known today about who was behind it than was suspected the night of the attack, when an editor at *The New York Times* wrote the headline "Red Plot Seen in Blast." After so many months of Palmer raids across the country, someone had taken revenge in New York City.[12]

If you were to start to categorize terrorists and prioritize the threat they pose, which is what Cohen had to set about doing, you'd recognize there are certain types that might strike in any town and who, acting without any real organization, are almost impossible to stop. The United States has a long, sad history of crazed loners slaughtering the innocents around them: Charles Whitman firing his Remington 700 hunting rifle from the Texas Tower in Austin in 1966; Timothy McVeigh blowing up the Murrah Federal Building in Oklahoma City in 1995; Seung-Hui Cho wielding his Glock and his Walther video-game style to cut down fellow students at Virginia Tech in 2007. And those are only some of the more memorable. There's a whole subgenre of high school slaughter epitomized by the Columbine killings in Colorado in 1999. Variations on the theme of random mass murder are disconcertingly commonplace just about everywhere in the country, and have been for as long as anyone can remember.

In New York City, a badly disabled and insanely disgruntled former employee of the Consolidated Edison utility company waged a one-man wave of terror for sixteen years in the 1940s and 1950s. George Metesky, known as "the Mad Bomber," repeatedly planted explosives in Grand Central Terminal, Penn Station, Radio City Music Hall, the New York Public Library, and the Port Authority, not to mention the subway. But a man like Metesky might just as easily have carried out his bombing campaign in Minneapolis.

Radical political groups using terrorism are a very different category and are likely to choose their targets more logically. They may have incongruous and delusional reasons for planting bombs, but they have convinced themselves and a few accomplices that some day thousands, even millions of people will see the righteousness of their cause. To impress their constituents they think a lot about the message for which terrorism is the medium, whether they are fighting for "national liberation," revolution in America, or the reestablishment of the Islamic caliphate. So they want publicity. By striking in and around the hometown of the most powerful news organizations in the world, they can always be sure that their ideas, in one form or another, will get out.

In the years since World War II, plagues of true believers have descended on New York City with their explosive messages, most of which are long since forgotten. A few city maps, for instance, still mark the address at 18 West Eleventh Street in Greenwich Village, where an elegant town house stood until March 1970.[13] That is, until young Cathlyn Wilkerson, the daughter of the advertising executive who owned it, invited in her friends from the Weather Underground Organization while her father and his wife were on vacation in St. Kitts.[14] The Weathermen, as they were called, held their truths to be self-evident. Their cause, to overthrow the government of the United States, and their approach, urban guerrilla actions, seemed to these privileged revolutionaries the only way to go. So they planned to bomb an officers' club at Fort Dix, New Jersey, as a gesture of solidarity with the Vietnamese fighting against American troops on the other side of the world.

The bomb-making skills of the Weathermen were not as refined as their ideological debates. They accidentally detonated the explosives in the Greenwich Village basement, killing three of the plotters and destroying the house. Wilkerson and another woman, Kathy Boudin, who had been taking a shower and was completely naked, ran into the street and then away from the law for many years afterward. Over time, the Weathermen came to seem quaintly anachronistic and deeply quixotic. The poet James Merrill, who had lived in the house on Eleventh Street when he was a little boy and saw the depressing irony of what had happened there, wrote that "the Aquarians in the basement / Had been perfecting a device / For making sense to us . . ."[15]

The legendary thief of the 1930s, Willie Sutton, supposedly said that he robbed banks because "that's where the money is." Terrorists have targeted New York City many times for the same reason. Its special curse is to be a symbol of the power that is money, the epitome of Mammon that drew the fire of anarchists at the beginning of the twentieth century, jihadists at the beginning of the twenty-first, and many others in between. When the Fuerzas Armadas de Liberación Nacional Puertorriqueña (FALN) launched their terrorist campaign to win independence for Puerto Rico by bombing five banks in midtown on October 26, 1974, their first communiqué declared the city was targeted as the center of "yanki monopoly capitalism."[16] The FALN went on to plant more than one hundred bombs. It hit Chicago and Washington, D.C., too, but it kept coming back to Manhattan and Brooklyn until, on New Year's Eve 1982, the Puerto Rican nationalists went on a bombing spree that left three cops maimed for life.

Twenty-five years later to the day, Commissioner Ray Kelly dedicated a plaque at the entrance to police headquarters, where one of those bombs had gone off. While bagpipes played and ranks of uniformed cops stood at attention, the three aging, injured members of the force sat in the front row listening to Kelly and others pay tribute to their bravery.

There was about that ceremony, as there often is at NYPD functions, a sense of family coming together. Detective Anthony Senft, a member of the bomb squad who was blown fifteen feet in the air by one of the FALN devices and was blinded in the right eye, still served with the department at the end of 2007—and his son was on the bomb squad. Detective Salvatore Pastorella, blinded in both eyes by the same blast that injured Senft, did not retire until 1993, and two of his sons went to work on the force. After the ceremony, Detective Rocco Pascarella, whose leg was mangled by one of the bombs and who lost an eye, but who also remained on duty, tried to explain to a reporter from *Newsday* what it had been like to live with scars inflicted by fanatics the world has forgotten. "When you talk to people about what happened, they don't connect it to 'terrorism,' " he said. "When they think of terrorism, they think of Islamic terrorism."[17]

THE BATTLEGROUND

Manhattan and Megiddo

Suicide bombs have particular signatures. Would-be martyrs in the Middle East might carry their explosives in a backpack or stitched into a vest they can wear close to their bodies. Crime scene investigators know right away which delivery method was used: a backpack tears the bomber's body in half; a vest destroys the torso and leaves mangled limbs, but the head tends to remain intact like some gory guillotine exhibit in a wax museum. The explosive itself is usually a volatile, homebrewed concoction called triacetone triperoxide, or TATP, packed and sealed inside steel pipes. But different groups will arrange the components of the bomb differently. The early Hamas bomb makers, for instance, liked to tape dozens of four-inch nails around each exploding pipe to serve as shrapnel. A second Hamas giveaway: no timer. The pipes were attached to nine-volt batteries with toggle switches.[1] The bomber had to make a very conscious decision to die. Eventually, the Hamas model became the blueprint for everyone else, so tiny variations, if detected, could be significant. What an investigator wanted was for the signature of the bomb to take him to the bomber, and onward.

In the first weeks after David Cohen took over the Intelligence division at the NYPD, he needed that kind of information and much more. He needed to know the who and what and when and where and how of suicide bombings, and he needed all that very damn fast, because the echoes of suicide bombings in Israel were rolling toward New York City like the violent thunder of an approaching storm.

For years, the madness of the Middle East's many conflicts had threatened New York, and if the worst attacks had been prevented before September 2001, the reason had less to do with good intelligence or smart police work than plain dumb luck. Those near misses could be very instructive if you studied them closely. But few people had.

In some cases, the clear and present danger to New York City came from Washington's muddled policies in distant lands. After the Reagan administration bombed Libya in 1986, the dictator Muammar Qadhafi, who had every reason to believe the strike was aimed at him personally, immediately set out to take revenge on Americans. This was perfectly predictable and borne out by terrible facts, yet for years afterward officials in Washington would claim that the air raids on Tripoli and Benghazi intimidated the dictator. What they would not or could not—in any case, did not—say was that Qadhafi merely shifted his support away from Palestinians attacking Israel and gave it to other groups directly targeting the United States and the United Kingdom.

From the time the Reagan administration took office in 1981 it had gone gunning for the Libyan dictator. Ronald Reagan was determined to show how tough he was on state sponsors of terrorism. But Iran and Syria were the countries that really counted: the Iranians had carried out the U.S. embassy seizure and then worked with the Syrians to organize years of terror in Lebanon, including the Beirut embassy bombing, the Marine barracks bombing, and many kidnappings. Qadhafi had no apparent connection to any of that. No matter. "When you want to scold the dog, beat the chicken," goes an old Arab proverb. Syria and Iran were big dogs. Qadhafi was not. By humiliating the Libyan leader, or worse, the administration hoped to teach a lesson to the Ayatollah Khomeini in Tehran and Syria's Hafez Assad in Damascus.[2]

After Palestinian terrorists attacked El Al ticket counters in Rome and Vienna at the end of 1985, leaving an American child among the dead, Washington blamed Libya. U.S. warships attacked Libyan naval vessels, shot down Libyan fighter planes, and blasted Libyan antiaircraft batteries. Reagan's conspiracy-minded aides like CIA chief Bill Casey and Oliver North were taunting Qadhafi and watching for a reaction. When terrorists planted a bomb in a Berlin disco, killing an American and a Turkish woman, Washington announced it had intercepted the message from Libya ordering the attack. That triggered the biggest U.S. bombing raid since the Vietnam War. British-based American F-111s targeted all those places where Qadhafi was known to live, work, and sleep.[3] If they didn't kill him, it wasn't for lack of trying. "Today we have done what we had to do," President Ronald Reagan said. "If necessary, we shall do it again."[4]

Such talk rang tough and true to many Americans. The shoot 'em up showed them a bad guy would get his just deserts. But on the ground in the Middle East you could see very quickly how counterproductive the raids had been. The next year, 1987, was "the bloodiest year for terrorist incidents since we began compiling such figures," the State Department concluded.[5] Qadhafi started sending massive weapons shipments to the Irish Republican Army to attack the British. By 1988 groups linked to Qadhafi had shown their ability to strike all over the map, from Indonesia to Spain. They attacked a hotel in Sudan and slaughtered a British family of four. They blew up an American service club in Naples, Italy, killing five people, including a U.S. servicewoman. And they set their sights on Manhattan.

In order to murder Americans without drawing attention directly to Libya, Qadhafi had turned to a small but infamous terrorist organization called the Japanese Red Army.[6] In March 1988, one of its members, thirty-five-year-old Yu Kikumura, flew into New York City using a stolen passport, bought a used Mazda in the Bronx for cash, and set out on a seven-thousand-mile drive through the American heartland—Chicago, Kentucky, Tennessee, West Virginia, and Pennsylvania—buying components along the way for the bombs he was building to attack Manhattan.[7] Kikumura's target date was April 14, the second anniversary of the U.S. air raids that had just missed killing Qadhafi. The hired gun from Japan packed gunpowder and makeshift shrapnel into emptied fire extinguishers so the bombs could be positioned in public places without attracting attention. This wasn't the kind of apocalyptic plot that thriller writers had conjured for Qadhafi in *The Fifth Horseman*. There was no nuke, far from it. But the carnage would have been horrible nonetheless as first one bomb, then another, then another went off. The focal point of the planned attack appeared to be a U.S. Navy recruiting office in midtown.

Kikumura must have been tired, or maybe he was getting shaky as he drove up the New Jersey Turnpike with the bomb components in the back of his car. Sometime late on April 11 or early on April 12, he pulled into the Vince Lombardi Service Area, the last rest stop before you head into the city. At about seven in the morning, New Jersey State Trooper Robert Cieplenski noticed Kikumura "loitering." As the trooper approached, the terrorist ran for his old Mazda and tried to speed away through the parking lot, but Cieplenski quickly caught up with him. The trooper later testified the explosives and bomb components were in plain sight on the car's backseat.[8]

In an unusually secret trial, federal prosecutors allowed Kikumura to plead guilty to illegal transport of explosives and other relatively minor counts. There was no jury, and the government carefully avoided presenting information in court about Kikumura's motives or his planned target. He was convicted in November 1988 and sentenced to jail for thirty years.

That same November, the State Department's ambassador at large for counterterrorism, L. Paul Bremer III (who would later be pro-consul in occupied Iraq), gave a speech at George Washington University about terrorism in the 1980s and the way he thought it could be fought in the 1990s. He had to admit that the recent record of attacks against Americans had been horrific, but "these data do not reflect a failed policy," he insisted, and the Tripoli bombing was "a watershed event in the world's fight against terrorist-supporting states."[9]

A month later, Pan Am Flight 103 exploded over Lockerbie while en route from London to New York City. The date was December 21. Many of those aboard were headed home for Christmas. In all, two hundred seventy people died. Years later a member of Libya's intelligence service was convicted of their murder.

As David Cohen looked at the news coming from Israel in early 2002, the suicide bombings there were crossing one threshold of atrocity after another. In late January, a young woman named Wafa Idris had blown herself up in a shoe store in Jerusalem, killing only one other person but injuring scores more. She was the Palestinians' first female suicide bomber. She was not known for religious fanaticism. Idris normally worked with the rescue teams of the Red Crescent Society (the Muslim version of the Red Cross) and she may have gotten past Israeli checkpoints in an ambulance. When she died, the twenty-six-year-old reportedly was dressed in a stylish overcoat with a muffler wrapped around her neck and chin, her long curly hair was uncovered, her makeup was perfect, her nails were manicured.[10] Someone like Idris would fit in easily almost anywhere in New York: in a theater, at a crowded restaurant or at Bloomingdale's.

And why wouldn't bombers hit targets like those in a city so intimately tied to Israel; a city where many more Jews lived than in Jerusalem?[11] At times the Holy Land's battle lines seemed to snake from the West Bank to Williamsburg, from Gaza to Crown Heights, and that was before Osama bin Laden decided to declare war on "Zionists and Crusaders" in 1996; that was before the attacks of September 2001 had stripped away whatever aura of invulnerability had helped to protect the United States. As mass communications brought scenes of Palestinian-Israeli bloodletting into the homes of Jews and Muslims in New York in 2002, the risk that an incident in Jenin would provoke murder in Brooklyn grew higher all the time.

"If you ask me, it all goes back to Nosair," a police sergeant said one night as we drove along Brooklyn's Atlantic Avenue, which is still talked about as the heart of the city's Arab community even though gentrification and real-estate speculation have driven many of the Arabs out. "You want to write the history of this terrorism thing, that's where you start it."

(The sergeant liked to use cop speak to simplify big issues. He told me an old homicide detective once told him, as they stood looking at a body in the street, that the motives for all murders "come down to three things: pussy, fear, and money." He paused. "And I've thought about that since, you know. And the older I get, the more I think, Yeah, that's about right.")

"Nosair." Sayyid el-Nosair. You have to be a real aficionado of Muslim Bad Guys in America to know what the sergeant meant, but if you are, then you think, Yeah, that's about right. To understand the story, you have to start in fact about twenty years before el-Nosair arrived on the scene. From the late 1960s onward, the Arab-Israeli wars had been looking to come to America. A first inkling was when the Palestinian Sirhan Sirhan, a crazed loner, murdered Robert Kennedy in Los Angeles the night he won the California Democratic presidential primary in 1968. But the real skirmishes began in the 1970s, when Rabbi Meir Kahane formed the militant Jewish Defense League in Brooklyn.

Its ostensible purpose was to fight anti-Semitism in the United States, but more often its members were just out for revenge, retaliating against soft targets in America for attacks on Jews in the Soviet Union or the Middle East. Such were the JDL's tactics that mainstream Jewish organizations like the Anti-Defamation League not only shunned the group and its leader, but some openly accused it of terrorism.[12] Eventually the State Department would reach the same conclusion, putting the JDL on its list of terrorist organizations, and the courts would uphold that judgment.[13]

As JDL followers beat Arabs senseless with wooden clubs or bombed the office of the Soviet airline, Kahane would say he "approved of" such actions while offering pro forma denials of responsibility. In 1973 the FBI reported that JDL members had plotted to use "a drone airplane" to bomb the Soviet mission to the United Nations. A federal indictment of five JDL members accused them of using pipe bombs and firing shots into buildings in 1975 and 1976. Kahane meanwhile did jail time for arms smuggling. The bombers told themselves their zeal for terror was equivalent, in its way, to the actions of the Irgun and the Stern Gang when Israel was fighting for its independence in the 1940s. In 1979, Kahane's partisans talked about the need for an armed Jewish-American "underground" to "quietly and professionally eliminate those modern-day Hitlers who are becoming an ever-increasing threat to our existence."[14]

In the 1980s, Kahane was in and out of courts in Israel while his Kach party was in and out of the Knesset. In the Jewish state he found himself increasingly isolated from mainstream Jewish life. In 1988, Israel's election law banned Kach as a racist party. But in the United States the JDL kept going.

Kahane's hate-filled rhetoric might have inspired a few Jews with pride, but it galvanized a lot of Arabs with anger. Kahane told a college audience in California in 1988 that Arabs were "dogs" who "multiply like fleas" and they would have to be expelled from Israel or eliminated: "I don't intend to sit quietly by while Arabs intend to liquidate my state—either by bullets or by having babies." Proudly, he told the kids who were listening, "It's important that you know what the name 'Kahane' means to the Arabs. It means terror."[15]

Kahane was an irresistible target. An Arab who killed him might well expect the admiration of his people, and if a righteous murderer died in the process, he could count on a quick trip to paradise. A thirty-four-year-old Egyptian living in New Jersey thought so, in any case. His name was Sayyid el-Nosair.

In November 1990, Kahane was in New York addressing a small group calling itself the Zionist Emergency Evacuation Rescue Operation, in the Marriott Hotel on Lexington Avenue between Forty-eighth and Forty-ninth streets. Kahane was just sitting down at a table when a man walked up to him and fired at point-blank range with a .357 Magnum revolver. The bullet entered the left side of Kahane's neck and blew out the right cheek. As the gunman scrambled to make his escape, he bumped into an elderly bystander and shot him in the leg. Out on the street, whatever getaway plan he had fell apart. Witnesses outside the hotel saw him get in a cab and then jump out, surprised, as if it wasn't the one he wanted. On the run, literally, at Fifty-third Street and Third Avenue he tried to commandeer another taxi at gunpoint. But a postal service cop on duty in front of the big post office there drew on him and ordered him to freeze. The shooter winged the cop and the cop shot back, catching Sayyid el-Nosair with a bullet in the chin.[16]

El-Nosair was arrested on the spot, the .357 beside him. But, incredibly, the prosecutor couldn't make the murder charge stick. Although the room at the Marriott had several people in it, none of them seemed to have seen the killer pull the trigger. No paraffin tests were taken of El-Nosair's hands to link him to the revolver found next to him, an oversight that allowed his defense lawyers, William Kunstler and Ron Kuby, to claim the gun was a plant. "The police basically did not give us enough," one juror told *The New York Times*. "We felt there was evidence to find him guilty on some counts, but not enough to find him guilty of killing the rabbi. We could not speculate."[17]

In fact, El-Nosair was at the center of a small collection of Arabs and African-Americans who had been dreaming for several years of waging violent jihad somewhere against someone. They were disorganized and inept—almost literally a gang that couldn't shoot straight—but they were trying hard to learn. Several were associated with the Al-Kifah Refugee Center, which worked out of a mosque on Atlantic Avenue, recruiting fighters for the war against the Soviets and their puppets in Afghanistan. In 1988 the FBI-led Joint Terrorism Task Force got a tip that some of these men were training at shooting ranges. The FBI put the group under surveillance, and what followed is one of the sources of deep suspicion between the NYPD and the three-letter guys.

The night of the El-Nosair shooting, NYPD Lieutenant Eddie Norris went with police in New Jersey to search the suspect's apartment. Waiting there were a red-haired Egyptian named Mahmoud Abouhalima and an empty-eyed young Jordanian named Mohammed Salameh—yes, the same dim-witted Mohammed Salameh who would try, three years later, to get the deposit back on the Ryder truck blown up beneath the World Trade Center. Both men were cabdrivers and both admitted they were outside the Marriott that evening. Norris figured they were the ones El-Nosair was looking for. What Norris didn't know at the time was that the FBI had spotted them and photographed them along with El-Nosair at the shooting range.

Back on the thirteenth floor at One Police Plaza there was a meeting with the Feds. As Norris recounted the story later, the NYPD's chief of detectives asked him if he thought Nosair acted alone. "Absolutely not," said Norris. "We have two other people we think were involved."

"Shut up," said the chief. "You handle the murder. They"—he nodded toward the FBI guy—"handle the conspiracy."

"We have no evidence to indicate anyone else was involved," said the FBI agent.

Later on, the chief of detectives gave the Feds authorization to haul away twenty-four boxes of evidence Norris had stored in his office, much of it seized in El-Nosair's apartment. The agents came while the NYPD lieutenant was taking his lunch break. Norris later told the *New York Daily News* that aside from numerous documents in Arabic, the files contained a bomb manual, military training guides, and an assassination list. There were also photos of New York landmarks, reportedly including the World Trade Center.

In the "joint investigation" that followed, Norris found himself running down leads the FBI had checked already without informing the NYPD. Among the relevant bits of evidence not shared: a 1990 phone intercept of the blind Egyptian cleric Omar Abdel-Rahman talking to Nosair about "attacking big buildings," saying he should "attack skyscrapers."[18] Then a few days after the Feds walked out with the files, they lost control of them to Manhattan District Attorney Robert Morgenthau, who took over the Kahane case. He favored the lone gunman theory. His team wound up with the no-gunman verdict.

The conspirators kept at it. During El-Nosair's trial, his cousin Ibrahim el-Gabrowny traveled to Saudi Arabia to get a twenty-thousand-dollar contribution for the defense fund from a then-little-known jihadist named Osama bin Laden.[19] After El-Nosair was sent to Attica, Bin Laden's former private secretary, Wadi el-Hage, visited him there. The FBI tried to recruit Abouhalima. He blew them off. A former Egyptian military officer named Emad Salem, working as a paid informant for the FBI, penetrated the group and by several accounts helped to give it better structure and a stronger sense of purpose (sometimes the borderlines between informing, inciting, entrapping, and even organizing are very hard to discern). Then the FBI decided to take Salem off the payroll. He wasn't producing enough, said his handler.

With Salem gone, the would-be jihadists had to find another mastermind. Precisely how they made contact with Ramzi Yousef has never been made clear, but he wasted no time from the moment he landed in New York in September 1992 (dressed as an Afghan and claiming political asylum as an Iraqi refugee), until he had pulled together the elements of the first World Trade Center bombing in February 1993.

In the meantime, peace—or something that was supposed to be peace—had begun to take over the headlines in the Middle East. The Oslo Accords, signed by Yasir Arafat and Israeli Prime Minister Yitzhak Rabin on the White House lawn in September 1993, seemed to mark a whole new era of reasonable negotiations between Arabs and Israelis, and perhaps an era of good feelings, as well. But the followers of Kahane, whose party was now called Kahane Chai, "Kahane Lives," would have none of it. They and other zealots believed any talk of returning West Bank lands to Arab control was a betrayal of the nation and of God. Many of these rejectionists were from the United States, and in fact, from Brooklyn.

Whenever I would go to Israel in the early 1990s I would talk to the well-armed Flatbush-born settlers at their heavily guarded compounds in the middle of Arab cities like Nablus and Hebron, or at the freshly erected outposts on hilltops overlooking Arab villages. There was about these men and women a strange Wild West aura, a cowboys-and-redskins attitude that kept them running on zeal and adrenaline. I remember one settler from Brooklyn telling me, as we sat in a newly established outpost one evening with an Arab town squarely in our line of sight only a few hundred yards away, that what he really loved about this place was the sense that no other human beings were around.

On February 25, 1994, a Brooklyn-born physician named Baruch Goldstein, an ardent follower of Kahane and longtime resident of Kiryat Arba, a Jewish settlement near Hebron on the West Bank, made his way to the Cave of the Patriarchs, known to Muslims as the Ibrahimi Mosque. There are few places in the world with deeper histories of more profound religious significance. Tradition holds that Adam and Eve, Abraham and Sarah, Isaac and Rebecca, and Jacob and Leah all are buried in the caverns beneath the hillside. The rectangular stone walls around the entrance to the caves date to the time of Herod the

Great; other parts of the structure were erected by the Byzantines. Salah el-Din built the minarets at the corners.

Like the Temple Mount and surrounding city of Jerusalem, the Cave of the Patriarchs and the city of Hebron are at the center of those millennial narratives in which each faith remembers its victimization and claims vengeance as self-defense. In 1929, during the British mandate over Palestine, sixty-seven Jews in Hebron were slaughtered and the rest evacuated. For centuries before that, Muslim rulers had prevented Jews from entering the mosque. After the 1967 war, one of the first Israeli settlements established in the West Bank was in the heart of Hebron. The interior of the mosque was divided to allow both Jews and Muslims places of worship.

Dr. Baruch Goldstein, whose faith had brought him from Brooklyn to Israel and whose pioneering zeal had brought him to Hebron, could not bear the presence of Muslims at the Cave of the Patriarchs—the cave of *his* patriarchs. Nor could he endure the talk of a peace that would surrender control of Hebron to Arabs once again. So Goldstein plotted his attack and waited for a propitious moment. During the Muslim holy month of Ramadan, the mosque would be filled with worshippers. The date he chose also coincided with the Jewish festival of Purim, commemorating the defeat of a plot to slaughter the Jews in ancient Persia.

On February 25, 1994, Goldstein went to the mosque in his Israeli Defense Force uniform carrying his American-made M-16 assault rifle, a weapon that settlers wear easily and everywhere. He entered the room where hundreds of men were crowded together at prayer. "We were down on the floor and we heard shooting," one survivor told me the next day. "If you see the mosque, it is like when they were slaughtering sheep," said a twenty-three-year-old with bullet wounds in his legs. People lay down flat, hoping to avoid the fusillade, but that only made them easier targets. Emptying one clip after another, Goldstein sprayed one hundred and nineteen bullets into the crowd in a matter of seconds, killing twenty-nine people and wounding a hundred and fifty before one of the Palestinians managed to hit him with a fire extinguisher (none of the Arabs were armed), and others crowded in to bludgeon the doctor to death, ending the shooting.[20] Shortly afterward, Goldstein's wife tried unsuccessfully to have his killers charged with murder. A monument to his bravery was erected by other settlers at Kiryat Arba.

The slaughter at the Cave of the Patriarchs inflamed the whole Muslim world, but the first real violence outside the Holy Land came on the Brooklyn Bridge four days later, when someone opened fire on a van packed with fifteen rabbinical students headed from Manhattan to the Lubavitcher Hasidic movement's headquarters in Crown Heights. The killer sprayed them with fire from a submachine gun, then pursued them across the bridge, shooting from his blue Chevrolet with a pistol as they tried to flee. One of the students, sixteen-year-old Aaron Halberstam, was killed. Another suffered massive brain damage. Two others were injured less seriously.

The incident happened at about 10:25 in the morning within a few hundred yards of the FBI offices at 26 Federal Plaza and in sight of NYPD headquarters at One Police Plaza, but the shooter got away.

His name, in fact, was Rashid "Ray" Baz, the son of a Druse father and Palestinian mother in Lebanon who had fled the violence there to become a gypsy cabdriver for the Pioneer Car Service in Brooklyn. He had a reputation as a hothead, but not a Muslim fundamentalist firebrand. Whatever anger had been building inside him for whatever reasons, the Hebron killings set him off. During his shooting spree that morning, he blew out part of his own windshield and one of the windows in his Chevy. When he pulled off the bridge he drove straight to Hilal Auto Repair in Red Hook and told the mechanic there, an Egyptian immigrant named Amir Abudaif whom he'd dealt with many times before, that he needed the brakes fixed. He also told Abudaif, "I've just killed four Jews on the Brooklyn Bridge."

The mechanic, now very scared, took a quick look at the brakes and said they seemed okay to him. Apparently Baz wanted the car up on the rack as quickly as possible so passersby wouldn't see the bullet-shattered glass. Baz grabbed a gun off the front seat and pointed it at the mechanic. "Fix the brakes!" he shouted.

As soon as Abudaif could mollify Baz and get away, he went to a nearby Dunkin' Donuts and called the FBI, offering to help capture the shooter from the bridge. But the agent on the phone wanted information, lots of information, and Abudaif was terrified he'd be discovered while trying to answer all the questions. "Forget about it," he said and hung up. Then he tried again from another phone. The second FBI agent said he would send someone to meet Abudaif at the corner of Eleventh Avenue and Sixty-ninth Street in Dyker Heights at seven that night, many hours later. Abudaif went and waited, but nobody showed up.

Finally Abudaif went to the NYPD's Sixty-second Precinct station house in Bensonhurst at about eleven at night and began telling his story to a civilian near the entrance. The civilian seemed uninterested and gave him papers to fill out. A reward had been offered, which always attracts crackpots. Disappointed and desperate, the young Egyptian was getting ready to leave when a cop in plain clothes caught some of what he was saying and took him straight to a lieutenant. "I told him I know who shot the kids on the bridge," Abudaif later testified in court. "I handed him a handful of spent shell casings I had taken from the car and told him the car's license plate number." The cops took Abudaif to the Pioneer Car Service, where he fingered the suspect. "That's Ray," he said, "the guy who shot the kids."[21]

Precisely forty days after the Hebron massacre, when the period of mourning for those slaughtered in the mosque came to an end, the Islamic zealots of Hamas carried out their first suicide attack—the first of so very many—inside Israel.[22]

Three years later, a young Palestinian from Hebron came within hours of carrying out the first suicide attack in the New York City subway. The case was another of those near-miss precedents largely forgotten outside the NYPD, and half-forgotten inside. But as the tempo of bombing in Israel picked up in the spring of 2002, the record of the attack that nearly succeeded in Brooklyn in 1997 seemed full of portentous warnings. Not least was the fact that, like the arrest of Ray Baz in 1994, the capture of the suicide bombers in 1997 owed more to divine providence than solid police work. "The information received, some people attribute to good luck and good fortune," Mayor Rudolph Giuliani said afterward, putting an elegant spin on the facts. "Some people attribute it to an act of God, or maybe to an act of a conscience that ultimately unites all men and women when they realized that beyond racial, religious, ethnic, and even political differences, we are all united as people and human beings and that we have to protect each other and help each other."

In fact, the city was spared because an Egyptian university graduate recently arrived in the United States after winning a green card through the State Department's lottery system had wound up sharing a small, filthy apartment in a makeshift structure behind a Park Slope tenement on Fourth Avenue with several other Arab immigrants. The living conditions were horrendous in the dead of summer, the rooms airless, putrid with the smell of garbage—much like what Jacob Riis had described in the alleys of lower Manhattan a century before. But after the extraordinary good luck of winning legal entry to the United States, Abdel Rahman Mosabbah was willing to endure. All he wanted to do was earn enough money to bring his wife and children to join him, and to stay out of trouble. He had no idea he was about to be caught up in the Middle East conflict.

On the morning of July 30, 1997, in faraway Jerusalem, however, two suicide bombers detonated their explosive vests in the packed Mahane Yehuda market, killing sixteen people and wounding one hundred and seventy-eight. And that night in Park Slope one of Mosabbah's roommates, a young Palestinian named Gazi Abu Mezer, to whom he rarely spoke and whom he hardly knew, proudly showed him something he'd constructed in a satchel with bits and pieces from hardware stores. There were segments of pipe about five inches long wrapped with four-inch nails. Wires ran from them to toggle switches and nine-volt batteries.[23] Inside the pipes was gunpowder bought on a short trip to North Carolina (no need to home-brew TATP when you can get the good stuff over the counter). "Did you see what happened in Jerusalem?" the Palestinian asked. "Well, tomorrow it will happen here."[24]

Abu Mezer's personal odyssey to Brooklyn made disconcerting reading at the time and seems appalling today. He had applied for asylum in the United States after repeated failures to get a legal visa or to sneak into the country from Canada. He said on his asylum application he feared persecution in Israel because he was identified as a member of

Hamas, but that really he wasn't. Thus was he able to plot mass murder in New York City while waiting for the federal bureaucracy to process his various applications.

Abu Mezer's plan was to emulate a favorite Hamas tactic: two bombs in quick succession. The first would go off and create mayhem, while the second, larger one would detonate as people tried to rescue the dead and wounded. As his sidekick, Abu Mezer had enlisted another Palestinian roommate, Lafi Khalil, who came from a relatively well-to-do family near Ramallah.

The two Palestinians planned to target the crowded transportation hub underground at the Atlantic Avenue stop, where the commuter trains of the Long Island Rail Road and six subway lines come together. With luck, they hoped to get on the B train, typically used by Orthodox and Hasidic Jews commuting from Brooklyn to work in the midtown diamond district. If the bombs could be set off while the cars were passing under the East River, rescue work would be complicated enormously. Scores of people would die, possibly hundreds. As the Egyptian Mosabbah listened dumfounded, Abu Mezer sprinkled some of the gunpowder on the floor and set it alight. "This is how the Jews will burn," he said.[25]

The young Egyptian excused himself to go for a walk. He was petrified. He wanted to warn somebody. But he had only been in the States a few weeks. He had no idea who to call or how to make himself understood. Outside the Atlantic Avenue station he saw two men in uniform standing near a white car with lights on top and the word "police" on the side. They weren't the FBI or the NYPD or the JTTF or the Marines or the Green Berets. They were a couple of young Long Island Rail Road cops making their rounds. Mosabbah tried to explain what he'd seen. He kept repeating the word *"bomba"* and making the noise of an explosion.

The clock was ticking on toward eleven and the LIRR cops might easily have turned Mosabbah away as another pitiful late-night nut case. But he was just so scared. Sweat poured off his body. "It was warm but not that hot," one of them said afterward. "Anyone who looked into his eyes that night would have known how serious he was."[26] Instead of sending him on his way, the LIRR cops accompanied Mosabbah to the Eighty-eighth Precinct house, where detectives left him sitting alone in an interview room while they tried to figure out what to do with him. Finally, they called One Police Plaza. Alerts went out, the brass came in. The members of the Emergency Service Unit got ready in case Mosabbah's story turned out to be true and they had to lay a siege or storm the bombers' apartment. But nobody could really figure out what Mosabbah was saying. Eventually a rookie cop with a North African background from the Thirteenth Precinct near Gramercy Park was hauled over to Brooklyn to translate, but the two men didn't speak the same dialects and communication remained excruciatingly imprecise. Hours later, an FBI translator was rousted out of bed, but he arrived slowly and reluctantly at the scene.

Mosabbah described the devices Abu Mezer had shown him in as much detail as he could. He drew a diagram of his apartment showing where everyone slept. But doubts about his story continued. It was almost five in the morning, seven hours after he had first made contact with the police and just ninety minutes before the B train would be packed with commuters, that the armored and helmeted team from the Emergency Service Unit opened the door of the apartment with Mosabbah's key and crept inside.

Abu Mezer grabbed the first cop who came into his bedroom. The E-man fired his pistol without hesitation. The first shot grazed Abu Mezer's face, then a second one hit him in the midsection and threw him back across the room. Khalil dived for the bomb, but the cop caught him with two rounds and took him down. A second E-man was now through the door of the room. He pumped another round into each of the Palestinians.[27]

In the end, both of the would-be Muslim martyrs survived. Everybody in the room survived. But it was a miracle. If Abu Mezer had not bragged to the Egyptian, if the Egyptian had not gone for the police, if the LIRR cops had not taken him to the NYPD and if the NYPD brass had not acted on the sketchy information he was providing through unreliable translators, if Mosabbah's descriptions of the rooms and the bomb had not been so accurate, if Abu Mezer or Khalil had moved a little faster—those were not the kind of ifs you liked to think about. And even five years later when Cohen came to the NYPD there was no good answer to the most central question of all: did somebody send Abu Mezer to New York as a terrorist, or did he just get worked up on his own?

Samuel M. Katz, who has written the most thorough account of the case in his book *Jihad in Brooklyn,* leaves the question up in the air: Mezer had thrown rocks at the Israelis, he had been in and out of Israeli jails, and he had connections not only to Hamas sympathizers but to people who knew how to build bombs to Hamas specifications. In the trash outside his house police found the torn pieces of a two-page handwritten note laying out all the components and how to put them together.[28] But when Abu Mezer lived in Hebron, he hung out with the more secular boys around the Popular Front for the Liberation of Palestine. His efforts to enter the United States had been determined but disorganized. When he was detained by the Immigration and Naturalization Service he posted a five-thousand-dollar bail with money sent from Saudi Arabia through the informal *hawala* system, which leaves no paper trail. But *hawala* transfers are used by immigrants from the Middle East and South Asia whether they are terrorists, trash collectors, or, for that matter, doctoral students.

If all these ifs and unknowns still applied to a bomb plot in 1997, what dangers waited for New York in 2002 as the thunderous drumbeat of suicide blasts continued to build in Israel? Suicide bombers attacked there on March 2, March 5, and March 7. On March 9 they hit the laid-back Café Moment in the heart of West Jerusalem, killing eleven people and wounding fifty-four, only about a hundred yards from the prime minister's residence. More suicide bombings came on March 17, March 20, March 21, and then, on March 27 at a Passover holiday seder at the Park Hotel in Netanya, a bomber walked in carrying a suitcase that blew up in the middle of the crowd. Thirty were killed and a hundred and forty injured. Mostly they were old people; several of them had survived the Holocaust.

William Nolte, the deputy assistant director of Central Intelligence, was a little surprised to hear Cohen's voice on the phone. "Hi, David, what can I do for you?" Cohen came right to the point. He was looking for some of the information he didn't have about the whos and hows of the suicide attacks in Israel. This stuff could mean life or death for the people of New York City, and in his new job, they were his responsibility. Nolte, an old friend and colleague from the Directorate for Intelligence, said he'd see what he could do. He'd get back to him.

The next morning, Nolte got another call from Cohen. "Did you get me that stuff I asked for?" he asked.

"I'm sorry, David, they haven't gotten back to me."

"I knew it! Hah! I knew that's the way it would be," said Cohen. "But I got it already." Apparently he had gone straight to the source: Israel.

Cohen's old employers were about to get information that he needed even more urgently. Hours after the Netanya bombing,[29] as it happened, CIA operatives thousands of miles away in Pakistan captured a man they thought held the keys to Al Qaeda—"the concierge," as one jihadist who knew him told me—Abu Zubaydah himself. At secret locations in Afghanistan and Thailand, interrogators and psychologists, contractors and physicians were about to start wringing him out like a towel twisted until it dries. He would be talking about plots and plotters. Sometimes he would talk about New York City. And no threat seemed greater, barely six months after 9/11, than what Al Qaeda planners liked to call "the second wave."[30] The NYPD needed to know everything. And it would.

THE BLACK SITES

Ways of Making Them Talk

There were so many blind spots, so many new threats, as if September 11 had opened a seismic fissure in some lunatic netherworld and pure evil poured out. Starting just a week after the attacks on New York and Washington, someone mailed envelopes laced with anthrax to journalists in New York City and Florida and then to senators in D.C. The bacterial spores infected twenty-two people; five of them died. All of the letters appear to have been sent from Princeton, New Jersey, and all concluded with the same message:

> DEATH TO AMERICA.
> DEATH TO ISRAEL.
> ALLAH IS GREAT.

But the rest of the wording suggested someone trying to sound like a jihadist, not a genuine *mujahid* steeped in the pious rhetoric of radicalism—perhaps someone trying to warn the United States of vast horrors to come by giving it a little taste of mass destruction: "09-11-01 . . . THIS IS NEXT. . . . TAKE PENACILIN NOW," read the first notes. "YOU CAN NOT STOP US. . . . WE HAVE THIS ANTHRAX. . . . YOU DIE NOW. . . . ARE YOU AFRAID?" read the second ones. Investigators traced the bacteria's DNA to a strain that originated at the U.S. Army's biological weapons research facility at Fort Detrick, Maryland, and an American scientist eventually was named as "a person of interest" to the investigation, but the case went cold.[1]

Then in December 2001, just three days before Christmas, American Airlines Flight 63 from Paris to Miami made an emergency landing in Boston. Two female flight attendants had discovered a thoroughly unsavory-looking passenger holding one of his thick-soled trainers on his lap and trying to light a fuse attached to it. He was a big guy, more than six feet tall, but one of the women tried to grab the shoe away from him with all the ferocity of an insulted schoolmistress. He bit her thumb. She screamed for help. Finally other passengers subdued him, tied him up with seat-belt extensions, and tranquilized him with Valium from the first-aid kit.

The terrorist's goofy face and the general weirdness of the incident would give comedy writers something to joke about on late-night talk shows, but all one hundred and ninety-eight people on that Boeing 767 came very close to dying that day. "The Shoe Bomber" Richard Reid was a half-Jamaican, half-English convert to Islam who fancied himself a tough guy (as his pseudonym he used the name Van Damme, after the Belgian star of martial-arts B movies, Jean-Claude Van Damme). The sole of his shoe had been cobbled out of the plastic explosive component PETN, with a detonator made of that terrorist favorite, TATP. If Reid had had a cigarette lighter instead of crappy matches from a cheap hotel, he would have blown the plane apart high over the Atlantic, where traces of the bomb and the way it was smuggled aboard would have been all but impossible to find. We might still be trying to solve the mystery of what happened.

In the immediate, uncertain aftermath of those crimes, Ray Kelly's basic goal was to know everything about *anything* that could threaten New York City. Clearly the big danger remained Osama bin Laden and his fellow travelers on the jihadist trail. But the sixteen branches of the federal government's "intelligence community"—the FBI, CIA, NSA, and others—were jealous of one another and essentially contemptuous of local police, including the NYPD. It was a story as old as terrorism. And they had a lock on the surveillance and spying both at home and abroad to which Kelly's force needed instant access. No matter how much Kelly reorganized his shop, the three-letter guys weren't going to open up theirs unless he could crack the federal bureaucracy.

In the spring of 2002, as fears grew that Osama bin Laden was positioning his assets for a new strike at the United States, and very likely at New York City, there was no time to lose. "We brought on tough professionals," Kelly said proudly as he looked back on those early days. They were all experienced men, picked not least because they knew how to batter their way through the federal labyrinth. "We wanted information—and we got it any way we could get it," Kelly told me. "We were grabbing it and pushing it and shoving it."

Kelly appointed as deputy commissioner for counterterrorism Frank Libutti, a retired lieutenant general from the Marine Corps who "had a lot of credibility, a lot of gravitas." As Kelly saw it, the situation inside the FBI-run Joint Terrorism Task Force was a "total catastrophe." So Libutti got the job of packing scores more NYPD detectives into the JTTF and bringing them under his direct supervision. "Just by sheer presence we were getting information," Kelly said. But the FBI was all about catching criminals after the fact, and that just wasn't going to be enough.

Terrorists had to be spotted and caught, or at least scared off, *before* they acted. Anticipation and prevention had to take precedence over arrest and conviction. And in Kelly's scheme of things, that's precisely where Cohen came in. Not only could he organize a police intelligence division with extraordinary capabilities of its own, he could tap into Langley directly. "Dave has, of course, great contacts with the CIA," Kelly told me. The FBI and the CIA were notoriously bad about communicating with each other, as *The 9/11 Commission Report* and subsequent investigations would document in excruciating detail.[2] But the NYPD was out to get solid information from both. "In the early days, we've got it coming in from a lot of different sources. That's what we wanted," said Kelly. "So we're getting it through the JTTF, we're getting it through other federal sources. So, were we in the loop? Yes. And when we weren't in the loop we complained." He smiled. "And we had enough clout to stay in the loop."

"We knew everything," Cohen told me when I asked him about those early years. In fact, the NYPD had worked out a very special relationship with the CIA.

Cohen declined to go into details, perhaps because a key figure was another veteran from the Agency who managed to join the NYPD without actually leaving the CIA. Lawrence H. "Larry" Sanchez and Cohen had been acquainted through the years at Langley. They had not liked each other. Sanchez was one of the people from the Operations Directorate who thought Cohen's name was "Fucking." But they got to know each other better when Sanchez was the Agency's main man at the United Nations and Cohen was running the Agency's office in New York City.

Physically it would be hard to imagine two men more different in appearance and personal style. Where Cohen is quintessentially gray, fading into the background, Sanchez is square-built, thick-necked, and bullet-headed, with "powerlifting and boxing titles," according to one brief biography, and qualification as a master scuba diver.[3] He's also an accomplished and extremely competitive skydiver whose body, as a result, is wired together in several places. Having joined the CIA as an intelligence officer in 1984, he served in Afghanistan and Egypt before returning to Langley to serve as assistant to Executive Director Nora Slatkin while Cohen was DDO. In 1998 Sanchez was seconded from CIA to the Department of Energy to head its Office of Intelligence. Sanchez was supposed to try to clean up the mess created by the hunt for a mole suspected of giving China critical atomic secrets.

The point man on that same investigation was an FBI agent described in one press report as "an espionage troubleshooter": Edward J. Curran—the same FBI agent accused by veteran CIA operatives of laying to waste the clandestine services of the Agency after the Aldrich Ames case in the early 1990s. Detailed to DOE as head of counterintelligence, Curran had inherited a botched inquiry in which the main suspect, a Chinese-American scientist at Los Alamos named Wen Ho Lee, learned before he should have that he was under suspicion.

(In the end, Sanchez and Curran at DOE and several agents from the FBI never found enough evidence to mount a prosecution for espionage in a case that seemed of enormous importance to national security. Had the Chinese really gotten their hands on crucial details of nuclear weapon design? Wen Ho Lee took a plea-bargain deal for mishandling classified documents on his office computer.[4] Was there someone else feeding the Chinese vital information about the W88 warhead? If such a person was found, he was neither named nor prosecuted.)

By the spring of 2002 it was time for Sanchez to wrap up at DOE, and his old friend Cohen went to see him. Cohen wanted him to join his shop at the NYPD in a very particular capacity. The deal struck with Langley would detail Sanchez to the NYPD to be "the CIA's guy in New York City on terrorism," as one of his colleagues put it. This would be in addition to anything the CIA was doing with the JTTF, where relationships were still "in the process of building, changing, evolving, whatever," according to the same cop. Sanchez's job was to provide the New York City Police with everything they needed to know to make their program effective, including "all the detainee debriefings." "Do you know what Larry means to me?" Cohen told one of his colleagues long afterward. "Without him in those days, I would have had nothing, *nothing* to show Kelly."

Through the Sanchez connection, as well as his own contacts and his own analysis, Cohen kept Kelly informed about the size, nature, evolution, and mutations of the Al Qaeda threat—at least insofar as anyone could make them out. The ability of Bin Laden's followers to adapt and learn stunned the intelligence analysts, especially in the first two years after 9/11. "Their capacity to respond to situations was phenomenal," as one put it, and what were called "the detainee reports" seemed the only way to keep track of that evolution.[5] "We were able to stay ahead of it in New York City," said the same analyst, "because we had access." But the information was often obscure and occasionally delphic. By way of example, Kelly recalled, "We had 'the bridge in the Godzilla movie.' "

The public probably never will see the suffering or hear the screams of Abu Zubaydah. The CIA destroyed the tapes. And maybe "scream" is not really the right word. What does a man sound like when cloth has been wrapped around his eyes and nose and mouth and he is strapped to a tabletop or to boards so that his feet are higher than his head, which is completely immobilized, and then . . . someone starts to pour water onto his bound face? He cannot see it coming and then, when it does, he feels like he is drowning, smothering, choking all at once. The technique used by the Americans was carefully—one hesitates to say "scientifically"—designed not to kill. By one account Saran Wrap or a similar plastic film was placed across the mouth so water wouldn't actually go into the lungs. But the air would be cut off, the gag reflex triggered, and panic would set in immediately. Before the technique could be administered (reportedly by CIA officers or contractors who had trained for several weeks in this and similar inquisitional arts), top officials at the Agency, including the deputy director for Operations, had to sign off on it.[6] Whether or not it was legal, it was all extra legalistic.

The writings of the neoconservative brains behind the secret executive lawmaking of the Bush administration would make "waterboarding" seem a limited and almost innocuous measure, a mere simulation of drowning and, indeed, a paradigm for torture lite that would be called, in the jargon of the moment, an "enhanced interrogation technique."[7] One infamous memorandum, written by the Justice Department's Office of Legal Counsel after Abu Zubaydah's initial interrogations, pretended to justify any method that did not result in organ failure or death.[8]

None of this torture was the responsibility of the NYPD. Far from it. Yet the intelligence product that came out of it was potentially vital to the puzzle the cops were trying to fit together. Abu Zubaydah was supposed to be a prize catch for the CIA, and waterboarding was supposed to have worked on him very effectively.

Reports that came out about Abu Zubaydah's interrogation clocked his time on the board at under a minute. One said that he lasted precisely thirty-one seconds.[9] And then he talked and talked. "In the next day or so," as a CIA veteran who was on the case at the time claimed to ABC News, "he told his interrogator that Allah had visited him in his cell during the night and told him to cooperate because his cooperation would make it easier on the other brothers who had been captured. And from that day on he answered every question just like I'm sitting here speaking to you."[10] But even if that is the case, you have to wonder: Of the many things he said, how could you know which ones were true and which false? Certainly some of the things said about Abu Zubaydah just after his capture did not ring true at all.

Zayn Al Abidin Muhammad Husayn, for such was the birth name of Abu Zubaydah, was a man who clearly had connections. I'd been hearing about him for years. His nom de guerre had come up in the case of an Al Qaeda facilitator named Fateh Kamel, whose case I'd covered in Paris, one of so many money movers, people smugglers, forgers, and petty criminals across Europe who helped would-be fighters make their way to wherever the jihad seemed hottest, whether Afghanistan, Bosnia, Chechnya, or eventually Iraq.[11] The name of Abu Zubaydah also loomed large in the testimony of Ahmed Ressam, the Algerian caught trying to smuggle explosives into the United States to blow up part of Los Angeles International Airport in 1999 on the eve of the millennium. In Jordan, the courts convicted Abu Zubaydah in absentia of plots to carry out terrorist attacks against tourist hotels. But court records and Arab intelligence agencies tell you only so much. A veteran of the Arab Afghan movement in the 1980s and early 1990s gave me a clearer idea of the man.

Abu Zubaydah had been another of those kids throwing rocks in the 1987 Intifadah against Israeli occupation in Gaza and the West Bank. Then he joined the battle against the Soviet occupiers of Afghanistan just as it was drawing to a close in the late 1980s and new battles were beginning among the mujahideen themselves. My Arab *muj* acquaintance knew Abu Zubaydah well in those days. He didn't consider him a leader, but a recruiter and fund-raiser who sometimes traveled in the guise of a merchant selling Afghan honey.[12] Abu Zubaydah's main function, in fact, was running guest houses in Pakistan for jihadists on their way to the Khalden training camp in Afghanistan. Was he "the number three in Al Qaeda," as the White House wanted to claim and many journalists repeated after his capture? Not by a long shot.

Then again, if you want to know about the people who pass through a hotel, you don't ask the owner, you ask the guy at the desk. In that

sense, Abu Zubaydah knew a lot. The frustrating problem for interrogators was the way he talked—even the way he thought. He liked to
write poetry and he tried to look at the world as a poet would.[13] He kept
a diary in the voices of three different people that told the story of his
quotidian travails with wannabe mujahideen. And then there were the
physical problems. He still had shrapnel in his head from a war wound
in the early 1990s that, he said, impaired his memory. And he almost
died the night he got caught. Fleeing a Pakistani special operations team
working with the CIA and the FBI in the city of Faisalabad, he jumped
off the roof of the villa where he was staying and took three shots to his
gut, his groin, and his leg.[14]

Five years after Abu Zubaydah's capture, when he appeared before
a military commission hearing "on board U.S. Naval Base Guantánamo
Bay, Cuba" (the heavily censored transcript of which was the closest
he'd come to making a public appearance), he did not plead for his life
or his freedom, but for the return of the diary he had kept for half of his
life: "When they take it, I feel they take my child." He also begged for
socks, which apparently are forbidden to prisoners at Guantánamo. He
told the commission he had lost one of his testicles and that his left thigh
"is not complete."[15] Abu Zubaydah said he often had chills and seizures
and tried to keep his left foot warm by putting the skullcap he used for
prayers inside his shoe. One of the Bush administration techniques for
"enhanced" interrogation is to keep a suspect standing and sleepless
for days at a time. In Abu Zubaydah's case, that would have been more
excruciating than the waterboard.

The president of the Guantánamo commission, an air force colonel,
asked Abu Zubaydah directly about the treatment he'd gotten before
his transfer to Guantánamo in September 2006. "In your statement,
you mentioned months of torture," said the colonel. "Has anything that
you provided us today regarding your written statements [been] related
to those times that you have been tortured?"[16]

"No," said Abu Zubaydah, but the rest of his reply about what had
come before is suddenly much more rambling than other passages in the
transcript. Given that it is delivered in halting English and censored in
several places, it is hard to tell, reading it on the page, just how much
of the incoherence comes from the way his body and soul react to the

memory of trauma. But the essential point comes through clearly: Abu Zubaydah would have said anything to get his interrogators to stop the torture.

"I was not afraid to die, because I do believe I will be *shahid* [a martyr]," he said, but "as God make me as a human and I weak," he went on, he would do whatever his interrogators told him to do. They kept demanding more information. "I say, 'Yes, I was a partner of Bin Laden [REDACTED] and I am partner of Ressam.' I say, 'Okay, but leave me.' " The interrogators would write that down. "But they want what's after, more information about more operations, [but] I can't." According to Abu Zubaydah's testimony at Guantánamo, he and Bin Laden had fallen out to such an extent that Bin Laden closed down the Khalden camp in 2000. Bin Laden didn't approve training facilities that were not under his direct control, and Abu Zubaydah and the others who actually ran the camp would not subordinate themselves.

As years passed and other figures were captured, the U.S government stopped talking about Abu Zubaydah as if he were of vital importance to Al Qaeda. In 2006 the carefully hedged biography of High Value Detainee Abu Zubaydah prepared by the Director of National Intelligence called him merely "a leading extremist facilitator." It noted that when he was captured he was raising money for an attack on Israel that he was trying to coordinate with the Jordanian terrorist known as Abu Mus'ab al-Zarqawi, who was soon to become infamous in Iraq and eventually died there. But in 2002 both of them were independent operators who had never pledged allegiance to Bin Laden. Yes, it was true that Ressam and three of the 9/11 hijackers had received training at one of the camps where Abu Zubaydah worked, but as he told the Guantánamo commission, the camps were like "supermarkets." People came and trained and took away from the experience what they wanted. According to the DNI biography, published almost five years after the event, and four years after his much-heralded capture, Abu Zubaydah was "not believed to be directly linked to the attacks on 11 September 2001."[17]

So in those first days of captivity, what did Abu Zubaydah talk about? In the first hours, badly wounded, covered in blood, tied down with torn sheets on a bed in a Faisalabad hospital, he asked the CIA interrogator to smother him with a pillow. The interrogator declined, of course. The smothering would come later, on the waterboard. Before the torture began, Abu Zubaydah talked philosophy, poetry, and elementary metaphysics. "He was a very friendly guy," the interrogator, John Kiriakou, said several years later, but "he was unwilling to give us any actionable intelligence."[18] Then he was taken to one of the CIA's ultrasecret "black sites," which had been set up in Thailand, Poland, Jordan, and elsewhere specifically to keep prisoners beyond the reach of American law or mercy. Once he'd been tortured he seems to have started talking about anything he'd ever heard or imagined; he was talking too much, in fact. Dan Coleman, the FBI's lead authority on Bin Laden at the time, looked over Abu Zubaydah's diary and other papers and concluded, "This guy is insane, certifiable, split personality."[19]

The headline in the *New York Post* on May 22, 2002, helped set a paranoid mood in the city as the Memorial Day weekend approached: "Lady Liberty in the Cross Hairs—B'klyn Bridge Also a Target: Terror Stoolie."[20] The public was only just beginning to get used to the way Kelly poured police through the streets in frequent shows of force. Cops suddenly seemed to be everywhere. Kelly stationed an Emergency Service Unit truck—what other police forces would call a SWAT team—on the bridge itself. Choppers fluttered overhead. Police boats patrolled conspicuously.

The information that two of New York's most famous landmarks might be targeted by a new Al Qaeda plot was first reported to have come from an unnamed detainee at Guantánamo, but then, quickly, it was attributed to Abu Zubaydah singing his poetic heart out at one of the CIA's secret facilities.[21] Indeed, he seemed to have the American government dancing to his incoherent tune. For weeks, each vague warning of potential threats to oil refineries and nuclear power plants, each hint of plots to put poison gas in office building air ducts, shoot down U.S. airplanes with shoulder-mounted missiles, or to send suicide bombers into the midst of American crowds had spiked the adrenaline levels in Washington. Now Abu Zubaydah had spit out something about plans to attack "the statue in the water," which seemed fairly straightforward, and he talked about hitting "the bridge in the Godzilla movie."

That reference was to the 1998 Roland Emmerich remake of the campy Japanese imports of an earlier generation. When the film came out in the States it sank faster than a dead dinosaur in New York Harbor. But like some of Emmerich's other apocalyptic epics (notably *Independence Day*, in which the White House and other monuments are blasted by alien death rays), it was huge with Third World audiences. In Pakistan and Afghanistan people watched it on pirated videotapes. They loved the spectacles of destruction, and some of Al Qaeda's acolytes clearly found them inspirational. At the end of *Godzilla*, the enormous monster is lured onto the Brooklyn Bridge, where he is ensnared by the web of suspension cables, almost bringing down the entire structure before he is finally killed by jet fighters. Abu Zubaydah's interrogators, none of whom actually had seen that box-office bomb, reportedly had to rent a tape to figure this out.[22]

As the Memorial Day weekend came and went without any terrorist attacks or any evidence of specific plots, doubts grew among the press and public about the seriousness of the threat. Under the glare of growing skepticism, the Bush administration and New York Mayor Michael Bloomberg started sniping at each other. So did the FBI and the NYPD. It suited some in the federal government to make it seem as if the city authorities just couldn't be trusted with "unsubstantiated and uncorroborated information" that the FBI had shared with them "out of an abundance of caution." *Newsweek,* apparently drawing on FBI sources, reported, "The Feds, using arcane lingo, told the locals that they were going to put out a 'terror line' on the threat. If the warning was 'above' the line, it could be released to the public; anything 'below' the line had to be kept quiet. But the jargon confused the New York cops, who believed they'd been authorized to spread it around."[23]

What Kelly believed, in fact, was that he couldn't take chances, so he drew a line in the asphalt instead of the shifting bureaucratic sand. He had his secret CIA channel taking shape to help him decide how serious the threat was, or was not, and he judged it was worth making a show of force, even if that made the public a little nervous. "There are notions, concepts, ideas out there that we have to be aware of," Kelly told the press. Al Qaeda's Afghan camps had trained people who were now in place in the United States and they might have operational instructions. "We think this detainee has some credibility," said the NYPD commissioner.

Kelly suggested the abundance of overstatement was in Washington. There, the drumbeat had been going on for weeks. In rapid succession one administration official after another had raised alarms. New attacks, said Vice President Dick Cheney, were "not a matter of if, but when." There were real fears, to be sure, heightened by a sample of anthrax found in an Al Qaeda house in Afghanistan and the dissemination of nuclear weapons technology by a network of scientists based in Pakistan and Europe.[24] But Bush administration officials also were going out of their way—way out of their way—to push their theory that the greatest danger to the United States lay not with creative low-budget terrorists like the 9/11 hijackers, whose only weapons of mass destruction were box cutters, but with the Axis of Evil—North Korea, Iran, and most especially Iraq—denounced by President Bush in his State of the Union address a couple of months earlier. As Defense Secretary Donald Rumsfeld put it to the Senate on May 21, "We have to recognize that terrorist networks have relationships with terrorist states that have weapons of mass destruction, and that they inevitably are going to get their hands on them, and they would not hesitate one minute in using them."

"Inevitably"—that was the key word.

Adding to the sense of confusion and fear was the frantic way the Feds tried to cover their asses. News had broken that FBI higher-ups, including the Osama bin Laden Unit and the Radical Fundamentalist Unit at FBI headquarters, had ignored a potentially vital memo from the Phoenix office that tried to raise an alarm about the "possibility of a coordinated effort by Osama bin Laden" to send students to flight schools in the United States, then use them to carry out terrorist attacks. The frighteningly prescient memo, sent in July 2001, wasn't even read at FBI headquarters until after September 11. It had also been sent to two agents on international terrorism squads in the FBI's New York Field Office that summer. What they did about it was exactly nothing.[25]

So, when FBI Director Robert Mueller jumped on the paranoia bandwagon in May 2002 and told an audience in Virginia that new atrocities were "inevitable"—that "there will be another terrorist attack, we will not be able to stop it"—Ray Kelly found the remarks unhelpful.[26] "I would not have used the word 'inevitable,' " Kelly told reporters in a public rebuke to Mueller. "Certainly, after 9/11, anything is possible. [But] I think we are doing the best that we reasonably can to prevent another incident and to respond if, God forbid, there is one."[27]

In fact, a second wave of attacks on New York City and other American targets *was* being planned, and in many different forms. Even if Abu Zubaydah could only half guess what was going on based on endless bull sessions with mujahideen passing through his guest house, he was close to the truth. He also gave up the name of an American, a Brooklyn-born, Chicago-raised former gang member named José Padilla, who might or might not be involved with new attacks, including one using a radiological bomb. (The witless Padilla was tailed from Pakistan to Chicago's O'Hare Airport and nailed as he got off the plane). And, most importantly, Abu Zubaydah confirmed something that analysts already suspected: The Al Qaeda operative who was being talked about in jihadist communications as Mukhtar—"the Brain"—was indeed the man behind 9/11, and his real name, already well known in counterterror circles, was Khalid Sheikh Mohammed.

THE SECOND WAVE

Not the Best-Laid Plans

"KSM was a strange one to me," Cohen said when we talked about Khalid Sheikh Mohammed's terrorist history and signatures. "He didn't swear allegiance to Al Qaeda and Bin Laden until very late in the game, as you know. He was kind of out there generating a lot of stuff, and it seems to me that he would be willing to commission lower-level work, and Bin Laden says, 'No, we want the really big one.' But I'm personally convinced that KSM would have been willing to commission a *lot* [of] lower-level stuff: 'Yeah, I like the planes. I'm going to do *them*. But there are other things we can do as well!' I think Bin Laden was sort of more purist. But I think the players below him and Zawahiri were much more willing to do second, third, and even fourth-tier terrorist events in terms of sponsoring, encouraging, saying, 'If you can pull this off, it's a good idea.' And a lot of them don't cost any money. Just do it.

"A guy like KSM was in the business of producing terrorist operations. That's what he did for a living, so to speak."

* * *

Khalid Sheikh Mohammed and members of his extended family created, in fact, the modern métier of terrorist impresario. His nephew, only three years younger, was the lean-faced and hungry-eyed Ramzi Yousef, who took the gang that couldn't shoot straight around Meir Kahane's assassin and organized it to build and detonate the enormous bomb beneath the World Trade Center in February 1993. Yousef and KSM together in the Philippines in December 1994 plotted "Operation Bojinka," the bombing of a dozen American-flag airliners taking off from different points in Asia while they were out over the Pacific.[1] An accidental fire in the apartment where KSM and his minions were brewing explosives attracted police attention. A laptop found there exposed their plans, and Yousef was caught shortly after that in Pakistan.[2] But KSM took refuge in Qatar for a while, holding down an office job with the Ministry of Electricity and Water. In 1996, as the Americans closed in on him, he made his escape to Afghanistan just at the moment the Taliban were taking over.[3]

KSM, unlike most of his cronies, had a firsthand feel for American life. In the mid-1980s, after graduating from high school in Kuwait, he enrolled at Chowan, a little Baptist junior college in Murfreesboro, North Carolina, which is set among farmers' fields about sixty miles southwest of Norfolk, Virginia. With a population of only two thousand people, it's a town proud of its few antebellum houses and its annual watermelon festival. The school didn't require proficiency in English, which may be one reason KSM applied. But it did insist on attendance at Sunday services in the Baptist church each week.

KSM didn't last long. He transferred after a semester to North Carolina Agricultural and Technical State University in somewhat more cosmopolitan Greensboro.[4] Among these North Carolina Aggies, and especially among fellow Muslims at the school, KSM came across as the class clown. He was religious, wore a long beard, and ate meat-free Whoppers because fast-food beef wasn't halal, but when he walked into a room he would just crack people up. Because his family came from Baluchistan and, yeah, because he had a little bit of that round-bodied, square-faced mien remembered from the late star of *Animal House*, classmates called him "B'lushi."[5]

The North Carolina years were not a bad time for KSM, by most accounts. He later said that he had no personal animus toward the United States, that he plotted 9/11 and persuaded Bin Laden to back it only because of his anger at American support for Israel.[6] But KSM certainly thought his time in Greensboro gave him special knowledge about how Americans lived, and how they could be killed, that few other Arab exiles in Afghanistan shared. Partly because KSM seemed to know how Americans thought, Bin Laden valued him as a media consultant.

During the planning for 9/11, whatever insights KSM had into the American mind and the American way of life were complemented by the intelligence and discipline of the lead hijacker, Mohammed Atta. The thin-lipped, ascetic young Egyptian stayed focused. He checked and rechecked every detail. But once Atta was gone, KSM quickly ran into problems pulling together the "second wave" of attacks on U.S. targets that he had planned. He simply made too many miscalculations. And the people he relied on made even more.

KSM had not expected the Trade Center towers to crumble as spectacularly and catastrophically as they did, or for so many people to die, and for that reason he hadn't anticipated an American counterattack on anything like the scale that toppled the Taliban and evicted Al Qaeda from its safe havens in Afghanistan. He hadn't counted on the extent to which new security measures would complicate hijackings. No more box cutters—not even nail clippers were allowed onto planes. All of a sudden, it became obvious the talent pool of people who could turn his grand visions into explosive realities just wasn't very deep.[7]

KSM had assumed from the start that anyone with a passport from an Arab country would be under such intense scrutiny by police and security after 9/11 that he or she would be useless for further missions inside the United States. In fact, KSM had planned the hijacking to focus future attention exclusively on Arabs, and not on other Muslims. Among those who took over the four planes on September 11, one was from Egypt, one was from Lebanon, two were from the United Arab Emirates, and the other fifteen, most of "the muscle" attacking and intimidating the crew and passengers, were Saudis.

For the second strike: no Saudis, and no Arabs at all. KSM wanted recruits whose passports came from France, Canada, Malaysia, or Indonesia.[8] He had started organizing this second mission in 1999, almost at the same time as the first. But months passed, and then years, and his Asian contacts didn't deliver. As the moment for the first strike approached, KSM had only two potential second-wave hijackers with the right profiles: a recently naturalized Canadian of Moroccan origin known as Faruq al-Tunisi[9] and a highly unstable French citizen of North African descent named Zacarias Moussaoui. Then Al-Tunisi backed out in the summer of 2001, and Moussaoui, unbeknownst to KSM, got himself arrested in Minnesota that same August.[10]

The evil genius of 9/11 had thought that for the second wave security might be more lax on the West Coast than the East, so he'd toyed with the idea of flying planes into the Library Tower in downtown Los Angeles and a high-rise bank in Seattle. He also liked the idea of hitting the Sears Tower in Chicago—but New York still tempted him. He wanted to take a shot at the Empire State.[11]

Now all those plans had to be dropped. So he shifted gears and pulled together the shoe-bomb plot with two British operatives: a young man from Gloucester named Saajid Badat, who was known as educated and sensitive, and Richard Reid, who was neither. Badat pulled out of the plot at the last minute in December 2001, e-mailing his handler, "I will keep you informed, but you will have to tell Van Damme [Reid] he could be on his own."[12] Then Reid flew, and failed to light the fuse. So by the beginning of 2002, KSM was looking for some new approach to the second wave, and new recruits. And whomever he could find, whatever they might do, New York was going to be a prime target once again. KSM knew where to go to get headlines.

Geneva Bowling, the ex-wife of Iyman Faris, still remembers Iyman as a fun-loving guy in his early thirties with long wavy hair and a ready smile who charmed the customers, and especially the ladies, at the Columbus, Ohio, gas station where he worked as a cashier. Faris had a good relationship with Bowling's ten-year-old son from an earlier marriage. Faris and the boy would watch action films together. One favorite was *Air Force One*, with Harrison Ford playing the president and Gary Oldman leading a bunch of terrorists who take him and his family hostage. Another was Steven Seagal's *Under Siege 2: Dark Territory* ("a top-secret satellite with nuclear capabilities, a team of international terrorists, a government held hostage"). The man and the boy would play video games, and Faris especially liked the helicopter simulation of "Comanche II: Maximum Overkill." Nothing special there, really. Welcome to the suburbs.

But there was something deeply wrong with Faris, Bowling told a reporter years later. He got himself a trucker's license and started earning good money. At first he didn't seem outwardly troubled. Then one day in 1997 or 1998, Bowling did not remember precisely when, Faris tried to commit suicide by jumping off a bridge above a highway. When Bowling got to him at the hospital he seemed to be out of his mind. He was talking about a strange "half man," a midget twin who looked like him from the waist up, and who had followed him around since he was a little boy.[13]

Faris recovered and went back to his job. As Attorney General John Ashcroft described him later, he "appeared to be a hard-working, independent truck driver" who "freely crisscrossed the country making deliveries to airports and businesses without raising a suspicion." Nothing about Faris really set off any alarm bells—a fact that might seem odd. He was born in the Islamist-nationalist battleground of Kashmir in 1969, then came to the United States in 1994 on a student visa and never seemed to take any classes. But that's just the way immigration works sometimes: he got married before he got caught without a valid visa, then after four years of marriage he got his American citizenship; after another year he got an amicable divorce—and then he went to Afghanistan to meet Osama bin Laden.

Faris's introduction to the dark side came through a "long-time friend" who was supposed to be "the right foot" of Bin Laden and played "a critical leadership role in providing supplies and materials needed by al Qaeda." Court documents refer to him only as C-1.[14] In 2000, Faris did some research and odd jobs for this terrorist-logistician buddy. He looked into ultralight aircraft that might be used for a getaway after an attack. He also helped pick up two thousand sleeping bags in Pakistan for Bin Laden's fighters across the border.

As an American citizen, Faris was able to commute between Ohio and Pakistan. And, on his trips back home to the United States, Faris started networking with other Al Qaeda sympathizers. In mid-2001, the hardworking truck driver visited the Khan family in Catonsville, Maryland, near Baltimore. They'd come to the United States from Pakistan in 1996 when the father, Ali Khan, bought a gas station and made other local investments. That night at their house, Faris talked with one of Ali's sons, Majid Khan, about the religious duties of a Muslim. That led, naturally, to talk about jihad and Afghanistan.

The alleged conspiracy that started coming together that night eventually would involve at least four of the "high-value detainees" captured by the Central Intelligence Agency in 2003 and known to have been interrogated at its black sites. Other players, including a woman neuroscientist, would simply disappear. But that spring of 2002, even with the help of C-1, none of the American intelligence agencies could say exactly what the second wave would target. Or when. Or how. It looked like the NYPD might be plugged into a circuit with no juice.

Majid Khan had graduated from a Maryland public high school for gifted students in 1999. His teachers remembered him as very serious. He was devout and he spent his spare time teaching computer skills to younger kids at a large Islamic center. Khan was Americanized enough to tell people he dreamed of becoming a rapper, but he was a geek. According to his family, he took advanced computer courses and eventually landed a seventy-thousand-dollar-a-year job as a database administrator with the Electronic Data System Corporation in Virginia.[15] Yet in his quiet way he seemed to have been kindling the sort of fire in his gut that Al Qaeda finds so useful.

In early 2002, Majid Khan left Catonsville for Karachi to get married. While he was there, relatives introduced him to KSM, who must have thought his prayers had been answered. This Khan kid's American English came easily and idiomatically. He knew his way around the States. He knew how *not* to draw attention in the West. The biggest challenge seemed to be finding the right mission for him. At one point early on in his talks with KSM, Khan volunteered to carry out a suicide attack against Pakistani President Pervez Musharraf—to catch him inside a building somewhere and set off an explosive vest.[16] That was good of him, but KSM must have seen what a waste that would be of Khan's potential talents. The kid needed a handler.

KSM turned to another member of his terrorism-prone extended family from Baluchistan. Ali Abd al-Aziz Ali, known as Ammar al-Baluchi, was a young computer programmer who had been mentored by none other than Ramzi Yousef. With KSM he moved money around for the 9/11 hijackers. During and after the American counterattack in late 2001, Al-Baluchi helped organize the evacuation of Al Qaeda's leadership from Afghanistan to Pakistan. He also served as KSM's go-between with the shoe bombers Reid and Badat. Now he would work with Majid Khan.[17]

The list of possible fallback targets for the "new" second wave was just taking shape. Khan's family owned a gas station, so maybe he could find a way to turn subterranean gasoline tanks—or gas trucks—into massive bombs, just as airliners filled with jet fuel had been turned into human-guided missiles. In Pakistan, Khan trained to make explosive timing devices. KSM also liked the idea of poisoning reservoirs. The kid could look into that, too.

With his head full of Al Qaeda's jihad and KSM's conspiracies, Majid Khan left his wife in Pakistan and flew back to Baltimore to earn some more money and to lay the groundwork for attacks to come. Once again, Faris showed up on the doorstep of the Khans' house in Maryland. Khan bragged to him that he'd met KSM and boasted that he'd volunteered to kill Musharraf. Faris was impressed. He would remember his young friend's sudden status as a *mujahid*. But the delights of matrimony seemed to tempt Majid Khan almost as much as martyrdom.

In the fall of 2002, Khan went back to his new wife, Rubia, in Pakistan, which was not a smart move for a would-be "sleeper" in Al Qaeda's American underground. Khan had applied for political asylum and these return trips to his home country could make it impossible for him to go back to the United States as a legal resident. Immigration officials weren't likely to believe his claim that he feared political persecution in Pakistan if he kept making conjugal visits to his homeland.

KSM and Al-Baluchi appear to have been testing Majid in late 2002. They sent him to Thailand to deliver fifty thousand dollars in cash to a man named Zubair, who was part of the network behind the bombing in Bali, Indonesia, that killed more than two hundred people in October that year.[18] They also wanted some sort of proof from Majid that he would complete a suicide mission if he got such an assignment. Dropouts like Al-Tunisi and Badat had plagued the plans for a second wave all along. KSM didn't want to have to put up with another one. According to a single-page biography of Majid Khan published by the director of National Intelligence in 2006, "Khan passed a test that KSM orchestrated which showed that Khan was committed to being a suicide operative."[19] But what good was all that if Khan couldn't get back into the United States?

Even filtered through censored American government transcripts and court papers, you can get a sense of KSM and Al-Baluchi trying to figure out what the hell to do with this young man. They want him to go back to the United States, and they want his paperwork there to be in order. So Al-Baluchi enlists the help of an extraordinarily well-educated young woman named Aafia Siddiqui. Her mother was one of the rare female members of the Pakistan parliament, a woman very prominent and well connected in political-religious circles. Siddiqui had studied at the University of Houston and the Massachusetts Institute of Technology, where she took her degree in biology before going on to Brandeis to study neuroscience. In school in the United States in the early 1990s, Siddiqui had raised money for some Islamic charities helping victims of the war in Bosnia. Her house in Roxbury, Massachusetts, doubled as an office for a nonprofit group called the Institute of Islamic Research and Teaching, which distributed copies of the Qur'an. But for the most part she and her first husband, a Pakistani anesthesiologist at a hospital in Boston, seemed to be living quietly with their young children.

U.S. officials eventually said they feared that Siddiqui's scientific background would give her the expertise to help Al Qaeda build biological or chemical weapons. But that sounds like sensationalist spin. What's known is that Al-Baluchi dispatched Siddiqui on a more mundane assignment. She was supposed to go down to Maryland to rent a post office box in Majid Khan's name so he could start to get mail there and create the impression he was still living in the United States. Shortly after that, Siddiqui and her husband went back to Pakistan themselves. The FBI had taken an interest in some of the things that they were shopping for on the Web: night-vision equipment, body armor, and military manuals.

So now Al-Baluchi came up with another option for Majid Khan. He introduced him to a well-connected Karachi businessman named Saifullah Paracha, who owned a half interest in a company in New York's garment district that imported cheap clothes from Pakistan for Kmart and other outlets in the United States. Paracha's son, Uzair, was about the same age as Khan and could pretend to be him, charging things on his credit card and creating an electronic trail that might trick the authorities into believing Khan never left the United States. Then Khan could sneak back in and no one would be the wiser. That was the idea anyway.

That the Parachas were bringing containers full of clothes from Pakistan into the heart of New York City was also of interest to KSM. The containers could prove useful for smuggling explosives and guns, and conceivably even a weapon of mass destruction, if and when the opportunity came. Government documents suggest KSM had hundreds of thousands of dollars put into one of the Parachas' accounts to underwrite their activities on Al Qaeda's behalf.[20] The Parachas have steadfastly denied any terrorist connection.

But, still, KSM needed somebody on the ground in the States to reconnoiter. He needed someone to help him decide which plots had the best chance of success, and to push them ahead. What he needed was another team leader like Mohammed Atta. But those were not so easy to find.

Khan suggested his friend—the hardworking truck driver with an American passport, Iyman Faris. He had trained in Afghanistan; he had met Bin Laden; he knew his way around the United States—he could be good. So a meeting was set up in Pakistan. KSM told Faris he was working on two new scenarios, one for the West Coast and one for the East Coast—specifically, New York City.

When KSM would run down the list of targets there, he would include the Stock Exchange and other financial targets and, yes, the

Brooklyn Bridge—with a new twist that seemed, in retrospect, wildly delusional. The idea was to cut the cables on the suspension bridge and bring it down. "Cockamamie" was the word used in one *Newsweek* article describing the plot.[21] But KSM's plans were always crazy. That was part of his signature, and that's why most of them failed or never materialized at all. But one, of course, had succeeded in changing history.

Remember that KSM had gotten his degree from North Carolina Agricultural and Technical in engineering. Although he hadn't calculated that the World Trade Center towers would crumble as they did, he certainly would have realized afterward that the key to their collapse was the way a catastrophic event shattered their finely balanced structural tensions. What is more finely balanced than a suspension bridge? It is tuned almost like a piano. Cut the wires in the right place and maybe you could start a cataclysmic glissando.

So KSM asked Faris to see about buying acetylene torches, what he called "gas cutters," that could slice through the web of cables that kept the bridge standing (the same web that had ensnared Godzilla). Faris also had to eyeball the bridge himself. What sort of security was there?

Faris didn't like what he saw. In the past, the Brooklyn Bridge had never been watched very closely. The Rashid "Ray" Baz shooting spree in 1994 had taken place in sight of One Police Plaza, and still Baz managed to drive away without being identified. But now that wouldn't happen and couldn't. There were cops everywhere, some readily visible, some not. Sometimes they swarmed over the bridge at unpredictable hours. Faris sent a thinly coded e-mail back to Pakistan: "The weather is too hot."

"I have Iyman Faris's pictures here," Kelly told me when I asked him about all this. Part of the hardworking truck driver's job was to make a photographic record of potential targets mixed in with a little tourism. "Iyman Faris was all over town, including a Pakistani restaurant," said Kelly. In one of the photographs, the police commissioner was surprised to see Faris next to his own apartment building in Battery Park: "He's standing next to my house downtown!" Kelly rattled off some of the other places Faris took pictures: in the rotunda atrium of Grand

Central Terminal, down by the World Trade Center site, around One Police Plaza. "And he had pictures of the Brooklyn Bridge." The FBI had passed along the snapshots. "I took a look at his pictures and said, 'Holy shit, this guy was all over the place.' " But all that came well after the fact, and after some bitter confrontations between the NYPD and the three-letter guys.

While Osama bin Laden was lying low in 2002, presumably in the sere mountains along the Afghanistan-Pakistan border, Khalid Sheikh Mohammed was putting himself on the line in the teeming city of Karachi. His mission was all about Al Qaeda's image, keeping it in the headlines, promoting the cause of global jihad. Mass murder was just a form of mass communication as far as he was concerned. But the murder business wasn't going as planned. So in the spring of 2002, after many disappointing efforts to launch a second wave of spectacular violence against the United States, KSM went for a more conventional PR tactic. He gave an interview.

Yosri Fouda, a reporter from the Qatar-based Al Jazeera satellite network, was working on a documentary to be aired on the first anniversary of the 9/11 attacks. KSM got wind of this, and after an exchange of mysterious faxes and phone calls, got Fouda to Pakistan. There were more intrigues. Fouda was blindfolded and taken on a long, roundabout drive through the outskirts of the city. Finally he found himself in a six-room apartment on a back street in one of the dusty warrens of Karachi. And there, at last, was KSM. With him was Ramzi bin al-Shibh, a member of the Hamburg cell of hijackers who was only saved from martyrdom on 9/11 because he couldn't get a visa to the United States. Bin al-Shibh proudly displayed a suitcase full of memorabilia belonging to Atta, for whom he and KSM clearly felt a great deal of nostalgia. Bin al-Shibh also showed off an array of laptops and other electronic gear that was keeping him in touch with the global jihad.[22]

The Al Jazeera appearance was a bold, desperate move to keep Al Qaeda's terror alive in the media, which it did. It also put the surviving plotters of 9/11 squarely in the sights of the Americans.[23]

Precisely on the first anniversary of the slaughter at the World Trade

Center and the Pentagon, the CIA caught up with Bin al-Shibh in Kara-chi. Despite a blaze of gunfire, the Pakistanis took him alive. But KSM, if he was there, managed to get away. The police hauled KSM's two young children into custody. Afterward, other prisoners held in the same adult facility as the little boy and girl claimed to have heard stories that they were tormented by interrogators, who put ants on their legs hoping to scare them into telling where their father was hiding.[24] Another ver-sion of the story from a source who was there is that the children were captured along with a caretaker who felt very close to them. Sometimes they were simply brought into the room where the caretaker was being questioned, just to remind him that the interrogators now controlled their fate. But, even if all that were true, the cell phones and computers captured with Bin al-Shibh would have been a much more useful source of solid intelligence.

Certainly KSM could feel the circle tightening around him. While his contacts launched attacks in Bali and elsewhere in the world, noth-ing seemed to be working in KSM's strategy to strike the United States a second time. Young Majid Khan couldn't get back. Aafia Siddiqui had been compromised. Iyman Faris thought the weather was too hot. Plan B had given way to Plan C, and D, and E, and F. Bin Laden and his number two, the Egyptian physician Ayman al-Zawahiri, might well have been running out of patience with KSM's failures and his ever-less-ambitious fallback plots. By some accounts they vetoed a plan to set off cyanide gas bombs in the New York subway: not spectacular enough.[25]

And then, the end. On or before March 1, 2003, the Pakistanis and the CIA finally captured Khalid Sheikh Mohammed. An informer re-portedly cashed him in for a reward that, by that time, had risen to twenty-five million dollars. The stories that have come out since about KSM's interrogation suggest that he refused to talk and that, after some delay, the CIA used waterboarding to loosen his tongue. Michael Shee-han, who by then had replaced Libutti as the NYPD's deputy com-missioner for Counter Terrorism, would later say that "KSM is the poster boy for using tough but legal tactics. He's the reason these tech-niques exist. You can save lives with the kind of information he could give up."[26]

But even if the CIA used the same kind of "legal" torture on KSM that was used a year before on Abu Zubaydah—and CIA Director Michael Hayden eventually told Congress that, yes, indeed, that was the case—the nature of the interrogation had changed.[27]

The key to grilling a suspect is to exploit any information you possess to make him think you know even more than you do and to catch him out when there are contradictions and lies. When Abu Zubaydah was captured in the spring of 2002, the CIA had very little information. A year later, it had a lot. ("Of all the tools an interrogator can use to win a good statement, nothing beats having some of the truth already in hand," wrote crime-fighter Jack Maple, a flamboyant former deputy commissioner of the NYPD. "The more information a detective has, the more creative, authoritative, and effective he or she can be."[28])

Intelligence Chief Hayden would tell Congress that waterboarding was no longer used after the KSM sessions precisely because the agency knew enough by then to make it unnecessary.[29] But many would argue it never was needed at all. As the late Jack Maple would have said, "Forget that smacking somebody around is illegal and just plain wrong, it's also the quickest way to ruin the chances of getting a statement of any kind."[30] Professional interrogators talk about building empathy and dependence. Maple put it another way. "If you can get them to laugh, you'll get a statement. That's always true."[31]

But nobody wanted to be seen laughing along with Khalid Sheikh Mohammed. According to one senior CIA official I interviewed, part of the reason KSM was waterboarded was for revenge, pure and simple. "People said, 'This guy killed three thousand Americans.' They said these people were just scum and they wanted to waterboard them every day forever."

In any case, the events that followed KSM's capture suggest he talked very quickly. Pakistani police picked up Majid Khan four days later and, soon, Ammar al-Baluchi, as well. According to the little biography of Al-Baluchi issued by the director for National Intelligence, he had married the recently divorced Aafia Siddiqui not long before his capture. That same month, March 2003, Siddiqui and her three children, ages seven, five, and six months, climbed into a taxi outside her mother's house in Karachi. They were not seen again for more than five years. Some human rights activists believed they were arrested and held in one of the secret prisons run by the CIA and its allies. But in August 2008 Siddiqui was reportedly detained in Afghanistan and extradited to New York.[32]

The FBI, meanwhile, picked up Iyman Faris in Ohio. Faced with the threat he might be sent to Guantánamo, Faris agreed to cooperate through days and weeks of debriefings at Quantico, Virginia, filling in details on his contacts with KSM, Majid Khan, Ammar al-Baluchi, and the plans for the Brooklyn Bridge. The FBI and NYPD also descended on the garment district offices of Saifullah Paracha to arrest his son, Uzair, then lured the father from Pakistan to Thailand and arrested him there. Uzair is doing time in federal prison. Saifullah Paracha is at Guantánamo.

In March 2003, New York City could have had a celebration. The battle against the September 11 terrorists—the war, if you want to call it that—had been won. The operational cell responsible for carrying out the attacks on New York City and Washington, D.C., had been rolled up. The second wave, or waves, had been stopped. Bin Laden and al-Zawahiri were still at large, but on the run, and whatever little semblance of command structure they once had was hugely disrupted. As Ray Kelly understood quite clearly, wise policy would have been for the United States to continue building intelligence and law enforcement cooperation with the rest of the world while doing everything possible to reduce the sense of injustice and anger felt by Muslims. It was that collective sense of victimization that generated the fury, funding, followers, and fighters for violent jihad. You wanted to play that down; you wanted to try to dry up the pools of potential recruits.

The most important lesson of the second wave was that it didn't happen. The most skilled and imaginative terrorist organizers in the world had been unable to find people committed or competent enough to carry out even third-tier and fourth-tier attacks inside the United States. Years later, an author of the National Intelligence Estimate on threats to the homeland would try to put his finger on the critical reason Al Qaeda and other groups had such trouble finding operatives inside the United States. "People who come here have greater opportunity to integrate themselves into American society, to prosper in a way that takes advantage of their talents," said Edward Gistaro, the National Intelligence officer for Transnational Threats. "You know, the idea that the American dream is something real does help us."[33]

A deputy inspector at the Counter Terrorism division of the NYPD felt pretty much the same way. He'd met a lot of cops from Europe worried about the immigrant populations there. "Do Moroccans from the third generation join the Dutch police? Or the Dutch military?" He would answer himself, "No. But in the States, they do join the police. You know, in New York Mom and Dad live in Bay Ridge, then the kids buy in Suffolk County."

Unfortunately the same month that KSM and his cronies were captured, March 2003, the Bush administration launched its wildly miscalculated invasion and occupation of Iraq. Washington's "global war on terror" would go on with no real end in sight. The American dream in the eyes of the world, especially the Arab and Muslim world, would devolve into the nightmare spectacle of Americans humiliating prisoners at Abu Ghraib prison and tales of fatal torture at Bagram Air Base in Afghanistan. Bit by bit, the stories of what had gone on at the black sites began to surface. And the terrorist threat to New York City continued to grow.

BUILDING THE SYSTEM

SAFE STREETS

Cops on Dots

Commissioner Kelly has a notebook filled with ideas, quotes, criticisms, headlines, "points I like to carry around with me," he says. One is from an Op-Ed piece in *The New York Times* that appeared on November 11, 2001, as the city anticipated life without Mayor Rudolph Giuliani.

The former federal prosecutor had styled himself the city's top cop and taken credit repeatedly for a dramatic decline in crime rates during his two terms. New York's streets went from battlegrounds to fairgrounds. Then came 9/11. While President Bush was nowhere to be seen, Giuliani went straight to Ground Zero, calming a stunned population, coolly exemplifying a spirit of brave resolve in the face of unknown dangers to come. Without him, the *Times* seemed to be suggesting two months later, New York could look forward to a rerun of the relentlessly grim 1970s.

Kelly read the lines out loud as we sat with his deputy commissioner for Public Information, Paul Browne: "A return to the days of dirtier streets, legions of the homeless, an increase in the welfare population, a rise in crime, a plummet in the quality of life so sharp that people fled town."[1] Kelly's mouth twisted in an ironic smile.

"There were a lot of these scare headlines," said Browne. "There was this notion that Giuliani was out of power, so everything would go to hell."

That had been a dangerous perception at a delicate time. If the fight against crime lost its momentum and its credibility—if, that is, people began to feel the way the *Times* Op-Ed thought they might—the fight against terrorists wasn't going to work.

Richard Falkenrath, who came late to Kelly's team in 2006, long after the scramble-for-survival phase had passed, takes a detached and slightly academic view of the ongoing challenge. Before he got his job as deputy commissioner for Counter Terrorism, Falkenrath had worked at the Brookings Institution in Washington and before that at the George W. Bush White House as deputy Homeland Security advisor. He had spent most of his career at Harvard's Kennedy School, looking at the critical trade-offs vital to maintain security. So Falkenrath has few illusions. The operations that he and Cohen are running are "extremely specialized" in the overall picture of policing, he says.

The terrorist threat is persistent and potentially catastrophic, but the action is sporadic. The more successful a counterterrorist operation becomes, the less people hear about it. Cohen's intel shop is focused on events that may be taking place on the other side of the world, as well as in the five boroughs. People don't want to be paying out of pocket for what's out of sight and out of mind, especially if they start worrying about muggers and rapists. So if New York taxpayers are going to support counterterrorism, Falkenrath told me, "first of all, you've got to have your crime rate under control, because the populace—" (Yes, he uses words like that, then catches himself.) "The general public will not tolerate you to do things which they deem extraneous if crime is out of control.

"Second," said Falkenrath, "you need size." You cannot take a thousand cops and assign them to something that isn't about the immediate day-to-day safety of the community if you don't have tens of thousands of cops to begin with.

"Third, you need leadership." You need someone to say, "I'm going to do this. I'm going to bear this responsibility." Fighting terrorists is very expensive, said Falkenrath, "and not just in terms of outlays, but in opportunity costs."

Put simply, securing a big city has a lot to do with balancing big numbers: the crimes, the cops, the costs. You don't get those right, you'll leave yourself wide open to a handful of crazies.

Kelly, in his long career, has heard all the buzzwords and often had to deal with the passing fads of policing embraced by criminologists and politicians. But what they came down to in the end was an axiomatic bit of street math, as he saw it: "You can lock up a lot more people if you've got a lot of cops." When Giuliani came in, he liked to talk about "broken windows" theory and "quality of life" policing, often summed up in the notion of "Zero Tolerance" for even the most minor crimes. People would be nailed for panhandling, fare jumping, unwanted squeegeeing of car windows on the idea that this would change the whole feel of the city, turning it into a place where cops intimidated criminals rather than the other way around. But as a practical matter, every time you make an arrest, you're taking a policeman off patrol. "If you're going to have a guy in a radio car lock up a window washer, well, you don't have that radio car," said Kelly. "You need to have the resources to do that. You need the bodies to do it."

When Kelly was deputy commissioner and commissioner in the early 1990s, he'd helped then-mayor David Dinkins fight for a 12.5 percent income tax surcharge that finally raised the money to make the hires that had been needed desperately for almost twenty years. But by the time those recruits came on to the force, Dinkins and Kelly were out, and Giuliani and the new police commissioner, William Bratton, were in. "They had a lot of cops on the streets, which we never had before," said Kelly. "That enabled you to do a lot of discretionary things. It's not brain surgery."

To really stop crime in New York you also needed something more than could have been delivered in 1994 by Kelly, the consummate insider.

You needed an outsider.

* * *

That man was a fat, eccentric, middle-aged lieutenant from the much-disrespected Transit police force who liked to wear sharp suits, two-tone shoes, and a homburg hat. Jack Maple looked like he pined for the days of Damon Runyon's guys and dolls. But whatever Maple's sartorial predilections, his greatest passion was catching crooks and, more importantly, developing *systems* for catching crooks. He did that like no one else in living memory.

Bratton got to know Maple at Transit when Bratton ran the show there in 1990. After Bratton took over from Kelly as commissioner of the New York City Police Department in 1994, he created a special high-ranking position for Maple as deputy commissioner for crime control strategies. The promotion "was the equivalent of an ensign in the Coast Guard waking up as a three-star admiral in the Navy," Maple said.[2]

Once he went into action, Maple actually had no use for what he called the "mystical link between minor incidents of disorder and more serious crime." In Maple's witty and remorseless little memoir-cum-instruction manual, *The Crime Fighter,* he savages the whole "quality of life" concept as it's commonly understood: "The implication is, if the police would take care of the little things, the big things would take care of themselves," wrote Maple. But "rapists and killers don't head for another town when they see that graffiti is disappearing from the subway. The average squeegee man doesn't start accepting contract murders whenever he detects a growing tolerance for squeegeeing. Panhandling doesn't turn a neighborhood into Murder Central. In fact, panhandlers don't work in bad neighborhoods. In Midtown Manhattan, a beggar might be able to act like a bully. In a bad neighborhood, he'd be set on fire. Literally."

"Quality-of-life enforcement works to reduce crime because it allows the cops to catch crooks when the crooks are off-duty," Maple concluded.[3] Grab them for the little infractions—an open beer can, a cloned cell phone—and if you check for outstanding wants and warrants, you might well nail them for much bigger crimes. You can put pressure on them then to finger their pals. The real crime fighting can begin.

Out on the street these tactics work most effectively if you apply them where the malingerers already are thick on the ground. Maple liked wild animal analogies. If you wanted to catch these predators, you went to the watering holes where they stalked their victims. And to figure out exactly where those were, you used numbers and maps to show where they'd struck before. You put dots where the crimes were, you watched where they accumulated, and then you put cops on the dots.

The manifesto that brought on a revolution in New York City crime fighting was first written on a napkin at another kind of watering hole, Elaine's restaurant on the Upper East Side. Maple loved to hang out among the flamboyant and the famous who endured the mediocre pasta for the delectable pleasure of seeing one another. Often he'd stay until closing time, in the very wee hours of the morning, telling tales about catching bad guys while drinking espressos and watching everything that went on around him.

It was the way Elaine Kaufman ran her business that inspired his plans for the NYPD, he said. "On this particular evening," Maple recalled, "she was, as is her habit, making frequent visits to her desk officer, who sits to one side of the bar, signing every check as it's paid and tallying up the receipts. She knew at all times, from checking his tape, exactly how well the night was going. If the receipts were down, she'd look for her waiters: Were they loitering near the coffee service area or were they out on the floor, anticipating and attending to the customers' every need? Chances are, she would also hit a few tables herself to keep the joint hopping.

"How different business was in the NYPD, I thought. We didn't check our crime numbers hourly, daily, or even weekly. Headquarters gathered the numbers every six months, and then only because the department was required to report them to the FBI for inclusion in the national *Uniform Crime Reports*. I couldn't imagine that many of our precinct commanders checked the tape on their crime numbers every day. If the numbers were going the wrong way, would any of them be out on field inspections to determine what was going on?"[4]

The ideas that Maple sketched out on his napkin came down to four fundamental principles for redefining the objectives, methods, and outcomes to be expected of any police organization:

1. Accurate, timely intelligence
2. Rapid deployment
3. Effective tactics
4. Relentless follow-up and assessment[5]

Like all good management schemes, once stated it seems obvious. But the NYPD in 1994 was a very hard organization to move.

As Bratton and Maple saw it, the cops didn't trust their superiors and their superiors didn't trust them. Vital units, like the Narcotics division, barely talked to other parts of the department, like, say, the Detective Bureau.[6] The biggest lie in law enforcement, Maple said, is "We work closely together." And it was never a faint-hearted lie, he noted. It's never just "We work closely together." It's always "We work very closely together—very closely."[7] As for allowing police on patrol to log on directly to CARS, or CRIMS, or NITRO, or WOLF, or BADS, and other colorfully named databases—forget about it. "The standard excuse," according to Maple, "was that opening up access to the systems would open up opportunities for corrupt cops to sell information to the bad guys."[8] A survey Bratton commissioned showed the rank and file thought the department's *real* priorities were writing summonses, holding down overtime, staying out of trouble, reporting corruption, and so on. Fighting crime was way down the list.

So Bratton and Maple demanded numbers and maps in real time, and started holding long meetings twice a week that commanders had to attend, during which they'd be held accountable. The whole process came to be known as Comstat, or eventually CompStat. Even the geniuses behind it never completely agreed on its spelling or derivation, but over the course of a few months it developed a meaning all its own.

"One way to look at a Comstat meeting is as a live audit of overall police performance," said Maple, whose follow-up really was relentless. He embarrassed and brutalized a lot of tough cops at these sessions. The gathering and analyzing of timely intelligence "has to be quickened by the heat of accountability," he said. "The reason is simple: Most people in the world learn things faster when they know they're going to be tested on them."[9]

Maple was widely loathed inside the NYPD. But as the test scores came in from the street, they could hardly have been more dramatic. After two years, "total felonies were down 27 percent to levels not seen in the city since the early 1970s. Murder was down by 39 percent, auto theft 35 percent. Robberies were off by a third, burglaries by a quarter."[10]

By then, however, Bratton and Maple and the rest of their team were on their way out. The basic reason: jealousy. They had gotten too much credit in the press for their success. Bratton had been on the cover of *Time* magazine, and that's where Giuliani thought Giuliani ought to be. City Hall forced the resignation of Bratton's deputy commissioner for Public Information, John Miller, a veteran television newsman and close friend of Maple. The rest resigned a few months later. Crime had been the issue. Egos had been the issue. Terrorism had not. "There wasn't an idea that there was a global network," Miller told me many years later. "There was an idea that there were angry young men."

A new era began under the lackluster and luckless Howard Safir. He was a former federal narcotics agent and U.S. marshal who'd known Giuliani for decades. Giuliani had made him fire commissioner, and now gave him the slot as police commissioner. But his record commanded little respect. Bratton's first deputy, the tough, Irish-born John Timoney, told the *Daily News* he'd quit rather than work for Safir: "There's no way I'm gonna prop up a lightweight."[11]

On Safir's watch, the tough-guy image of the police swung wildly out of control. In August 1997 a Haitian immigrant named Abner Louima was picked up in a scuffle at a bar. Two cops took him into the bathroom at the Seventieth Precinct. While one held him down, the other sodomized him with the wooden handle of a plunger, tearing his bowels and puncturing his bladder. Both officers eventually did time, one for the assault, the other for perjury.[12] But just as the air cleared from that disaster, in 1999 an unarmed African immigrant named Amadou Diallo made the mistake of reaching for his wallet when four plainclothes officers from the Street Crime Unit approached him for questioning.

In the pre-Giuliani, pre-Bratton, pre-Safir days, only a few patrol cops were allowed to work in jeans and T-shirts or other civilian clothes, and their service weapons were .38-caliber revolvers. Now they had nine-millimeter automatic pistols that allowed them to squeeze off a dozen or more rounds in a couple of seconds, and Safir had expanded the Street Crime Unit from one hundred and twenty to four hundred officers operating in twenty precincts. Their motto: We Own the Night.

As Diallo stood in the doorway of an apartment building, maybe he looked like a suspected serial rapist the four cops had been searching for. What's sure is that when they approached him and he pulled out his wallet, one of the cops fired. One stumbled back on the stairs. The others thought their buddy had been shot. In eight seconds they squeezed off forty-one rounds. Nineteen hit Diallo. He died then and there. And so did Safir's career as police commissioner.

The next Giuliani pick was worse: a crony named Bernard Kerik who'd spent most of his career working in and running jails. That's not an easy job, but he was not the right man for the NYPD command. Although Kerik won headlines and praise in the aftermath of 9/11, he's now best remembered for the criminal corruption charges leveled against him by federal prosecutors. He steadfastly maintains his innocence.

Yet for all the decay in the NYPD in the later Giuliani years, when Kelly came back into the commissioner's job in 2002 the legacy of CompStat, with its focused exploitation of numbers and trends and its systems of relentless accountability, remained. "We left behind an organization that had adopted a process for perpetual self-improvement," said Maple, who died of cancer at the age of forty-eight in the summer of 2001.[13] Bratton put it even more succinctly: "CompStat cut through a lot of crap."[14] And common crime continued to drop.[15]

The computers and interrelated databases in operation now can turn out numbers, maps, and relational diagrams the likes of which Maple could only dream of fifteen years ago. Kelly has built an eleven-million-dollar Real Time Crime Center at One Police Plaza that gives detectives access to everything from criminal records to public utility bills, to a database of tattoos. Banks of computers fill the room and can project their findings on an array of screens along the wall. As crimes are reported, they're posted moment-to-moment. Much of the operation can be replicated in mobile units that are taken close to the action during a crisis or a big event. Cops on the street have BlackBerries. The public can access basic CompStat figures on the NYPD website.[16] And when it comes to tracking terrorists—discovering whether they are angry, lonely young men or part of global networks—the basic rules of policing are more important than ever: working each case systematically, looking for patterns, squeezing every last bit of information out of interrogations, then running down every lead. You pressure them to finger their pals. Then the real counterterrorism can begin.

But beyond all that, and in ways distinct from common criminals, would-be terrorists have to be deterred. No law and no threat of retribution will stop a man or woman planning a suicide attack. Only the threat of failure, capture, and humiliation is likely to be effective. Wannabe mass murderers have to be shown, as Iyman Faris was, that "the weather is too hot," and to do that the cops have to make themselves seem all-powerful and all-knowing. They have to infiltrate organizations and groups. They have to publicize their undercover operations sometimes to spread mistrust among potential conspirators. They have to show that they can make important arrests—and every so often they just have to put on a show. "Police work is largely a game of bluff," the great city reporter Jacob Riis wrote in 1901.[17] A century later, what European police call "the circus" would become a key part of Kelly's strategy.

SHOTIME

Surges and Scuba

The moon lingered high in the sky and the January sun was about to rise from behind the skeletal trees in Central Park when the police cars started to converge on Lincoln Center. They seemed to be coming from every corner of the city, and to be everywhere in *this* corner of it. Dozens lined up on Columbus Avenue near a communications truck that looked like a school bus painted in police blue and white. A large camper served as a mobile command center. Now the cops were out of their cars, some sipping coffee, trying to blink the sleep and the cold out of their eyes as they stood on the sidewalk waiting for roll call. A woman in uniform walked past me.

"What's going on?" I asked.

"Counterterrorist deployment," she said.

"Are there any terrorists around here?"

She shook her head, but I couldn't tell if she was saying no or just blowing me off. She checked in with the other officers, then there was another lull—having hurried up, they waited—and I asked her again. She was more relaxed now. "We do this every day in Manhattan," she said. "Different locations."

"Quite a show."

She looked around, smiling. "It's nice," she said.

"Nice" was not the first word that would have occurred to me, but it did kind of fit. What the police call "Critical Response Vehicle (CRV) surges" are now so common in Manhattan that they seem a normal part of daily life. There's none of the press drama or public consternation that accompanied the deployment against Godzilla back in 2002. At least twice a day on every weekday, and often on weekends, too, seventy-six patrol cars converge in a single spot near a possible terrorist target. The show of force is unpredictable and impressive, "a kind of shock-and-awe effect," said Deputy Inspector Brendan Sheerin when I caught up with him in the middle of another surge near the entrance to the Queens Midtown Tunnel. "Someone who has evil in mind doesn't know what to think," said Sheerin.

Maybe it was the Irish in him, maybe just the confident way he carried himself, but you'd have said Sheerin was an old-time New York cop no matter how much his job description changed under the new regime. "Crime fighting, policing, is central to my being," he said. "I've been doing this for over twenty-five years." For him there was nothing mystical about the terrorists. They were just more bad guys out there to be captured or deterred. And the critical response vehicles might help do that. "If anyone is assessing the subway system or gauging Macy's and all of a sudden seventy-six cars appear, that's going to make them think again."

But the surges aren't just there to keep the bad guys guessing, they're designed to keep the rank-and-file cops alert and informed and educate them about what's going on in the rest of the world that might play out on Manhattan's streets. (In some cases the surges just teach them how to figure out where they are. Cops serving in the outer reaches of the outer boroughs might spend years without coming into midtown or the financial district.) Some police commanders don't like to let their cops go on the surges. Some police officers don't want to bother. But the word came down from on high: "Commissioner Kelly made it apparent [that] this is very important to him." And for some, says Sheerin, "It's a nice change. You're not in the middle of a family dispute solving the world's problems for them. You're seeing all different parts of the greatest city in the world."

The reason seventy-six cars deploy in a surge is that every one of the seventy-six precincts in the city is expected to contribute a vehicle. Each vehicle is supposed to have two officers in it. A surge is run by one of the eight counterterrorism coordinators from the eight patrol boroughs.[1] (Inspector Sheerin was from Queens North, where big events like Mets games at Shea Stadium and the U.S. Open at Flushing Meadows often kept him busy.) Before the operation began, Sheerin "briefed the executives": eight police captains who then passed along relevant information to the sixteen sergeants and the one hundred and fifty-two police officers outside on the street.

"You want to keep everyone plugged into the counterterrorist theme," said Sheerin. This afternoon they were on the subway theme, later that night, the Times Square theme. "Sometimes the theme is hotels, financial interests, Jewish-associated properties. There is an array of themes," said Sheerin.

All through the operation, bystanders will ask, as I did, what the hell is going on. The general responses are supposed to be well rehearsed. "It's not practice. . . . We do this regularly. . . . It's terrorist prevention." It's also a substantial mobile force able to move quickly. "Should anything happen anywhere in the city," said Sheerin, "I know I can take one hundred and fifty-two cops there and lend support."

A few minutes before the deputy inspector starts briefing the captains, he gets what he describes as "a time-sensitive package produced by our intelligence division." There is always one of these. In it are some details about the deployment, background on current terrorist threats, and an assessment of what it might mean for cops in New York. For instance, if Kashmiri terrorists get picked up in New Delhi with explosives hidden in stuffed toys, that doesn't mean kids with velveteen rabbits get stopped on their way to nursery school in Manhattan. But it does mean a man carrying a panda onto a bus might be worth a second look. At the meeting with the captains this afternoon in early 2007, Sheerin refers them to a sheet prepared by Cohen's shop. "This is information on the hanging of Saddam Hussein and how it might affect New York. You might want to take a look at that."

*   *   *

The "E-men" from the Emergency Service Unit have all the skills and equipment you'd find with any Special Weapons and Tactics (SWAT) team in the country, and then some. But nobody who knows them calls them SWAT, and they're proud to tell you, "We do rescue work," which is what Detective Jeffrey King said when I talked to him on top of the Empire State Building one morning. He and the three other E-men with him were in full battle regalia: Kevlar helmets; heavy body armor with ballistic plates front and back; M-4 carbines with collapsing stocks; and Smith & Wesson nine-millimeter sidearms with fifteen rounds in the clip and one in the chamber. American tourists tried not to stare. Europeans, who are used to cops carrying a lot of heavy metal in public places, barely gave them a second glance. Some Japanese tourists wanted to pose for pictures with the imposing officers. "I take off my helmet and ask five dollars a shot," joked one of the E-men. King looked around at the scene. "We do rescue work," he said again.

Their job that day was to be a Hercules team, performers in the same circus as the Critical Vehicle Response surges. Fully equipped and mobilized, they could move quickly to the scene of any emergency, it's true, and take plenty of firepower with them. But their main goal is to see and be seen at high-profile, potential targets like the Empire State Building. Plainclothes officers from the Intelligence division watch the crowd to see if the E-men in full battle gear provoke any unusual behavior. They also serve as a reminder that the bad guys are still out there; an antidote to the deep American tendency to forget any history older than the morning news. "They keep the story alive," Sergeant Joseph Salzone told me as we watched the parade of firepower around the observation deck. "They work against the amnesia."

At their daily eight o'clock meetings in 2002, Kelly and Libutti and Cohen had been grabbing ideas out of the air. Before they came up with the surges and the Hercules teams, "we started," said Cohen, "with Operation Nexus." The concept was to network with businesses that might be exploited by terrorists. Companies that sold chemicals like hydrogen peroxide or nitrate fertilizers, the stuff of homemade bombs, needed to have their consciousness raised. But so did self-storage warehouses (where components and chemicals might be hidden), exterminators (poisons and sprayers), propane gas vendors (the canisters can serve as ready-made explosives), cell phone vendors (mobiles work as timers and triggers), hardware stores (for all sorts of odds and ends), and eventually even plastic surgeons (for bad guys whose faces have gotten too familiar). Some eighty different categories of businesses were deemed of interest to the police.

Many of the specific cases for concern came from the files about known plots. After Ramzi Yousef's attack on the World Trade Center in 1993, his shopping lists that were entered into the court record became good examples of the way banality can translate into extraordinary evil. At a chemical supply company in the same Chelsea neighborhood where many NYPD and federal law enforcement operations now have office space, Yousef picked up a couple of thousand dollars' worth of alcohols and acids, another couple of thousand dollars' worth of urea, and some storage drums. The whole bill was about seven thousand dollars. The clerk threw in some sodium carbonate, another important component for homemade bombs, free of charge. And why wouldn't he? It's what used to be called washing soda. Eventually Al Qaeda's textbooks, its "terrorist encyclopedia," also served the police in New York. Bin Laden's checklists became their checklists.

In the middle of 2002, Operation Nexus focused first on what seemed to be the most immediate threat, one against which there'd been very little preparation. "We were worried at that time about maritime terrorism. Scuba gear. Marinas," said Cohen. "Kelly gave orders, 'Get a team out, identify every marina, and go out there,' and then we kept learning and learning and learning."

The basic concern was well founded. Al Qaeda had an admiral, of sorts. In 2002 the name Mullah Bilal kept turning up in CIA and FBI dossiers. Though less well-known than KSM, he was almost as imaginative and ambitious—a semi-independent operator who waited years before pledging his loyalty to Bin Laden. He wanted to carry out actions with global reach and in 2002 he was on the move, not holed up in Pakistan like Al Qaeda's other operatives.

Bilal, whose real name was Abd al-Rahim al-Nashiri, had as much hands-on experience with massive terrorist attacks as anyone on earth. He'd played a key role in organizing the simultaneous bombing of the United States embassies in Kenya and Tanzania in 1998, which killed 224 people, including a dozen Americans, and wounded thousands more. Bilal's first cousin was the suicide driver in Nairobi.[2] As one of the few Saudis besides Bin Laden at the top of the organization, Bilal had vital contacts inside the Kingdom, just waiting for the signal to launch a wave of terror there.[3] "Nashiri does his job very patiently," a senior Arab intelligence officer told me while he was working the Mullah Bilal case. "Nairobi was three years in the planning." And seaborne operations were his specialty.

Mullah Bilal plotted the attack on the American guided-missile destroyer the USS *Cole,* anchored in the Yemeni port of Aden in October 2000. A Boston Whaler filled with explosives blew a forty-foot hole in the warship's hull and killed seventeen sailors.[4]

Before the U.S. invasion of Afghanistan in 2001 broke up Al Qaeda's bases and disrupted its communications, Bilal dispatched a small group of Saudis to Morocco to prepare the logistics for an attack on American warships in the Strait of Gibraltar. Their mission was to rent a safe house and acquire Zodiac rubberized speedboats to use in a hit similar to the one against the *Cole.* But a tip from one of the captured Moroccans held at Guantánamo in early 2002 was passed on to the security services in Rabat.

At first the Moroccan intelligence chief had doubts about the tale. But because General Hamidou Laânigri had a close working relationship with the CIA, the Americans allowed his people to talk directly to the Moroccan prisoners at Guantánamo. The information they gathered checked out on the streets back home and communications intercepts led to the arrest of the key organizer on the ground, Zuhair al-Tbaiti, in June 2002.[5]

In October 2002, Bilal directed a suicide attack on the French supertanker *Limburg* off the coast of Yemen—and seems to have given himself away in the process. He was tracked to Dubai, where the locals picked him up and handed him over to the CIA, which quickly dispatched him to a black site and put him on the waterboard.[6] The CIA, in its way, was learning and learning.

Bilal wanted to train pilots to fly small aircraft from small airports with lax security, then launch them against ships like Japanese kamikazes in World War II. And this is what caught the attention of the NYPD: Bilal wanted to use martyrs who could attack from beneath the surface. Before 9/11 he had sent a Tunisian with a Dutch passport to Morocco to set up what amounted to an Al Qaeda diving school, but the Tunisian security services identified him as someone suspicious and the Moroccans expelled him from their country. In 2003, the dive master was still at large and presumed to be in Great Britain.[7]

So, yes, Cohen was very worried about maritime operations. With Operation Nexus, the NYPD hoped anyone who sold Zodiacs or filled air tanks would report anything remotely suspicious about new customers. But later on, anxious to check out the risks a little farther afield, NYPD detectives from the intel division started phoning dive shops on the Jersey Shore. According to Leonard Levitt's muckraking blog "NYPD Confidential," the detectives pretended to be suspicious characters: they wanted to pay cash for scuba lessons, but they didn't want to fill out the required paperwork. The idea was to see if the dive shops would contact the proper authorities, which they did.

The problem, according to Levitt, is that the New York cops hadn't contacted the proper local authority, which at that moment was the New Jersey Office of Counter-Terrorism. This operation of about seventy people, many of them state troopers, had been created after 9/11 and was run by two heavyweights retired from the FBI. One was Sidney Caspersen, whose many assignments had included the investigation of the 1998 embassy bombings in Africa. When Cohen was the CIA station chief in New York City in the late 1990s, Caspersen had overseen electronic surveillance activities there. The other was FBI veteran Edward J. Curran, whose path just seemed to keep crossing David Cohen's.

New Jersey's cops spent "days trying to figure out where these calls are originating, whether they're from Osama's guys," according to one of Levitt's unnamed sources, "only to discover they are from detectives in intel." Caspersen put out a terse communiqué, leaked to Levitt, saying his office "was not aware that the tests were being conducted and has since informed the NYPD Intelligence Division to cease and desist all such activity in the state of New Jersey."[8]

You might remember castor oil from old *Our Gang* reruns, a vile liquid employed as purgative and punishment for wayward children. The beans from which it is made have been used for millennia as herbal medicines. But they are also the source of ricin, which can be extracted with relatively little effort or expertise and is one of the most toxic natural substances known to sorcery or science. In 1978, a Bulgarian dissident was murdered in London with a tiny pellet shot into his leg from the tip of an umbrella. The fatal dosage was an infinitesimal 0.2 milligrams.

In 2003, ricin became a serious worry for the NYPD. Just before the beginning of the year, the Algerian security forces picked up a militant named Mohammed Mergueba, who claimed to know about a plot to commit mass murder in Britain. Interrogated by one of the most experienced and savage services in the Arab world, which is saying something, Mergueba told his tormentors that he had been recruited while working as an immigrant waiter in Ireland, had trained at the Darunta camp in Afghanistan, then went to England on a mission for Bin Laden. He got arrested on immigration charges, jumped bail in Britain, and returned to Algeria to join the guerrillas fighting the government there—but got caught. Mergueba told his interrogators that one of the men who trained with him in Afghanistan was a compatriot named Kamel Bourgass, who was now living in London without papers. Mergueba said Bourgass had brewed up a horrifying poison that he kept in jars of Nivea cream.

When the Algerians passed this story along to the British, many of the preliminary details checked out, including the address for Bourgass. When police raided his London apartment they found instructions for the production of poison and some raw materials, including apple seeds, cherry pits, and twenty-two little spotted castor beans. But there was no ricin. And no Bourgass.

He turned up in Manchester, England, a few days later when police went to arrest another man on other charges and found Bourgass staying with him. Bourgass grabbed a kitchen knife and tried to break out, slashing and stabbing four policemen. One of them, Detective Constable Stephen Oake, died at the scene.

The NYPD was getting firsthand reports on all this from a veteran Manhattan detective and member of the narcotics squad that Kelly and Cohen had just detailed to Scotland Yard. Taking up his post on January 13, the day before Bourgass was arrested, he was in a position to offer some balance to headlines about a "poison factory" in London and the "desperate manhunt" for the men behind it. In practical terms, what could the NYPD do? It started searching quietly for the little beans central to the threat. "The Nexus team went out to every organization in the tri-state area that stores, processes, or moves castor beans," Cohen told me with the shadow of a smile. "And it was said that Commissioner Kelly knew where every castor bean in the city was."

The scare would not die, however. The alarmist headlines continued, now with ominous international implications. A month after Bourgass's arrest, when Colin Powell addressed the United Nations to present the American case for war against Iraq, he linked Saddam Hussein to the Jordanian Abu Mus'ab al-Zarqawi, and Zarqawi to a "network" that was "teaching its operatives how to produce ricin and other poisons." He cited the unearthing of the "British cell" as a proof of the danger that Washington was sure it saw.

"Let me remind you how ricin works," said Powell. "Less than a pinch—imagine a pinch of salt—less than a pinch of ricin, eating just this amount in your food would cause shock followed by circulatory failure. Death comes within seventy-two hours and there is no antidote, there is no cure. It is fatal."[9]

Years later, when the Bourgass trials were over and the British lifted censorship, readers could discover that "the ricin plot" never presented much of a threat. No ricin was produced. Bourgass had a notion that he could kill people by smearing the stuff on door handles. But that wouldn't have worked. You can't absorb ricin through your skin (it would be more effective in, say, a salt shaker). As a murder weapon, ricin can be very deadly. As a weapon of mass destruction, it is risible.

Because the British police had arrested eight other people in connection with the ricin plot, the description of a terrorist "cell" sounded credible. But four were found innocent and the government dropped the charges against the others. Bourgass is serving a life sentence for killing Stephen Oake, but the only charge that stuck to him in connection with his "poison factory" was "creating a public nuisance."[10]

As for Iraq, no poison factories were discovered there. But the NYPD still watches the market for castor beans.

RED CELLS

The Counter Terrorism Bureau

"Al Qaeda is simply not very good," said Mike Sheehan. It was the late spring of 2003 and he had only been on the job a short time as the new deputy commissioner for Counter Terrorism. He figured this wasn't exactly what Kelly or Cohen wanted to hear, but he thought it was something that ought to be put on the table. Al Qaeda has a small and determined group of killers, he said, but under the intense pressure brought to bear against them in 2002 and early 2003, they just couldn't get the job done. "We underestimated Al Qaeda's capabilities before 9/11 and overestimated them after," said Sheehan.

Sheehan, who tends to lean forward and look up at people, looked up at Kelly. At Cohen. He could see they were taken aback. It wasn't so much that they disagreed. They'd all learned over the previous year that Al Qaeda could blunder, and badly. But they also knew the terrorists only had to get lucky once to precipitate a catastrophe out of all proportion to their action. They all understood only too well the way the public and politicians would react if headlines started to read "Commissioner Disses Qaeda." Support for counterterrorism would start to crumble. The armor would start to rust. Amnesia would settle in like a poisonous fog. And then, if the bad guys got lucky . . . Kelly, Cohen, and Sheehan agreed it would be better if Sheehan kept this estimate to himself for a while.[1]

Michael A. Sheehan was another one of Kelly's prizes hires. Frank Libutti, the first deputy commissioner for Counter Terrorism, had left after about a year on duty with the NYPD. The retired Marine general decided to head back to Washington, where his wife was happier than in New York and where he'd been offered a senior position in the newly created Department of Homeland Security. So Kelly looked for a replacement with a strong background and a strong personality who could handle the three-letter crowd.

Sheehan was just up the street at the United Nations, where he was serving as assistant secretary general for peacekeeping operations. Stabilization forces and nation building were part of his expertise. In the early days of the Clinton administration, he had been a special advisor on peacekeeping missions and one of those was in Haiti, where Ray Kelly, not long after leaving the NYPD, had tried to set up a decent national police force under UN auspices.

But most of Sheehan's career had been spent, in fact, in counterinsurgency and counterterrorism. A graduate of West Point, he was a Green Beret advisor to local troops at a remote base deep in guerrilla country during the Salvadoran civil war in the mid-1980s. He earned a master's degree writing about irregular warfare at Georgetown University, where Madeleine Albright was one of his professors. During the George H. W. Bush administration, Sheehan went to work on the National Security Council staff dealing with "the War on Drugs" and other low-intensity conflicts. Albright brought him into several positions during the Clinton administration, both when she was ambassador to the United Nations and after she became secretary of state. Then, in 1998, in the wake of the Al Qaeda bombings in Nairobi and Tanzania, Albright picked Sheehan to be ambassador-at-large for Counterterrorism. Along with John O'Neill at the FBI and Richard Clarke at the White House, Sheehan's voice had been one of those raised most often, most loudly, and—as it seemed until September 2001—most redundantly warning of the Al Qaeda threat.

Sheehan was wiry, intense, hot-blooded, and confrontational, and he was inheriting a fractious empire. The Counter Terrorism bureau that he headed was one of those elements of the NYPD that Kelly had sketched out on butcher-block paper in 2001. It had never existed before, as such, and even now it was a bit of a grab bag. A big part of its function was managing the extremely difficult relationship with the FBI through the Joint Terrorism Task Force. Another part was supervising the counterterrorism inspectors like Brendan Sheerin, who ran the surges around Manhattan and oversaw the gritty details of operations in the eight patrol boroughs and the transit system. The CT bureau would be responsible for extensive training programs, and run its own small "terrorist threat analysis group." It would make sure—or as sure as possible—that New York City's complex infrastructure, from the water supply to the subway trains, was well protected and that its landmark buildings were secure.

CT oversaw training and exercises and meetings of state and local agencies to talk about everything from defending against radiological and nuclear attacks to surviving pandemics. (Cops were the single biggest component of the Office of Emergency Management in New York City.) And then there was the more secretive stuff that went on in a low building in southern Brooklyn that flies no flags and, in fact, has no identification at all on the outside: the Counter Terrorism bureau's Counter Terrorism division.

If any of the hundred and thirty cops and civilian analysts at the CT division wanted to take a very long stroll through some low-rent neighborhoods and grungy industrial sites, they could eat a hot dog among the dilapidated attractions of Coney Island's boardwalk: the Wonder Wheel, the Parachute Jump. Maybe they could squeeze off a few rounds of paintball at Shoot the Freak, which advertises "Live Human Targets." But the fun fair at the division HQ is much more exotic and varied.

In the parking lot there's an old Ford Econoline van painted in the usual Ryder truck rental scheme: "One Way," it advertises. If you were paying close attention you might notice that the license plate says "WTC 1993," but not until you opened the rear doors would you understand why the truck is there. Inside are what look like a couple of sandboxes: two wooden frames holding what appears to be granular fertilizer. On top of them are three large steel bottles, a little like elongated scuba tanks, each labeled "HYDROGEN." This is a model of the bomb that Ramzi Yousef built—a teaching aid pulled together in 2002 for cops training in counterterrorism. Inside one of the Econoline's doors are posted photographs of the sites in New Jersey where the chemicals were mixed and stored and the bomb assembled. They're just low-rent row houses and what looks like a gas station, nothing special at all—which is the point.

On the other door are mug shots connected to the '93 blast. Their stories provide an instructive narrative: Omar Abdel-Rahman, "the Blind Sheikh," who preached violent jihad against the United States from the mosques in Brooklyn and New Jersey; Ramzi Yousef, the mastermind without whom the other conspirators would have been unable to organize an outing to Shoot the Freak, much less the bombing they carried out; and Mohammed Salameh, the terrorist who went to reclaim his deposit on the van.

Mostly when the tale is told outside the ranks, it centers on Salameh's stupidity. But inside the department, with the details, the story of Salameh's arrest is emblematic of the blue-collar experiences that give the men and women in blue uniforms a special edge on the street.

The Feds had been all over the Trade Center bomb site in the immediate aftermath of the explosion in 1993, but it took an NYPD bomb technician named Don Sadowy to come up with the key piece of evidence: a mangled chunk of metal. Sadowy had graduated from New York's Automotive High School in Brooklyn, and he knew it was part of the back of a truck. His former partner had worked auto theft, so he knew that there were hidden vehicle identification numbers on those pieces. That's the kind of street smarts you don't find so much among the three-letter guys. Then the NYPD lab, with maybe a little help from an FBI technician, managed to raise the numbers. Those took them to the Ryder agency and to Salameh.[2]

But, of course, a lot of that was luck. It was amazing that first-time terrorists could build such a massive bomb. Then again, getting the components had been so easy in 1993.

And when Mike Sheehan came on board at the NYPD, it still was.

* * *

Inside the brightly lit cubicles of the windowless Counter Terrorism division headquarters, which has a vaguely subterranean war-room feel to it, a small group of NYPD cops specialize in plotting terrorist attacks of their own. This is the Special Project Group, or "red cell" unit, which tests the methods and exploits the sources employed by mass murderers. "We always plan on the basis that we're fighting the smart terrorist," said Deputy Inspector Hugh O'Rourke, the CT division's executive officer. "We have to defeat the smart guy, the Mohammed Atta, not that guy who went back to get the deposit on the Ryder van."

Although the New Jersey authorities blamed Cohen's intel division for the bogus phone calls to scuba shops in their state, that sort of action is the stock-in-trade of CT undercover officers like Chris, who took part in what was called Operation Kaboom a couple of years later. Far from ceasing and desisting, under Sheehan they stepped up their activities outside New York City and, indeed, outside the state.

The idea was to take several cops who had no particular experience with explosives and see what they could pull together from information on the Internet and from suppliers within a few hours' drive of Manhattan. "We built a device that would destroy a building," Chris told me with a certain note of pride.

The model they used was not an Al Qaeda construct or the one cobbled together by Timothy McVeigh to blow up the federal building in Oklahoma City in 1995, but the massive bomb detonated by the Irish Republican Army in Manchester, England, in June 1996. The truck packed with some three thousand pounds of explosives was the biggest terrorist bomb ever detonated in Great Britain, and that was the kind of thing Chris and his crew thought New York City should worry about.[3]

The day before Thanksgiving they drove to an Agway farm supply store in upstate New York to buy ammonium nitrate fertilizer, which was essentially the same stuff used by Ramzi Yousef, McVeigh, and the IRA. There are about eighty Agways within a hundred-mile radius of midtown Manhattan, but the red cell team wanted to get outside the area where the Nexus program was supposed to have raised some awareness.

"I called ahead of time on the phone so they were expecting us," Chris told me. He didn't identify himself to the clerks in any particular way, and certainly not as a cop. To transport a thousand pounds or more of ammonium nitrate, you need a special license from the Department of Transportation. So Chris ordered nine hundred and ninety pounds. A woman clerk met him and his partner when they drove up. Neither of them looked even vaguely Middle Eastern or South Asian. Chris clearly works out a lot and bore himself in a manner that might suggest a military background. The woman was suspicious. "You could be a terrorist for all I know," she said. "You look like Timothy McVeigh." Another man working at the Agway wouldn't even shake Chris's hand.

"I think the New York City plates kind of spooked her," Chris said. "I told her I was picking up the fertilizer for my boss who had a farm." After about twenty minutes of "joking around," he recalled, she said okay. He loaded the fertilizer in the back of his pickup and drove away, looking in the rearview mirror to see what the woman and the man were doing. Chris thought they might call the local police. For the first several miles of the drive back to the city he worried he might hit a roadblock where he and his partner would have to come clean about who they were or risk a fatal misunderstanding. "That's how spooked I was," he said.

He should have been. According to Sheehan, the clerks in upstate New York, like the dive shop owners in South Jersey, did the right thing. The woman called the local cops and the federal Bureau of Alcohol, Tobacco, Firearms and Explosives called the NYPD (must have been those New York City plates). "We waved them off," said Sheehan.

More often than not, though, the buyers went unreported and undetected by other police agencies. The same team picked up twelve hundred more pounds of ammonium nitrate in Pennsylvania without incident. Shortly after that, on a freezing winter afternoon, the NYPD's terrorist bomb was assembled at its firing range on Rodman's Neck in the Bronx. It exploded with the force of more than a thousand pounds of TNT, short of the Manchester bomb, but enough to have killed hundreds of people if it had been detonated in Manhattan.[4]

In the months and years that followed, the members of the Counter Terrorism division kept discovering to their consternation just how easy terrorist supplies were to come by, even when you went out of your way to look suspicious. Sheehan assigned an Egyptian-born undercover cop and an Egyptian-born woman who worked in his office to arrange a buy of one hundred and ten gallons of industrial-strength hydrogen per-oxide. At high levels of concentration, this is one of the most important components of the extremely volatile TATP explosive that terrorists use in all kinds of infernal devices, from suicide vests to incendiary sneak-ers. But it's also used for plenty of innocuous purposes, like cleaning the water in swimming pools. The undercover officers said they would pay COD—cash on delivery. They gave a nonexistent address, and waited for the truck to show up at the closest street corner.

Sheehan had told the two cops to make it easy for the driver to say no to them. He told them he wanted to give the guy every chance to report a suspicious incident. "Make it easy for us to get nailed here," he said. "I want you to do everything but wear an Osama bin Laden T-shirt." The woman wore a long white coat with wraparound sun-glasses. "She looked like Mata Hari," said Sheehan. "It was hysterical." But the sale went through without a hitch, and without anyone so much as presenting an ID. The driver just left the chemicals where they told him to on the sidewalk. Clearly, more outreach to the private sector was going to be needed.

Sheehan installed a large trailer that became known as "the Van" at the back of the CT division headquarters. Inside it, terrorist hideouts that had been discovered in other cities and other countries could be repro-duced in great detail, a little like movie sets.

One of the rooms was modeled on the apartment in Leeds where the bombs were prepared for the murderous attacks on the London Under-ground in July 2005.

Another was a copy of the apartment of a twenty-one-year-old Uni-versity of Oklahoma engineering student named Joel Hinrichs. You may never have heard of him. I had not. But on October 1, 2005, Hinrichs put two or three pounds of homemade TATP in a backpack and headed in the direction of the crowded stadium where the Sooners were play-ing Kansas State. A couple of hundred yards from the gate, he sat down on a park bench and started fiddling with the backpack. The explosion blew off his head.[5]

Hinrichs's Oklahoma apartment was a textbook bomb factory, and it is reproduced in New York down to minute details: the mixing bowls, the slow cooker, plastic containers, a five-gallon can of acetone, large bottles of peroxide, and a lot of white powder. As a CT instructor explained, one of the first lessons for cops visiting the Van is that "white crystalline powders don't always mean narcotics." A police officer naturally would think he'd come on a drug operation, maybe someone cooking crack. "But places where they cook crack are very clean," said the instructor, "because all this white stuff is money." The cops are told that if there's any suspicion that what's being brewed is TATP, they need to call in the bomb squad.

In Hinrichs's room authorities found almost half a pound of the stuff, some of it crammed in a pill bottle, some of it in a Tupperware container. It is so unstable that a match can detonate it from several inches away. The heat from friction—feet sliding over the powder on the floor—can set it off, too. "If you see something like this, our punch line is very simple," the instructor said. "Get out."

We're never going to know what Hinrichs's motive was, whether he intended to kill only himself or to slaughter as many people as possible inside the stadium. The FBI discovered no link to any terrorist group, organization, or ideology. His father said he only meant to take his own life. Perhaps. But his case, little noticed outside Oklahoma, represents another concern for the NYPD. The American public has become grimly accustomed to the angry loner with his personal arsenal of rifles and pistols. But for such killers, homemade high explosives are now an option, too.

In the Van, an open laptop sits on the desk in the re-created Hinrichs room. The original had a document on the screen when police arrived. The cursor pointed to what probably were the last sentences the bomber wrote before setting out toward the stadium: "Fuck all this. None of you are worth living with. You can all kiss my ass."[6]

GREEN CLOUDS

Weapons of Mass Disruption

I was surprised the first time I visited the CT division headquarters that the commanders there didn't seem very worried about the stomach-turning stench that had settled over a large part of Manhattan. It was the talk of a very worried town that morning. People described the smell as something like rotten eggs or like cooking gas. The PATH trains to New Jersey were stopped as a precaution. An F train in midtown was evacuated. At least one woman succumbed to the stink and was rushed to the hospital. On a normal day in New York City, the 911 calls come in at a rate of about five hundred an hour but on this day the rate was three thousand. People wanted to know if it was the terrorist attack they'd been taught to fear.

It wasn't. Technicians from the city's Department of Environmental Protection went into the streets with sensors and laptops and quickly determined that the odor, while vile, was not a health hazard. No certain cause was determined, but the most common theory blamed an atmospheric inversion for trapping the putrid air from rotting New Jersey marshlands over lower Manhattan. "Belching Bog Blamed for City-wide Gas Stink," headlined the *New York Post,* while *The New York*

Times blandly told its readers, "Mysterious odors come and go in the New York City area, sometimes never identified." Mayor Bloomberg called the whole incident "good theater" for reporters and late-night comics.[1]

If the officers at the CT division were not exactly blasé about the odor, they didn't spent a lot of time theorizing about it, either. The public reaction, all things considered, had been moderate and well controlled. The large, stationary chemical detectors permanently deployed around the city had functioned well, indicating there was no danger. Indeed, if there was any problem with the city's warning system when it came to chemical agents, it was the tendency of sensors to register false positives. A plan to issue cops with belt-size detectors had to be scrapped because substances as innocuous as nasal decongestant spray would set them off. So the stink of the morning finally wafted away, and by the afternoon when I arrived, the CT division was focused again on the real dangers that do exist from chemical, biological, radiological, and nuclear weapons. "A lot of people analyze the threat," said Inspector Michael E. O'Neill, the division commander, as he showed me around the situation room. "We try to analyze it and do something about it. That kind of makes us unique."

The idea, of course, is to use good intelligence to, as the cops say, "detect and interdict." "The most important thing to do is to learn about the plot while it's developing and then take it down. That's *the* most important thing to do," said Richard Falkenrath. "The rest is defense." But when information is less than perfect, and the threat mainly theoretical, how do you balance caution and alarm? How do you find the concrete resources to meet hypothetical horrors?

Chlorine gas is a case in point. It was the first of what have since become known as weapons of mass destruction. The Germans used it with devastating effect at the World War I battle of Ypres in 1915. When released from a container by opening the nozzle or setting off an explosive charge, it billows out as a heavy greenish fog that smells, not surprisingly, like chlorine bleach. When it mixes with the tears in your eyes, or the blood and soft tissue in your lungs and throat, it turns to searing hydrochloric acid. Outside, it settles into low-lying terrain—trenches during World War I. And in a closed space—a building or a subway—

the effect is both gruesome and lethal. Yet chlorine gas is available from industrial suppliers all over the United States.[2]

After 9/11, when Falkenrath was working in Washington, he became "sort of obsessed with it," he said, "and tried pretty hard at the White House to do something about it—and failed."

"Why?" I asked.

"Why did I fail?"

"Yeah. What was the resistance to doing something about chlorine?"

Falkenrath shook his head. "It hadn't happened yet."

That changed in Iraq in late 2006, as the insurgents started adding canisters of the gas to their suicide bombs. By early 2007, these crude devices began attracting some attention in Washington. One exploded at a military base in Ramadi in January. It killed sixteen people, but the U.S. claimed the casualties came from the blast, not the gas. Then in February the insurgents set off a truck with two big chlorine gas tanks in it at the town of Taji north of Baghdad, killing six people and sickening scores more. A day later, they blew up canisters with a car bomb along the Baghdad airport road, killing two and sickening twenty-five.[3] All of these attacks were in relatively open spaces. If they'd taken place in, say, the tunnels of New York, their impact would have been much worse.

In June 2007, Falkenrath had the CT division start pulling together another red cell to carry out "Operation Green Cloud." The cops created a phony construction company complete with a website, claiming it had a contract with the City of New York to restore and purify the water in Coney Island Creek. The police bought a private mailbox where they could get correspondence. Then they started shopping around for poison gas. From a list of five vendors they found on the Web, they picked the one that seemed to do the most business on the Internet with the least amount of actual human contact. They ordered three one-hundred-pound, high-pressure cylinders for delivery to the street address they gave as their construction site. They paid using a credit card on the Web. No one ever asked any of them for identification at the time of the purchase. No one asked for ID when the lethal gas actually was delivered in October 2007.

The NYPD made it a point publicly to send Washington a documentary film about Operation Green Cloud, along with the suggestion that "know-your-customer" rules be added to the guidelines.[4] By early 2008, the Department of Homeland Security at last was writing new regulations to govern chlorine manufacturing plants.

At least since the 1970s, thriller writers have toyed with the notion that terrorists could hide an atom bomb somewhere in New York City. President George W. Bush made the threat seem all too real during his rush to invade Iraq. "We have experienced the horror of September 11. We have seen that those who hate America are willing to crash airplanes into buildings full of innocent people. Our enemies would be no less willing—in fact they would be eager—to use a biological, or chemical, or a nuclear weapon," he said. "Knowing these realities, America must not ignore the threat gathering against us. Facing clear evidence of peril, we cannot wait for the final proof—the smoking gun—that could come in the form of a mushroom cloud."[5] All of which was possible, except that neither that smoking gun nor that awesome cloud were to be found in Iraq, where he claimed they were. As in pulp fiction, Bush confounded possibility with probability and willfully mistook intention for ability.

The *possible* scenarios for nuclear terrorism are infernal, insidious, and much broader than just the nightmare of Hiroshima hitting home, which is why fears that some sort of improvised atomic device will be used against the public have been around for so long. "To many people who have participated professionally in the advancement of the nuclear age, it seems not just possible but more and more apparent that nuclear explosions will again take place in cities," the *New Yorker* writer John McPhee warned us on the first page of his book *The Curve of Binding Energy*, published in 1974. "There is also no particular reason the maker need be a nation. Smaller units could do it—groups of people with a common purpose or a common enemy."[6]

"What will happen when the explosions come—when a part of New York or Cairo or Adelaide has been hollowed out by a device in the kiloton range?" McPhee asks. "Since even a so-called fizzle yield could kill a number of thousands of people, how many nuclear detonations can the world tolerate?" One of the conclusions from an expert McPhee interviewed: "I think we have to live with the expectation that once every four or five years a nuclear explosion will take place and kill a lot of people."

But in the three and a half decades since McPhee wrote his book we have not seen seven or eight atomic explosions that killed a lot of people. We have not seen any.

The proliferation foreseen by McPhee and his sources continued without interruption, and in some respects got worse than they or anyone had imagined. The number of declared nuclear weapons states has increased from five to eight, plus Israel, which does not acknowledge its weapons, and, soon, Iran, which seems to have adopted a similar guessing-game strategy. The breakup of the Soviet Union in the early 1990s provoked fears that corrupt officials would sell bits and pieces of its enormous nuclear arsenal to the highest bidder. The Pakistani scientist A. Q. Khan ran a for-profit, for-Muslims proliferation network in the 1990s that sold basic nuclear enrichment and weapons production technology to the likes of Muammar Qadhafi in Libya. The head of the United Nations' International Atomic Energy Agency, Mohamed ElBaradei, tells me he believes we will soon see dozens of "virtual nuclear weapons states," which have the necessary technology at hand but don't choose to use it. So, why haven't those bombs gone off every four or five years?

One reason is that the warnings about how easy a bomb is to build often have come from people like Theodore B. Taylor, a theoretical physicist and former atomic weapons designer for the U.S. government. "He knows how to do what he fears will be done," said McPhee. But among the pool of terrorist recruits, not one has been found with that kind of expertise. Cutting throats with X-Acto knives, mixing an explosive sludge of fuel oil and fertilizer, concocting TATP out of hair bleach, or blowing up a couple of bottles of chlorine gas—those are the technological triumphs of terrorists, and they've been operating at the very limit of their abilities. (The most sophisticated weapon ever created by apocalyptic crazies was the sarin nerve gas used by the Aum Shinrikyo cult in Japan. The organization had assets estimated at over one billion dollars. It had talented scientists on its staff. Religious freedom laws protected its secrecy. And it had the determination to carry out mass murder. "With the use of sarin we shall eradicate major cities," its leader proclaimed. The gas released in a coordinated attack on five lines of the Tokyo subway in 1995 killed twelve people, severely injured a few dozen more, and caused temporary eye problems for about a thousand.[7] A few shotguns and assault weapons would have been just as lethal.) The challenges of nuclear technology are such that even nation-states have massive problems. When the North Koreans finally tested their bomb, after fearsome international fanfare, it misfired. Iran's rhetoric generally has been way ahead of its actual success with enrichment activities. The United States used diplomacy and money to round up potential loose nukes from the old Soviet stockpiles. And states—even the most rigid tyrannies—feel a certain duty to their constituents, to history, and to their own survival. It is difficult to imagine any government risking an overt or even a covert attack on the United States using a nuclear bomb that, ultimately, would be traceable to its origins.

For all these reasons, the NYPD focuses less on the threat of atom bombs than on "radiological" weapons, which are no more complex than the devices created countless times by terrorists around the world. All that's needed is the added ingredient of radioactivity. That could be as potent as plutonium or polonium-210, which are very hard to find outside of government circles, or much more common isotopes like cesium-137, which has numerous industrial uses. The radiation released by such a bomb probably wouldn't kill many more people than a conventional explosion, but it could leave a much more enduring imprint on the place where it was detonated and in the mind of the public. The cleanup would be long and painstaking, the area out of bounds and out of use, and even after the Geiger counters showed the radiation threat was gone, mistrust and fear would linger. Imagine if Times Square were targeted, or Penn Station or Wall Street. "You lose one of these downtown hubs or midtown hubs, or one of the underwater tunnels or the George Washington Bridge," said Falkenrath, "I mean—the implications are just horrifically bad."

If there is good news, it's that radiation can be hard to hide. "Out of all the threats we face, this is the easiest to find," said David Kao, the detective in charge of the NYPD's hunt for weapons of mass destruction in the city streets. Unlike the small chemical detection devices, the "personal radiation detectors" or "radiation pagers" that have been worn by thousands of cops for several years are very effective at picking up minute traces of potentially dangerous rays—even if the record shows that none of those detected have had any link to weapons or to terrorism.

Most of the "positives" picked up by the pagers are, in fact, inside the bodies of people who have had medical treatments. "Ninety-nine percent of encounters with this device have been patients who come off some kind of table," said Kao. Most of the rest are cars or trucks transporting isotopes used in devices that test the density of earth at building sites.

I asked Kao if he didn't think that sort of record made the radiation pagers almost as unreliable as the chemical ones. Kao, who sometimes looks almost professorial, responded with a dose of police mystique. Detection devices were all well and good, he said, but "we need cops." He held the pager in his hand, weighing it. "This is a tool to trigger your cop sense, to make you come out and do the investigations. You read the Geiger, you look at the subject, you look into his eyes. Is he lying to you?" Kao smiled. "We want to take the science and combine it with our field experience." Another CT detective, David Goodman, jumped into the conversation. "The pager will help you figure out *what's* out there," he said. "The cop has to figure out why."

Indeed. On New Year's Eve 2006 in the area around Times Square, the cops stopped one woman visiting from India for medical treatment seven times because she set off their radiation detection equipment. "She kept moving," one of them laughed a few days later when we were talking about the incident at CT headquarters. "If she'd have stayed still we'd have checked her once, maybe twice." He shook his head. "We sure ruined her evening."

In August 2007, an Israeli intelligence tip sheet called Debka File published a report that "chatter" on websites sympathetic to Al Qaeda threatened an attack "by means of trucks loaded with radio-active material against America's biggest city and financial nerve center."[8] That would be New York, of course.

"We thought it was not very credible," one of the senior men at the CT division told me afterward, "but we ramped up." National and local news shows carried pictures of the police stopping trucks, sweeping them with detectors, questioning the drivers. "You'd have thought you couldn't drive into the city that day. That's what you call homeland security theater," said the cop. As a deputy inspector said about these highly publicized efforts to find radioactive threats, "I want them talking about it in Terre Haute, saying, 'Shit, they are doing trace detection in New York.' "

Not all the talk is good. In 2006, the Department of Homeland Security set up its "Securing the Cities" program in hopes it could use New York as a model for radiation detection in other urban areas. But by 2008, Congress was raising questions about national funding for the project. Washington bureaucrats go back and forth about whether the real danger is dirty bombs or, getting back to the curve of binding energy with, perhaps, an Iranian twist, whether the real threat is from high-enriched uranium bombs encased in lead shields, which would be harder to detect out on the street (but also pretty heavy to move around). In early 2008 a high-profile "secret" exercise to detect cesium-137 planted in the back of an SUV near Times Square was not entirely successful. Cops on the ground found it, but the chopper cruising above the area with new radiation detection gear in its tail couldn't quite get a fix on it.

And there is one subject the cops would prefer not to have the folks in Terre Haute talking about at all: biological weapons.

If the infrastructure in place to detect radiation sometimes turns out to be exaggerated, the technology to discover the presence of plagues and poisons before terrorists can use them is essentially nonexistent. "When it comes to biological agents, a lot of people say it's a question of detect-and-*treat*, not detect-and-interdict," one of the senior cops working the WMD beat told me. Since July 2002, Dr. Dani-Margot Zavasky, an infectious diseases specialist, has been working as an advisor to the successive deputy commissioners for Counter Terrorism. But her function is more to coordinate with public health authorities after an attack than actually to prevent one. Academic papers, of which she has authored many, tell us detection of bioterrorism will likely come either from the medical community or first responders, meaning police on the street.

So along with whatever sensors are available, cop sense now has to include the training and the instinct to tell you if you've just walked into the middle of a man-made plague, or poison gas, or lethal radiation. Police officers are a little bit like birds in a mineshaft or, as one cop in CT puts it, "blue canaries."

"You'll have to change your suit," Falkenrath told me when I said I wanted to go down into the subway shafts. He had just been touring the subterranean labyrinth beneath the city himself, and, figuratively at least, was still wiping the dust off his hands. "It's an immensely vulnerable system," he said, thinking about what he'd seen. "There's no question about that."

The ventilation towers are a vital part of the transit system. Some of them are obvious; some are hidden completely. At least one appears to be a rather elegant brick town house on a cobblestone street in a fashionable corner of Brooklyn. A special police unit responsible for watching over this infrastructure has to turn off the alarm before you go inside through the locked steel doors, because you go straight into the subterranean world of mass transport and potential mass destruction. The effect is more than a little disorienting, like stepping off the sidewalk into the set for some expressionistic horror film without quite knowing how you got there. The light inside is low and heavily shadowed. A fine layer of black dust—steel dust from the rails far below—covers everything. Flights of steel stairways descend to the tunnel itself, where walls are so tight around the train that it pushes a wave of air before it like a piston. Overhead are horizontal doors that can open to the sky like some 1950s missile silo.

At the core of the towers are enormous fans behind louvered walls. They can blow air into the tunnels or suck it out as needed to deal with fire and smoke or, Falkenrath told me, "in the event of an improvised chemical weapon attack."

"Like chlorine."

"Yeah."

Falkenrath said the venting capacity of the tunnels "is considerable," but wondered aloud what you do with the air that's contaminated. You can't just pump it into the sky above Brooklyn. "There's actually no one right answer on how to do it," he said without elaboration. "The complexity of the New York City subway is extraordinary," he said. "It's an open system. . . . An immensely vulnerable system."

It was then that I asked him about the Iranians.

Iranian Probes—2003

Alireaza Safi and Ahmad Safari were taking pictures and making little movies, and if it weren't for the time, ten minutes before one o'clock on an icy Saturday night in mid-November, and the place, near the Hunter's Point subway station in a lonely corner of Long Island City, Queens, the transit cop might not have taken much notice. But he did.

The two men had focused their attention and their lenses on the Number 7 subway line at the point where it ends its run as an elevated train crawling along Twenty-third Street and Davis Street past parking lots and half-abandoned buildings covered with graffiti, then plunges underground on tracks that take it beneath the East River, beneath the United Nations, and onward to Grand Central Terminal.

The cop asked Safi and Safari what they were doing. They looked puzzled, shrugged, said unintelligible things. Not a good sign, but not all that unusual in New York. It seemed the two might be from Iran. They'd been to some event in Queens, not clear what. They might be part of the mission to the United Nations. That's not clear, either. "No speak English," they say. "Only speak Farsi."

The Transit policeman thought, well, he'd let them go. But then he thought again and called for backup—a cop who spoke Urdu and Farsi, who arrived in short order. He grilled Safi and Safari for two and a half hours in their own language until, toward the end when it was clear they were in deep trouble, they discovered their English wasn't really so bad after all.

Who were they? They said they'd arrived in the United States less than a month before, and they would be leaving in another three months, so they were out taking pictures. They said they hadn't been doing anything wrong, but anyway they had diplomatic immunity.

Safi and Safari were not the first Iranians attached to the UN mission to be caught checking out New York's landmarks and, more importantly, its infrastructure. Two others who were under surveillance by the FBI while they were conducting their surveillance on the soft spots in the city got picked up in June 2002. They were both declared Persona Non Grata by the State Department and expelled. Nor would Safi and Safari be the last. Two more with diplomatic immunity were caught and PNGed in May 2004.

In fact, the Feds have gotten used to what one agent calls "this game of cat and mouse" with suspected agents attached to Iran's UN mission. It's almost like the spy-counterspy contests of the cold war. You watch them, they watch you watching them, you try to figure out their gambits, they try to get around yours. Those with diplomatic passports "might be security personnel, they might be chauffeurs, they might be cooks," says the FBI agent who's been in on the chase. He laughs. "I keep saying, 'Remember The Hunt for Red October!' " (That's a cold war gospel if ever there was one, in which the least imposing member of the submarine crew turns out to be the most dangerous.) With the Iranians, "It's the cook!"

Deputy Commissioner Mike Sheehan at the CT bureau had, and still has, doubts about how dangerous Safi and Safari really were. "It's not clear what they were really doing." Were they plotting an imminent terrorist attack? Probably not. Were they from Iran's Ministry of Intelligence and Security (MOIS) or from the sometimes-competing, sometimes-complementing Iranian Revolutionary Guard Corps (IRGC)? Sheehan asked himself the question. "I'm not sure which organization these guys are from," he said. "They send people to the United

States and they do things in the United States. And whether it's train-
ing or actually preoperational activity or both doesn't really matter to
us. Either one, it's unacceptable. Was this a really serious reconnais-
sance for a terrorist plot? I don't know. Could have been. Could have
just been for the files. They could have been just doing general recon-
naissance, general preparation: 'Know the potential battlefield.' That's
probably what it was. That and getting their people used to operating
in New York City. That's what I think they were doing. And that is very
dangerous activity and unacceptable."

The Iranians have done this sort of thing before in other parts of the
world, fattening their files with reconnaissance before wreaking havoc.

Iran's agents hit the Israeli embassy in Buenos Aires, Argentina, in
1992 and a Jewish community center there in 1994. The first attack
took twenty-nine lives, the second eighty-five. The apparent reason was
retaliation for Israeli strikes against Iran's top protégés in Lebanon's
Hizbullah militia. But Tehran's relations with the Argentine government of Carlos Menem were complex, and rumors floated of secret
deals gone awry. The investigations into the bombing stalled repeatedly,
even after voluminous evidence established the role of Iranian-backed
operatives in the attacks.[1]

The other relevant case is Khobar, the apartment complex in eastern
Saudi Arabia hit by a massive terrorist bomb in 1996, which killed nineteen American air force personnel and wounding hundreds. That was
on Cohen's watch at the CIA. His shop might have seen this coming,
but did not. Months earlier, Jordanian intelligence identified and the
Saudi security forces arrested members of the Iranian-backed branch
of Hizbullah in Saudi Arabia. The prisoners had admitted they were
conducting surveillance of the Khobar Towers complex, which housed
American military personnel flying missions over Iraq.

The CIA's relations with both the Jordanians and the Saudis are extremely close. John O. Brennan, the CIA station chief in Riyadh at the
time, was considered a high flier, and went on to be George Tenet's
chief of staff before running the national Counterterrorism Center. But
the Saudis seem to have felt they'd eliminated the threat. And if they
warned their friends at the CIA about it, the word never got to the soldiers living in Khobar Towers.[2]

The arrest of one of the group's cells in Saudi Arabia didn't faze the Iranian intelligence operatives. They merely activated another cell and kept the same target, Khobar, that their agents had been casing for almost a year.[3] They could see that no extra security had been put in place.

That's how the Iranians did these things. They and their agents observed, researched, recorded, organized. And sometimes they hit. And sometimes they did not. But they had the information they needed to act, and the cells they needed for action, at their disposal.

What may have been most interesting about Safi and Safari is that they were not in fact covered by diplomatic immunity. They were not on the list of the Iranian mission's employees given to the State Department. So the FBI was not looking at them as guards or chauffeurs or cooks. It was not looking at them at all.

It was the Transit cop out on the street that night who spotted them and the Farsi-speaking officer from the NYPD who nailed them.

THE WAREHOUSE

From Sharing to Trading

Cohen's years at Langley and in the New York office of the CIA had taught him "there's no such thing as information sharing, there is only information trading," as he told his colleagues at the NYPD more than once. If the city's needs were going to be addressed by Washington, or even within the Joint Terrorism Task Force, it couldn't wait for information handouts. "You go to the FBI and say, 'Tell me what you're doing,' they're going to say, 'Go fuck yourself,' " is the way another senior official with the NYPD put it.

Back channels to the CIA or other parts of the intelligence community could only take you so far. To get the stuff you needed, you had to be able to pull your weight. You had to be giving as well as getting. Otherwise you were going to be like the puny kid having sand kicked in his face by bullies in the old Charles Atlas body-building ads. But you couldn't order this muscle-building program out of a comic book or off TV. You couldn't really get anyone from the outside to tell you what was needed.

Cohen knew languages would be key. You can't run informers in immigrant communities, much less undercover cops, if you don't speak the dialects. That's true whether you are talking crime or terror or both, and out on the street you can't always tell the difference. You want to investigate a brothel run by gangsters who speak the Chinese language Fukienese? You aren't going to get through the door speaking Mandarin.[1] Moroccan Arabic isn't going to help you much with excited Egyptians, as the cops found out the night they busted the Brooklyn jihad plot in 1997. Mexican bad guys won't trust anyone speaking with a Caribbean Spanish accent. Cohen drew up a list of fifty different languages and dialects altogether, in order of priority: Arabic, Urdu, Farsi, Fukienese, Dari, Bengali, and so on, and presented it at the morning meeting.

Kelly thought he knew where he could find these people. Police work had always been an entry-level job for immigrants. The badge, the uniform, the authority carried a sense of belonging, as well as prestige, in a new country. The Irish, the Germans, the Italians had all joined the ranks in their first generation, and if their numbers still were strong—all those Kellys and O'Neills and O'Rourkes—a lot of new blood from scores of different countries was coming in, too. A search of the records showed about two thousand five hundred department employees had claimed on their job applications that they had some ability to speak a foreign language. "We sent out a notice asking for volunteers to participate in our language program, which would mean being tested, and I think about eighteen hundred put their names forward," said Cohen. Kelly hired Berlitz to grade them on reading, writing, and comprehension. About seven hundred tested as "expert," or relatively fluent. Of those, about two hundred got perfect scores, and were called "master linguists." A lot of them had been "white shields" in uniform out on the streets before that, or detectives in the precinct houses. Now they were very special to the department, and especially to Cohen: a unique asset in the fight against terrorists.

Remember, in 2002 the total number of undergraduate degrees granted in Arabic in all American colleges and universities—yes, *all* colleges and universities—was six.[2] Now Cohen had a trove of more than sixty cops who were fluent in Arabic and across a range of dialects. The tests had shown expertise in some forty-five languages, from Dari to Gaelic, Bengali to Spanish (in many accents). "In 2002 the Feds marveled at it," laughed a deputy inspector in the Counter Terrorism division. " 'How did you guys get your linguist program up so fast?' they'd say. 'Oh, you mean Ahmed and Mohammed? They were white-shield cops *before* 9/11.' "

The CIA is weak in linguists. So is the FBI. So is the U.S. military and the State Department. They have them, of course. They try to train their own. Very few are native speakers born in foreign countries, and there's a reason. If they were, they'd have a very hard time getting secret and top-secret security clearances. "For the top-secret levels they want to go knock on the doors of the places you were born, which gets dicey if you were born in Alexandria, Egypt," said the deputy inspector in Brooklyn. And because so much crap is classified, without that kind of clearance it's virtually impossible for the foreign-born linguists to work effectively within these federal bureaucracies.

The basic problem is an outmoded notion of "counterintelligence," or CI. The U.S. government's system for granting clearances dates back to the cold war and even before, when the risk of the United States defense and intelligence establishment being penetrated by agents of powerful foreign governments was very real and the preoccupation with counterintelligence obsessive. The mole hunts by James Jesus Angleton at the Agency and J. Edgar Hoover's decades of increasingly paranoid Red chasing helped raise the barriers against foreign employees. The grim housecleaning at the CIA that the FBI's Curran conducted after the treachery of Aldrich Ames (whose wife was Colombian, a foreigner) only helped to freeze the old security clearance procedures in place. And after 9/11, when it should have been clear that patriotic, naturalized Americans with firsthand experience on the ground in foreign countries would be invaluable for collecting vital human intelligence, there was a tendency at the federal level to look at foreign-born Muslims, especially, as unreliable. One stunning result: In late 2006, three and a half years after the United States invaded Iraq, of the one thousand American personnel at the enormous embassy in Baghdad, only thirty-three were Arabic speakers, and only six of those could be called fluent.[3]

In contrast, by 2003 the New York City Police Department had more than six hundred linguists, and not just in Cohen's intel division. Most—hundreds—are "marbled" through the organization, as he likes to put it. "I probably have about forty linguists that are foreign born," he said. "But it's a very critical element of the Intelligence program of the NYPD." Cohen scoffed at the federal clearance procedures: "Oooh, they grew up in Pakistan, what are we going to do?" he said, mocking the thinking at the federal level, "This is the most frightening thing. We got to go talk to their grandmother. What madrassah did they go to? Oh, do you mean you went home and visited eight months ago? Well, you know, you're finished. We can't use you."

Fighting terrorists and other criminals is not like the old chess game of espionage played against an almost theoretical background of nuclear war, nor the kind of intrigue by and against foreign governments that has caused embarrassing, sometimes painful, incidents with China, France, and Israel over the years, nor the Aldrich Ames and the Nicholson cases. The consequences of terrorist attack are much more immediate, as nearby Ground Zero constantly reminds people at One Police Plaza: "a cemetery about five blocks from here with three thousand people in it," as Cohen says. But by the same token, Osama bin Laden's ability to penetrate police operations is negligible. As one of Cohen's senior colleagues puts it, "There is zero counterintel problem with Al Qaeda and you can take more risks."

"James Jesus Angleton would be turning over in his grave," said Cohen. But if the NYPD intelligence and counterterrorism operation is called "the gold standard" by other police departments—and it is, both nationally and internationally, and even by some veterans of the CIA—Cohen credits his foreign-born, foreign-language-speaking staff, many of whom are Muslims, with helping to make that true. "To a person—to a *person*—they've been dedicated, loyal—and critical to what I think is this gold standard. . . . We have never been disappointed in the people we've brought in. Not a one. And to me, it's proof of concept. And I tell my colleagues around the world: Open up and you're stronger. Because you can deal with that threat better when you have the kind of workforce that understands where the terrorists came from, understands their language, can talk to them, will be able to spot 'em when they see 'em."

The NYPD's language capability was unique. "It comes from the size of the department and the diversity of the city," said Cohen. "And it distinguishes the NYPD from every other department—globally." So a pattern started taking shape very early on: Cohen's team would do— and more importantly could do—what federal agencies were not doing in the hunt for the bad guys. And that began to make the difference between "sharing" information and trading it.

If a terrorist comes to New York from overseas, where's he going to live? Most likely he'll be looking for an SRO, "a single room occupancy," a flophouse. But which one will he go to in a city with so many? "Terrorism comes in so many different ethnicities," said Cohen. "We put specialized debriefing teams together to talk to people: native born speaking to native born. And it's not spy work," said the former master spy. "It's just asking them, 'If someone wanted to come in to New York City and be unseen, where would they go and where would they spend their time? What SRO would they line up? If you've got to hang out for a couple of weeks with no one seeing you, where would you go?' " It was basic police work, in fact, another way to figure out what dots to put your cops on. "You have to have a local talking to a local about that," said Cohen, "so that they understand the subtleties and the nuances."

The same principle plays out in another part of Cohen's operation, the Cyber Intelligence Unit, where local, as it were, goes global. Its focus is not so much on catching hackers or fending them off, which is a hugely expensive and technically advanced enterprise handled by other agencies. The fifteen women and men Cohen has assigned to the cyber intel unit are chatters, stalkers, predators presenting themselves in countless digital disguises. They constantly visit the Web world of real and would-be jihadists. "The Internet has become the Afghan training camps of the new millennium," as Commissioner Kelly has been saying for years. "We've been in these websites," says Cohen. "We monitor them. We're familiar with them. We know the ones that are worth listening to or not worth listening to. They tell us about how the threat is evolving, the radicalization process, the recruitment process. You go to the Web to get indoctrinated, depending on who you choose to listen to." But that's just the beginning.

"You meet 'like-minded' people once you drop into the chat rooms. And you say, 'Hey, you and I think alike. Hey, there's another guy in Australia who thinks like us,' " says Cohen. "So you meet people from around the world and it gives you a sense of power: 'Here I am in New Jersey and this guy is in Belgium and the other guy is in Sydney, and we think alike.' " The cops are watching those chat rooms to see if the people start to form what they call "clusters," or, "groups of guys." "It could start out as an electronic cluster but then move outside the Internet and become real people meeting real people," says Cohen. Finally, if those people want to blow up their enemies and themselves, "the Web just produces so much in the way of how to build a bomb."

All of the members of the Cyber Unit are "U.S. citizen, foreign-born linguists," says Cohen, "and they can get into a chat room and talk to someone in Peshawar or Kandahar." And because the undercover cybercop is a native-born Afghan, "he can talk about the same street corners, the schools they went to," and get past the chat room administrators who are looking for cops.

"There's a sort of watchman for the site and he will create traps," says Deputy Commissioner Paul Browne. "They'll have somebody say, 'You know that mosque that burned down last year in such and such a square?' And if the linguist is somebody who's just been trained at Middlebury School, he'll say, 'Oh, I'm sorry to hear that.' *Our* guy will say, 'I was visiting family there last year and it was still standing. What are you talking about?' "

Very early on, Cohen had an idea that was diplomatically, politically, and operationally problematic, but that seemed to him fundamental: to put New York City cops in liaison positions working with overseas police forces that had strong counterterrorism units. You'd have NYPD officers in Scotland Yard, with the Israelis in Tel Aviv, maybe with the French at national police headquarters in Paris. But Cohen wasn't sure how to broach it to Kelly: "We didn't know each other very well," he recalled.

"I said, 'Commissioner we ought to think about putting people around key places.' He said, 'I like that idea.' And so, two weeks later at the morning meeting, I said, 'Commissioner, we should talk about this notion of putting people around the world.' And he turned to me—that's when I knew this was different than anything I'd ever experienced—he said, 'David, I thought we'd already made that decision.' And then I understood his decisiveness, his determination to change the paradigm, whatever that word means, and to think of what's best for New York City first."

The point of the overseas program was to cull details, to learn the operational, ideological, social, and technological signatures, not just of bomb makers now, but of any dangerous group. "What we're looking for are people, organizations, places. And you learn that from reading the intelligence as it comes across—*and* you learn it from having your people where the action is, so when something goes on, they're able to get it to you immediately: 'Here are a set of signatures.' Those signatures then inform our tripwire program on how to interpret what we see and how to know what to look for. Because absent an understanding of what those signatures are, you're just walking around doing things you shouldn't be doing."

But Cohen, who'd seen the FBI move into the CIA's overseas turf in the 1990s, must have known the Feds weren't going to take kindly to this. And they didn't. The NYPD had to fight a kind of guerrilla warfare against the FBI to put its people in place (about which more later). Yet in theory and in practice the functions, and especially the ways they operate, are quite different. The CIA deploys its people overseas to recruit agents inside governments, political movements, and businesses and gather information that way. The FBI under Louis J. Freeh grandly proclaimed that the scores of legal attachés it assigned in foreign lands were out there to build a paternalistic "global network of trust."[4] But the FBI "legatts," as they are called, worked out of American embassy offices and often lived in the opulent housing commensurate with diplomatic status. Whatever their intentions, they tended to get sucked into the semi-isolation of embassy community life.

Cohen wanted his NYPD cops overseas living and working with the cops in the countries where they were assigned, getting to know them personally, culling from those ties the day-to-day and minute-to-minute operational details, the granular stuff, that is so important to a city. But of course it didn't always work out like that.

Some of the cops were indeed working-class guys with that special street touch who could relate to other working-class guys who'd worked their way up in, say, the Canadian or French police. But others were from different backgrounds and made that pay off, too. When an NYPD lieutenant named Brandon del Pozo stationed in Amman, Jordan, heard breaking news about the train bombings in Mumbai, India, in 2006, he was on the next plane out.

"What balls, I got to tell you," said Cohen. "Dartmouth grad, I might add." Mumbai was "the Indian version of New York City" as far as Cohen was concerned, so he wanted a very damned granular picture of what went on there. But nobody had any real contacts. Del Pozo had met an influential young Indian at a course he attended at Harvard, however. Through that one contact, he was able to get the other connections he needed. "Within twelve hours, he's in a meeting with the police commissioner," said Cohen.

Mordechai Dzikansky, the NYPD's man in Tel Aviv for several years, worked out of the Israeli national police headquarters—and out on the street. "No U.S. law enforcement person has been on site at more suicide bombings," said Cohen. But from the beginning it was understood that terrorism in Israel and terrorism in New York City, while often parallel, were not equivalent. "We spend a lot of time talking to the Israelis," said Cohen. "And the Israelis have a different kind of threat. They have a constant suicide bomber threat that comes from a community that is very homogeneous, primarily Palestinian. When we look at the world, we have a much more diverse threat coming at us. You know, if I list it and wandered through the range—a mixture of Moroccans, Egyptians, Saudis, Bangladeshis, Pakistanis. . . . The jihadist community that is coming to New York is much more diverse. So the way we do our business has to be different than the way they [the Israelis] do theirs. What we do and the way we do it may not be appropriate for them and vice versa." The bottom line: "What we want from them is information, not 'lessons learned.' "

* * *

Settled into what Cohen calls "humble" offices in "a warehouse of sorts" are not only Cohen's linguists, but some of the best and the brightest young analysts he could attract from the academic world. "They are on a par with the best in the Agency—and many of them have been offered positions with the Agency," he told me proudly one morning. "In fact I would say most of them have. And they're here because they want to be in the game. They think there's high value added for their time and they want to be in New York City. And they have this urge for public service. And we've been able to tap into that vein very effectively."

In 2006 Cohen brought Sam Rascoff into the intel division not only to head up the analytical team, but to attract more wunderkinds to police ranks, and he did. Rascoff had gone to Harvard undergrad, then Yale Law School, clerked for Supreme Court Justice David Souter, and done a stint working for L. Paul Bremer in Iraq. And, oh, by the way, Rascoff spoke Arabic and he was not yet thirty-five years old. So he could set the tone. The hours were long and the pay was laughable compared to the worlds of corporate law and high finance. But the sense of excitement, the sense of *significance*—that, you couldn't beat. Rascoff told potential recruits that working in the NYPD's intel division was what it must have been like in the Office of Strategic Services, the OSS, during World War II, when you had a small collection of some of the best brains in the country dealing with issues of life and death and national survival, and just "making it up as they went along." Who could resist? The talent you wanted just couldn't.

Then you'd take, say, a woman who'd been at Harvard's Kennedy School, whose research had focused on Islamic radicalization and terrorism, military privatization, transnational law enforcement, and national security law. She'd graduated from Harvard magna cum laude, then got her juris doctor cum laude from Harvard Law. On her résumé was a tour at the Council on Foreign Relations working on nuclear nonproliferation, international trade law, energy policy, and biotechnology, not to mention her work in Paris with the Organisation for Economic Co-operation and Development on transatlantic biotechnology policy and France's nuclear energy industry. And—you took her and teamed her up with street-smart detectives and you said go out and look at groups of guys in Bay Ridge.

"You don't have that in other intelligence agencies," said Paul

Browne, "where the analysts and operators work side by side." But Cohen loved it—or at least loved the idea. Bit by bit, he really was building the kind of organization where he'd wanted to work when he was associate deputy director for Intelligence at the CIA, or for that matter deputy director for Operations. It was, yeah, the lost spirit of the OSS, where everything internal was transparent from top to bottom. "A young analyst will come in, and she will brief the commissioner on a core piece of intelligence analysis that will drive what we do, in a major way, in the Intelligence division for the next three to five years," he said proudly. "These are the people that work for Sam."

But the whiz kids and their older counterparts could be temperamental. "Working with analysts is harder than working with operators or collectors or detectives," said Cohen. "You send out the detectives and—it's kind of fun. They're out there. Analysts are a different breed. In many respects, their job is more difficult because they have to create insight and knowledge and findings from disparate pieces of information." It's the analysts who have to pull the pieces together and say, Yeah, that is the signature we should be looking for.

The analysts do make strange partners for hard-bitten detectives, but effective ones, according to Paul Browne. Your typical police officer, whatever his rank, "has a real aversion to writing anything," says Browne. "These guys became cops because they didn't want to have to sit in an office and write things. So they've embraced the analysts who put it all on paper. They like that."

"An analyst will tell them what's important about what you're doing," said Cohen. "What are the subtleties? What should you be looking for in addition to what you've already found? And it's the combination of the two that is extraordinarily powerful. And the appetite comes with the eating. The more they work together, the more they want to work together. It's been an absolute wonder to watch."

Cohen didn't disguise his sentiments. "It's like starting the CIA over in the post-9/11 world," he said. "What would you do if you could begin it all over again? Hah. *This* is what you would do." He was happy and proud. And widely hated.

* * *

The Intelligence division operated in ways fundamentally different than the rest of the department. It did not focus on making arrests and building cases. It was not required to keep normal statistics. While other divisions faced the continued, relentless matrix of CompStat, the Intelligence division's six hundred cops were exempted. This led to internal jealousies. But the real clashes were with the three-letter guys. By the middle of 2003, the frictions between Cohen's shop and the FBI had gotten ugly. Not only were the two institutions divided, even within the NYPD the detectives on the Joint Terrorism Task Force were "at war" with Cohen's operation, as members of the JTTF have told me. They talked about Cohen "running his own little CIA," which basically was true. They claimed they were tripping over Cohen's people all the time, that he wasn't telling them who he was watching, or how, or what he knew. And sometimes that was true, too. One of Cohen's friends and admirers at the NYPD used to tell him, "You've *got* to share this with the FBI." And Cohen would shake his head. "I know, but *fuck* these guys." Cohen's temper was as legendary as his enthusiasm.

In fact, the balance of power with the Feds had been shifting. At one point in 2004, ostensibly as a courtesy and obviously to serve notice about just how much things had changed, Kelly sent out letters to the CIA, FBI, DIA, and NSA offering help with linguists. "That's how you start," said one of his senior subordinates. "You open up the kimono a little bit." Meanwhile, the special relationship with Larry Sanchez and the Agency became less of a one-way street as the NYPD's operations came into their own. Cohen's shop was able to run undercover operations in New York, and sometimes elsewhere, like nobody else in the business, taking more risks and getting ever more intelligence to be traded. Whether in cyberspace or on the street, its people got deep inside immigrant communities, speaking their dialects, remembering whether the hometown mosque really had burned down or not, gaining trust, and identifying suspects. As the threat of homegrown terrorism began to loom larger than the threat of attackers coming from abroad, that sort of intelligence became hugely valuable to the FBI, the CIA, and other branches of the security establishment. And if they wanted it, they had to go to the NYPD—not over it, under it, around it, or through it—and they had to ask.

"Cohen couldn't share until he was strong enough," said one of his friends and admirers. "They would have shit on him." But by early 2006, said the same friend, perhaps thinking of the old Charles Atlas ads, "Cohen was muscle-bound."

THE FEDS

Against Them and with Them

Michael Sheehan wanted a Sensitive Compartmented Information Facility, known inevitably as a SCIF, or "skiff," and he wasn't the only one. Kelly and Cohen had been fighting this battle even before Sheehan came. It was a practical thing. The facility is a room or rooms where the computers are shielded from all sorts of electronic monitoring. Specially designed filing cabinets hold classified documents, the space itself is soundproofed, and you may have to go through various locked doors and cages to get in and out. A few people who might not have top-secret clearances themselves can be allowed to see select top-secret documents inside this hypersecret bubble. The idea, from a security standpoint, is a little like what they say about Las Vegas: What you see in the SCIF, stays in the SCIF. And if you don't have one, basically, you can't look at all the relevant traffic from the FBI, the CIA, the NSA, and other agencies as it comes in on the screens. Even if you print it out, you had to have a SCIF to store it. And then, as everybody understood, there was the prestige thing. "Information is power," said Sheehan.

The FBI had a SCIF at its downtown New York City field office, just a few hundred yards across Federal Plaza from police headquarters.

Before Sheehan came on board at the NYPD, there had been a time when the police detectives on the JTTF couldn't get in there.[1] That had changed. But the procedures still were cumbersome, time-consuming, and too far away for Sheehan. He had been "an intelligence guy" at the White House and the State Department. He knew the sort of intelligence available there, what one of his State Department colleagues called "a whole huge river of information," and he knew he wasn't seeing that at the NYPD. His detectives would come back to him with anecdotal stuff picked up in the SCIF, but not the kind of vital little details that you need to get the big picture. It was like trying to put together a jigsaw puzzle with all the edges rounded off the pieces.

So Sheehan pulled together seven of the hundred and thirty detectives he had at the JTTF and had them cull all the traffic going through the FBI's SCIF to prepare his own little equivalent of the daily brief the president of the United States gets (the PDB) from those same intelligence services every day. And along with the brief, his guys often brought printed copies of the relevant documents across the plaza. Sheehan had about half an hour to read through them, then had to give them back to have them returned to the SCIF at the FBI.

It drove Sheehan nuts. If somebody interrupted him, and that happened all the time, he wouldn't be able to finish the reading, and he'd never have a chance to get back to it. He wanted to be able to browse the cables while eating a sandwich at his desk, the way he'd done in Washington. But the FBI wouldn't budge.

So, in what was now almost standard operating procedure at the NYPD, he worked around the federal roadblock. The police would build their own SCIF at the CT division out in Brooklyn. It wasn't going to be convenient, but it would be theirs. "We were resisted. We had permission. The FBI blocked it," remembers one of the senior people involved. "They said, 'No, you can't have it, you've got this other access.'" But several of the top officers in the CT division were military reservists with good connections at the Pentagon. "We cut some deals with the DOD, the navy and the DIA," said the same official, "and *they* helped us build out a SCIF." It was cleared only for secret, not top-secret materials, but that was still a breakthrough. Sheehan would be able to search, store, and print at that level—even if he had to schlep for miles out on the Gowanus Expressway to get the job done.[2]

As Cohen was back-channeling to the CIA and Sheehan was back-channeling to the DIA, the FBI's fury about NYPD operations just kept growing. And that was only the beginning of the internecine clashes complicating efforts to protect New York City in 2003 and 2004. While Cohen's connections had given him about as good a picture of Khalid Sheikh Mohammed's confessions as anyone could get outside the waterboarding room, the FBI wanted direct access to KSM. It had its own questions it wanted to ask, and its own agents who wanted to ask them directly. Months passed, and then months more. The CIA would not budge. No direct access.

In the case of Iyman Faris, meanwhile, the Feds were shutting out the NYPD. The FBI had Faris down at Quantico talking about his plans to burn through the suspension cables of the Brooklyn Bridge. They had the pictures he'd taken while casing likely targets all over the city (including, perhaps, Kelly's apartment building). But they wouldn't let the NYPD detectives near him. "Iyman Faris says, 'Oh, I was gonna drive my truck over the Brooklyn Bridge,' " remembers one of the frustrated police investigators. "Well, any New York cop knows you can't take a truck over the Brooklyn Bridge. But the *FBI* agent may not know that, because none of them live in Long Island, they all live in New Jersey."

The related Paracha investigation case caused more bad blood, still, as Sheehan himself would acknowledge later. In March 2003 his detectives in the JTTF had gone with FBI agents to the offices of International Merchandise in the garment district, where the American-educated Pakistani businessman Saifullah Paracha and his Jewish partner had, over the course of the previous ten years, built their business importing cheap clothes.[3] Saifullah was out of the country, but his twenty-three-year-old son, Uzair, was working from a desk in the offices. The cops told him they just wanted to question him. He went peaceably. And question him they did. "We broke him down," said one of the police investigators. "He spilled out everything." He admitted to having contacts with Majid Khan and others in KSM's plot to bring a second wave of attacks to America's shores.

The interrogators had quite a bit to work with at that point. Information from KSM's confessions was filtering out and more details came from the Pakistani businessman known to the Parachas as "Mir" and in subsequent court documents as C-1—Confidential Informant 1.[4] The elder Paracha had met twice with Bin Laden in 1999 and 2000. By early 2003 Saifullah Paracha allegedly suggested smuggling explosives and chemicals to attack Americans. More frightening still, he proposed using nuclear weapons against U.S. troops and, as one U.S. government document alleged, "suggested a source for such weapons."[5] (At the time, the nuclear black market operations of Pakistani scientist A. Q. Khan were still extremely active.) Saifullah Paracha had a background in basic physics and had studied as a computer systems analyst at the New York Institute of Technology. He had lived in the States from 1971 to 1986, and during that time had established offices—mostly travel agencies—doing business in Washington, Chicago, San Francisco, and New York.[6] His clothing-importing company received consignments from Pakistan in shipping containers that might easily hide a crude nuclear bomb. You put all that together, and you had the outlines—potentially—of enormous and imminent danger to New York City. But young Uzair Paracha did not seem to have the details.

After Saifullah learned that his son had been arrested, there wasn't much question of his returning to the United States from Pakistan. But he still had his business interests in New York. In July 2003, some of his associates, working with the FBI and the NYPD, persuaded Saifullah there was an important deal to be made in Bangkok. As soon as he landed in Thailand, the Americans grabbed him. Unceremoniously but with all the increasingly common accoutrements—shackles, blindfolds, diapers, and so on—they took Saifullah Paracha to Afghanistan, to the infamous prison at Bagram Air Base.

The NYPD had been there before, and at Guantánamo, interviewing other suspects who had some connection to New York. But this time the FBI closed the door. "We wanted to get at him with the same guys who broke down his son," said one of the police investigators. "But we couldn't do it. Not only that, but we had delays in getting the information." This guy might have set a plan in motion to blow up New York, but the NYPD supposedly had no business in Afghanistan talking to him. Turf, it seemed to some of the officers, trumped everything else.

There were a lot of reasons, in fact, that a bunch of cops from New York City wouldn't have been wanted just then. This was the summer of 2003, when many members of the American security establishment, especially those rooted in Washington, still wanted to share in the glory of the mission just "accomplished" in Iraq, which was of course part of the great GWOT. Since the beginning of the year, bureaucrats, operatives, and agents had been positioning themselves as counterterror cowboys. In Italy, for instance, the CIA station chief insisted on mounting an elaborate "rendition" to Egypt of a minor Al Qaeda facilitator known as Abu Omar, even though Langley wasn't much interested in him.[7] Everybody wanted to be the toughest guy on the winning side, and the Paracha case looked like it could be a big one. Why share it?

There was something else going on, too. The abuse of prisoners at Bagram was out of control. On December 3, 2002, U.S. interrogators had beaten senseless a taxi driver picked up in the wrong place at the wrong time, kicking him as they questioned him until he died. A week later another prisoner, who the interrogators thought probably was innocent, died from what the autopsy report ruled as "blunt force injuries to the lower extremities." In both cases, the Armed Forces Institute of Pathology examiners wrote a single unadorned word, "homicide," after the heading "manner of death."[8] Internal military investigations into those killings were under way by mid-2003, and no outsiders, especially not outside cops, were welcome at Bagram with all that going on.

To Sheehan it made no sense at all to exclude some of the few interrogators who had the street smarts, the contacts, and the background to make a difference.[9] His detectives, in the Jack Maple mold, were just "very, very good" at making people talk. "They've been doing it for years. And we wanted to get our guys over there, because they knew things. They knew questions to ask. When you arrest somebody who has in his PDA a bunch of phone numbers, partial phone numbers and partial addresses, we want a guy who grew up in New York City to look at that list. Because he would identify phone numbers or partial addresses that would give information about New York City. And we're talking about a guy who is talking about a plot in New York City so we wanted access to that guy." Even years later, Sheehan shook his head thinking back. "That was in the early days of my time at NYPD, and yeah, did I make enemies with the FBI? You better believe it. I was pushing hard."

The real bête noire for the Feds, however, remained David Cohen and his little CIA at the warehouse downtown. The official line on all sides maintained that the FBI and the NYPD worked very closely together—*very* closely.[10] But the minute anybody talked off the record, you knew that wasn't true.

At a hotel bar where chic singles were drinking dirty martinis, one of the three-letter guys bent my ear about his frustrations with Cohen's shop. The problem wasn't between detectives (NYPD) and agents (FBI). On the JTTF the detectives were deputized as federal marshals. They had security clearances, and "you can't really tell them apart from the agents." It wasn't a case of cops on one side of the room and Feds on the other, he said, taking a solid swallow of beer out of the bottle. No way.

But Cohen. Cohen and his intel division. "They do stuff that would get us arrested." To hear this agent tell it, that part of the NYPD operated outside the regulations and laws imposed on the Feds, and maybe even beyond that. "The Constitution applies to everyone," the agent said. The First Amendment guaranteeing freedom of speech and religion and the Fourth Amendment protecting against unreasonable search and seizure still apply to "anyone who carries a badge."

Who wouldn't agree with that? But the agent was short on specifics. The Constitution? That had been pretty badly shot up already by the scholarly hit men from the Office of Legal Counsel and the staff of the vice president. What were we talking about here? The agent ran down a litany of grievances against Cohen: His officers tripped up FBI–JTTF investigations, and not only because the right hand wouldn't tell the left hand what it was doing. Sometimes the FBI would signal its interest in a suspect or possible informer, and the next thing you knew, the intel guys were knocking on the subject's door. The agent claimed the intel cops only cared about New York City, and might spook a potential terrorist to the point where he or she left the metropolitan area. "If they go out and bumper-lock one of our suspects"—that is, trail him so close he knows they're on his tail—"or knock on his door to the point where the guy leaves, to them that's a win. But to us it's a loss. Where did he go? He might be in another city. He might be overseas." Any way you cut it, the Feds' investigation is screwed.

But, even if those kinds of things happened, those weren't constitutional issues. What did the agent have in mind? What do they do that would get an agent arrested? My friend didn't like the red cell ops out of state, and he didn't like the efforts of the intel division to penetrate groups in other parts of the country. And then he talked about the tracers put on cars to track them. (One of the computer screens in the NYPD's unmarked chopper soaring over Manhattan follows the signals from these devices.) Without a warrant the FBI couldn't go on private property to place them, say, under the fender of an SUV parked in a suspect's driveway in Queens. The cops, according to the agent, didn't think twice about doing that sort of thing.

Later, I asked Sheehan about all this. As he listened to the litany in the lobby bar of a hotel in the Middle East, I thought he was going to knock over his orange juice. "That's ridiculous," he said. If the NYPD operated outside the city, the FBI complained. But if it operated inside the city and a suspect went outside, it complained. And anyway, nothing like that happened, said Sheehan. "If we ever found serious terrorist activity we were not going to push it away. We want to identify it and latch on to it, and also we are going to share the information with the FBI immediately. We would, and we did." As for the Constitution, Sheehan insisted the NYPD operated under all the constraints and guidelines of the Patriot Act, and then some.

By Sheehan's lights, the "war" between the FBI and the intel division that had greeted him when he first arrived in 2003, and quickly got worse over issues like Iyman Faris, Saifullah Paracha, and the SCIF, started to improve after he created working groups to address concrete questions. "I brokered a tripartite meeting," he told me. "I said, 'We are going to share, but we are going to share smart. There were ten working groups. In the meetings were FBI agents, NYPD guys in the JTTF, and Cohen's people. And they sat around a table and they worked these issues over. The first meeting was introductions: 'Fuck you,' 'Fuck you.' After that, fistfights. Then you got to work," said Sheehan. Eventually "they shared information. They shared operational activity. It wasn't perfect. There were egos and there were some issues, but generally it dramatically improved the coordination."

The agent from the trenches took another swig of beer and mulled over the problems with Cohen's shop. "Sometimes it's that we're jealous. We'd love to be able to operate without the oversight and restrictions," he said. "Since 9/11 the focus is on intelligence gathering to prevent another terrorist attack—but this has to be done with the idea that the information should be usable in court." And there you had it, I thought. The FBI was still, years after 9/11, in the process of reinventing itself, while the NYPD had accomplished that huge task in a matter of months. Sure, the cops wanted prosecutions, but from Kelly on down the priorities were clear: anticipation and prevention. The FBI wasn't so sure.

Just how slow the Feds were to catch on became painfully and publicly apparent after the Egyptian-born agent Bassem Youssef sued the FBI for job discrimination in 2004. He spoke Arabic and he'd been the legatt in Saudi Arabia with a lot of sensitive contacts there, but he wasn't brought on to any of the elite counterterrorism teams within the Bureau after 9/11. Instead, his superiors shuffled him off to a document processing unit. Depositions from top FBI agents made it clear that personal connections and experience with one another counted for more than understanding where the terrorists were coming from. Pasquale "Pat" D'Amuro, who was running the New York operation by 2003, had worked for several years with the late, legendary John O'Neill. He'd learned about terrorism on the job, he said.[11] Speaking Arabic wasn't really all that important. There were translators. Thanks to that approach, as of 2006, of some twelve thousand agents in the FBI, a total of thirty-three had "some proficiency" in Arabic. The NYPD had twice that many officers who were fluent.

* * *

As the intel division grew stronger, it continued to recruit the best people it could find from the federal government, and it didn't rule out former FBI agents. One was Dan Coleman, known as "the Professor" around the Bureau, where he'd been considered one of the great experts on Al Qaeda. He'd been detailed to the CIA's "Alec Station," set up to track Bin Laden when Cohen was DDO in the mid-1990s. Coleman had gone on to work with O'Neill, with D'Amuro, and with another member of that small FBI clique, Chuck Frahm, who had also been assigned to the CIA for a while. Sheehan approached Coleman about coming to work on the CT division's analytical team out in Brooklyn, which was looking at long-term threats. But in late 2005 Coleman decided he'd go with the intel division—until his first morning meeting at One Police Plaza.

As the story subsequently appeared in the *New York Post,* Coleman sat at the conference table as Cohen started outlining some antiterror plans, "which prompted Coleman to innocently ask Cohen whether he had spoken with the department's detectives on the FBI–NYPD Joint Terrorist Task Force who had global contacts," according to the *Post.* "Cohen responded with derision and swear words, saying at first he didn't want to talk with the 150 NYPD detectives because he did not want to deal with the FBI's terror division chief, Chuck Frahm, whom he cursed out.

"Coleman suggested Cohen needn't attack people personally, and that Frahm was a friend and former colleague. Then Cohen really erupted, broadening his assault to include the entire Bureau—railing about the ' "f——ing Bureau" this and the "f——ing Bureau" that, and going on about how the FBI was always withholding information,' a source said. Cohen was essentially saying, 'F—— the FBI, we do what we want!' the source added. After listening to the brutal diatribe, Coleman pushed his chair away from the table, calmly stood up and announced that he was resigning—before he ever technically started—and walked out."[12]

Mark Mershon, one of the most experienced agents in the ranks of the FBI, wanted to round out his career running the New York field office. It's a top assignment, with some two thousand bureau employees plus another five hundred from other agencies serving on the various crime and terrorism task forces. The office of the assistant director in charge, the top FBI position in New York, is in the tower at 26 Federal Plaza, downtown. It has a spectacular view, and the men who've served there could gaze out over the city with that peculiar sense of command that Manhattan's aeries give to the high flyers who occupy them. NYPD headquarters is only a couple of blocks away, and the Feds literally look down on the cops. But if you'd been around as long as Mershon—a onetime accountant who dreamed of being an agent when he was a kid in New Jersey, and who did his first stint with the FBI in New York City in the late 1970s—you knew better than to think you were in complete control.

Even in California, where Mershon was the special agent in charge of the San Francisco field office before and after 9/11, he had heard stories about the FBI's problems with Ray Kelly's NYPD, what he would later call "unacceptable breaches in communication and trust," especially at the "upper levels of management." But Mershon decided early on that if he were going to take the bureau's top job in its biggest office, he'd have to start, as he put it, "from the premise that not getting along with the NYPD is not an option."

"We have to find a way to pursue our mutual interests mutually," Mershon said in carefully measured phrases as we talked about the crises of the last few years. When he got the job in mid-2005, his first call was to his wife, he said, and the next one was to Ray Kelly. He wanted to tell the commissioner that he thought a lot of his style. "I said, 'Ray, I have profound respect for your command presence in New York and I dearly hope when the game is on, you and I will stand shoulder to shoulder reassuring the public that we're a team working this.' " As Mershon recalled the conversation, "There was a pregnant pause after that, because I don't think Ray expected that, but when he did respond it was very warmly. And I'd like to think that kind of calmed things down from the beginning."

As it happened, the first time Kelly and Mershon actually did stand shoulder to shoulder before the public, in October 2005, they were warning against a threat that turned out to be bogus. Reports had reached Washington from an intelligence source in Iraq that Al Qaeda planned to attack the New York subway system using explosives planted in baby carriages. Homeland Security passed on the information, and Mayor Bloomberg decided to take the report public in a press conference, followed by Kelly and then by Mershon, who claimed that "classified operations have partially disrupted this threat." Yet once the report of the plot was made public, a Homeland Security spokesman played it down, saying the information was a specific but "noncredible" threat to the New York City subway system. In fact the source of the allegations—"the allegator" as they joked around the JTTF—belonged to neither the NYPD nor the FBI, and later was deemed a complete fabricator. Shoulder to shoulder in the New York trenches, both the cops and the Feds wound up looking foolish thanks to Washington. But at least they were working together, or trying to.

In early 2006, FBI Director Robert Mueller went to New York to meet with Kelly, Sheehan, and Cohen. He and Mershon listened as Sheehan and Cohen briefed them about the way the NYPD ran its operations. The session went on for "about two hours, with power points and a lot of monologue," as Mershon recalls, "and the director and I left and came out thinking, 'Wow, that's pretty aggressive.'" When they got back to 26 Federal Plaza, Mueller sat down in one of Mershon's wing-back chairs, "and he looked at me and his brow wrinkled and he said, 'Mark, what do you think of Ray Kelly sending detectives overseas?'" Mueller waited for the head of the New York field office to fill the void left by the question. Mershon looked at the floor. Finally Mershon looked up and said, "Well, sir, two things occur to me. Number one: Ray Kelly is immensely proud that he has seven detectives overseas," which was the number in those days. "I know that I am not going to be able to go across the street, wag my finger and say knock it off. And, no offense, sir, but I don't think that you can either."

"Number two, and far more importantly," Mershon continued, "our agents overseas are assigned inside the embassy. They work as part of the ambassador's team. They have multiple liaison relationships not only in that country but I think it is fair to say for most of them they have road trips to other countries. We are not staffed, funded, or mission-oriented to do what Ray Kelly expects his detectives to do and that is to go sit in the bullpen of the host police agency, go out for coffee in the morning, go to lunch together. If it's a country where they drink, they go out for beers at night, and they are there to develop that relationship to the point when the bomb goes off they can get inside the [crime-scene] tape, light up a cell phone, call the department here, and say, 'Here's what I'm looking at'—and the department can react based on the assumption that there may be near simultaneous or copycat attacks carried out here in New York.

"Now, Director, as you well know, such early reporting is always erroneous, sometimes grossly erroneous, but that's what Ray Kelly wants. On the other hand, when the Israelis are looking for that financial fugitive that's kicking around somewhere in Miami Beach they're not going to call Ray Kelly to find him, they're going to call us. So we don't need to be fearful of being supplanted by the NYPD. I say let it go."

By this point, as Mershon recalls, FBI Director Mueller's expression was so wrinkled "his face was practically a prune." Mueller looked at Mershon and said, "The way you explain that, I agree." And from that point on, according to Mershon, "Institutionally, the objection to Ray sending detectives overseas ended." But not the objections from many of the agents. "You will still find individuals in the FBI who bristle at that," said Mershon, "but maybe they don't appreciate what it means being in a town where the towers came down."

From early 2006 onward, a new era was supposed to have begun. If suspicions and mistrust remained down in the trenches where the agents came up against the intel division's operatives, and they did, the FBI's top people weren't listening to them. Indeed, as one agent said, "Kelly picks up the phone and talks to Mueller any time he wants."

The Madrid Bombings—2004

Cohen got the call sometime between two and three in the morning New York time on March 11, 2004. Terrorists had just blown up commuter trains pulling into the main station in Madrid, Spain, at the height of rush hour. It looked like hundreds of people could be dead. Who did it and how wasn't clear. Could be the Basque nationalist group ETA, which had been bombing Spanish targets for decades. That was the first direction in which the Spanish government looked. But it could just as easily be Al Qaeda or one of its spin-offs, which would be a lot more worrisome for Americans, since ETA wasn't likely to target people in the United States. But Al Qaeda and its spin-offs certainly did. They never gave up—and whatever they learned in Madrid, they could turn against New York. So Cohen wanted to be very damn sure he learned the signatures fast enough to act. You couldn't rule out the possibility that the next round of commuter train bombings would be in Manhattan, maybe even later that morning.

So Cohen put his guys in motion. The officer assigned to Tel Aviv got on a plane from there. Another three officers, "an intel guy, a CT, and a Transit guy," scrambled to get the next flight out of JFK. By that afternoon, they were in Madrid and reporting back. The New York rush hour came and went. Nothing. But that could just be luck. Now at last the NYPD was in Madrid. "Within three hours of them landing on the ground, they were sending stuff back to us," said Cohen. "They're telling us about the attack. The nature of it. Not who did it. We want to know the M.O. How was it done? Where in the train?"

It didn't look like suicide bombers, it looked like they'd left sports bags on different cars and then gotten off at earlier stations. One of the bombs had failed to blow up. Inside it, the Spanish investigators found more than twenty pounds of powerful commercial plastic explosives, the kind used in mining. More than a pound of nails and screws had been worked into the lethal dough to serve as shrapnel. The trigger mechanism was a cheap Mitsubishi Trium cell phone with the alarm set for 7:40 a.m. Two little wires had been soldered to the mobile's vibration mechanism to connect it to the bomb's detonator and trigger the explosion when the time arrived. In twelve of the thirteen bombs this crude system had worked perfectly.[1]

As the reports came in, Cohen would brief Kelly and Kelly would order immediate changes in the security measures on New York City's trains and subways. It wasn't a good day to leave a sports bag lying around.

The FBI legatt at the U.S. embassy in Madrid was on the scene, too, and he was furious. Some of the Spanish authorities the cops needed to talk to were confused by the crossed signals coming from the Americans, after Cohen's people called them to clear the way for their arrival. The legatt called the intel division office in Manhattan. Cohen picked up. "We understand you're sending—"

Cohen cut him off. "Yeah."

"You're not authorized to send anybody."

"It's already been approved by the Spanish government," Cohen claimed. "They're already on their way." In fact, at that point in the early morning, the cops Cohen was sending from New York were still standing right next to him in the office.

Cohen still laughs when he tells the story. " 'They're on their way!' Boom. That's it. The Spanish loved them."

How bad was this deconfliction problem? The Feds will still tell you privately that it was a disaster, confusing the Spanish authorities, muddling lines of communication about a critical event at a critical time. But the NYPD felt it got what it needed. Based on what was learned about the bombers' behavior in Spain, the security perimeter around subway stops and commuter train stations quickly was pushed out by a couple of blocks. Madrid inspired a renewed focus on the "If you see something, say something" campaign and the Nexus program was ramped up. "We had our team out there in Madrid, and we knew that there were two civilians who saw that attack unfold and knew something was desperately awry but for whatever reason didn't pick up the phone and make a call," said Sheehan. "And we studied that case, we talked to the Spanish about it, and we came back and talked about it with Kelly, and we said we're going to amplify our message: If you see something, tell us."

As the Spanish investigation zeroed in on a handful of suspects, the narrative that emerged about who organized it and how became increasingly worrisome. The cell phone from the dud bomb was traced to a shipment of several Triums sold to one Jamal Zougam, co-owner of a little mobile phone shop in a mixed working-class district of Madrid. Zougam had come from Morocco to Spain as a kid and grown up looking as European as he did Arab. (When his hair was long and wavy and unkempt as it appeared in mug shots, there was a little bit of Jim Morrison there, a little bit of Diego Maradona.) Known among his North African buddies as "El Blancón," the big white guy, he could blend in perfectly with the native Spanish population, whether at a bar or on a train.

Zougam's terrorist connections were known, but not clear. The French and Moroccans had been looking at him since before 9/11. At one point in 2001 the French persuaded the Spanish authorities to search his apartment. In Casablanca in May of 2003, suicide bombers on foot had stunned the Moroccan security forces when they carried out simultaneous attacks on several targets, including a Jewish center, killing forty-five people. (Only four months before, the head of the Moroccan intelligence service had assured me that all radical groups in the country were totally penetrated and under control.) Zougam's name came up again after the Casablanca attacks. But still the Spanish secu-

rity services declined to move against him. Six degrees of separation is an interesting parlor game, but not enough to make an arrest.

In fact, Zougam didn't seem to be doing much of anything apart from running his little phone shop, where he might well be breaking a few laws (it was the kind of place that specialized in breaking the electronic locks on stolen mobiles), but nothing really out of the ordinary in the community where he lived.

What the Spanish police had not counted on was the way Zougam and a small group of his contacts would react to an anonymous manifesto published on the Internet in December 2003: "Jihadi Iraq: Hopes and Dangers: Practical Steps for the Blessed Jihad."[2]

By then, the insurgency against the American-led occupation in Iraq was well under way, and one of the emerging leaders was a Jordanian known as Abu Mus'ab al-Zarqawi. Brutal, street smart, and arrogant, he had been singled out by the Bush administration as a key figure linking Saddam Hussein to jihadi terrorism. But that wasn't true. Al-Zarqawi was playing his own game, building his own mujahideen pipeline into northern Iraqi territory out of Saddam's control before the invasion and moving his cells down to Baghdad after the Americans cleared the way for him.

Dating back to the Fateh Kamel case in France and even earlier to the days of the Bosnian war, European investigating magistrates like Jean-Louis Bruguière in Paris, Stefano Dambruoso in Milan, and Baltasar Garzón in Madrid had been monitoring many of these networks. But there was an assumption in Spain and in Italy, and even in Britain, that if these would-be jihadis decided to blow themselves up, it wouldn't be in the countries they used as logistical support bases. In France, which had seen repeated terrorist attacks on its territory since the mid-1980s, there was no such complacency. But all the authorities had an interest in watching the small fry to see if they'd lead somewhere else, even if the authorities only checked in on them occasionally.

After "Jihadi Iraq," Zougam and some of his friends started to move very fast. The strategy laid out in the forty-two-page document was to make the European countries in the "Coalition of the Willing" that sent troops to Iraq unwilling to stay there any longer. As the burden of fighting became heavier and heavier on the Americans, eventually they, too, would decide to leave. The conservative Spanish government of José María Aznar had cast itself as one of the Bush administration's closest friends, as willing as any member of the coalition, with 1,300 troops on the ground in Iraq. The move had been tremendously unpopular with the Spanish public, but Aznar had faced down millions of his people in the street to back his buddy Bush.

Now Aznar was stepping down and his successor was running on a platform to continue his policies. The Socialist opposition candidate, José Luis Rodríguez Zapatero, promised that if elected he would pull all Spanish troops out of Iraq. The race was tight. Could a terrorist attack turn the tide in those elections? A Tunisian scholarship student named Serhane Ben Abdelmajid thought it could. So did one of the men he'd met in Madrid mosques, a drug dealer who had become an Islamist zealot named Jamal Ahmidan, who became the driving force behind the operation. With drugs and drug money, he paid off an employee of a mining company hundreds of miles from Madrid and drove away with cases full of the plastic explosive known as Goma. Together with more than a dozen accomplices, they plotted the attack. Zougam and others placed the bombs aboard the trains. Their detonations, from 7:36 to 7:40 in the morning on March 11, 2004, which killed 191 people and injured 1,800, came just three days before the election.

If the conservative government had declined to speculate on who was behind the bombing until it had more evidence, or had looked more closely at the nihilistic nature of the crime, or had better intelligence on the Basque separatist movement, it might still have saved the election and kept its troops in Iraq. But the Aznar government repeatedly suggested in the first hours after the atrocity that it was the work of ETA—which would have been politically convenient for Aznar's party, raising no questions about its unpopular Iraq policy. As that story fell apart, however, so did the conservatives' chances. They looked like cynical liars manipulating a nation in mourning. Zapatero won, and within weeks the Spanish troops would be on their way out of Iraq. Al-Zarqawi rejoiced and so did the plotters in Madrid. But not for long.

Twenty-three days after the massacre at the Atocha train station, Spanish police closed in on the apartment where Ahmidan, Ben Ab-

*delmajid, and five others were hiding out. As the police prepared to en-
ter, the men inside blew themselves to bits.*

*For Cohen, all this narrative was useful for what it showed about the
way homegrown terrorists, who had little or no direct contact with Al
Qaeda's training camps, could improvise a monstrous terrorist attack
and possibly change the course of a country's history. And Cohen was
glad to have the FBI's take on all this in a study that had a great deal of
detail when it came out, even if the operational insights were a little late
to be of much use to the NYPD. "Listen to this," said Cohen. "Eighteen
months later we got a report from the FBI on the Madrid bombing,
which was terrific. It was great—it was fucking eighteen months later!
They tried the best they could. It's just not their job."*

NEIGHBORS

Other Cities, Other States

Whether you think New York is heaven and Washington is hell, or the other way around, for counterterrorism specialists, New Jersey is a kind of purgatory that lies in between. For terrorists, it has long been a staging ground for attacks on New York City, whether they were blowing up the arsenal at Black Tom in 1916, cruising down the New Jersey Turnpike with bombs disguised as fire extinguishers in 1988, packing explosives into a Ryder van in 1993, or serving as a temporary home to seven or eight 9/11 hijackers. United Airlines Flight 93 took off from Newark's Liberty International Airport.

So when Sidney Caspersen, veteran of a quarter century of counterintelligence and counterterrorism work at the FBI, took over in September 2002 as the new head of New Jersey's little Office of Counter-Terrorism, he had a very clear idea of where the state fit into the terrorist picture. "The bull's-eye may be on Washington, D.C., or New York City," he told a local paper, "but if you're familiar with a bull's-eye, it has ten rings. We're in both of their ten rings."[1]

Caspersen knew he was going to have to revamp the whole operation in Jersey, and with nothing like the resources Kelly would bring to bear in New York. New Jersey's governor, James "Jim" McGreevey, was going to let him have a staff of maybe seventy investigators, some of them new hires, some detailed from the state police (Cohen, by contrast, had six hundred). With a budget of $7.2 million, there weren't going to be any deployments overseas. And while the offices of the NYPD intel in Manhattan and the CT division in Brooklyn were hardly extravagant, Caspersen's was in a dreary corner of Trenton.

There was no question of Caspersen muscling in on the Feds the way Kelly did when he first put more than a hundred and thirty NYPD detectives on the New York JTTF; that was twice as many officers as Caspersen had in his whole command. The Newark field office of the FBI was one of the Bureau's great fiefdoms, as former Special Agent Caspersen well knew. It counted some three hundred and fifty agents. Depending on who was special agent in charge, Caspersen might have a good relationship. But with the FBI in so much turmoil, you couldn't count on that.

So Caspersen turned to another retired agent, Edward Curran, to help him out. Curran, after his job housecleaning at the CIA and then at the DOE, had left the FBI in 2000 with thirty-eight years of service. Together, Caspersen and Curran started looking for signatures and trip wires. The Office of Counter-Terrorism that existed before was mainly prosecutorial. Caspersen and Curran were thinking prevention. "Whatever a terrorist needs to do his duties, whether it be getting into the country, living in the country, the support, the logistics and actually going out and getting chemicals, or whatever, we're at those places," said Curran. "And when those unusual activities take place, we jump on it."

But as the NYPD got better at its job, it also seemed probable that the direct risk for New Jersey would grow. "Because of the hardening of the targets in New York City, the people trying to get them may be forced to do an attack somewhere else," Caspersen told the *Newark Star-Ledger*. "We are that somewhere else."[2]

All of New York City's neighbors saw that danger, in fact, as did many cities and states much farther afield. But at the same time many of the major police forces in the country wanted to emulate the NYPD's strategies in some way, recognizing them as the gold standard for what had come to be known as "intelligence-led policing" in the fight against crime, as well as against terrorists.

William Bratton, who had worked with Jack Maple to turn New York City's crime wave around in the early 1990s, became the chief of police for the city of Los Angeles in 2002. L.A. was another prime target for terrorists: Ahmed Ressam had meant to hit LAX in 1999, and KSM put the city at the top of his list in 2002. It is, like New York, a magnet for media coverage whenever there's a disaster, and, like New York, a city glorified as an international icon of sex, sin, and violence on the kinds of videotapes and DVDs you can get smuggled into Pakistan. L.A. is near a porous and poorly controlled border and home to many people who were not born in the United States and who live, because of their immigration status, on the outside margins of the law.

As Bratton was quick to note, the LAPD had to do more, geographically, with a great deal less in terms of manpower. (The NYPD had more cops on its rolls than the next five largest police departments in the country combined.) The LAPD can boast, and does, that it has the third-biggest civilian air force in the United States, but that's needed just to cope with the basic challenge of law enforcement when you've only got ten thousand officers in a city of three and a half million people sprawled across four hundred and seventy-three square miles. The LAPD also has to police a map full of jurisdictional holes. The barrios of East Los Angeles are patrolled by the Los Angeles County Sheriff's Department, not the LAPD. So the model Bratton worked on for countering terrorism turned strongly toward cooperation.

For "intelligence-led policing" to work in the Los Angeles environment, real intelligence sharing was vital both "horizontally"—among the various police and sheriffs' departments—and "vertically," with the three-letter guys. By 2006 Bratton thought he was making some progress. A consortium known as the Los Angeles Joint Regional Intelligence Center (JRIC) started operations that year with officers from the LAPD, the LASD, the FBI, and scores of other agencies. Like other "fusion centers" established around the country with the help of federal funds, it was supposed to break down communication barriers. But as Bratton wrote in an article coauthored with the academic George "Broken Windows" Kelling and published later that year, the Feds were still reluctant to play on the same team.

Bratton's argument, well understood by cops across the country, was that the seven hundred thousand police officers on seventeen thousand different local police forces in the United States ought to be the first line of defense and prevention against terrorist attack. But they couldn't very well do that if they arrested a suspected terrorist and didn't know anyone was looking for him—as happened when a Maryland state trooper stopped one of the leading 9/11 hijackers for speeding two days before the attacks on New York and Washington.

Communication with the Feds might have improved as the number of JTTFs across the country grew from thirty-four before 9/11 to one hundred in 2006, but even such joint programs specifically designed to spread information tended to dispense vital intelligence to the local cops as if through an eye dropper. "According to the way the system works now," wrote Bratton, "if a local officer interdicts someone who is of interest to the federal government, a 'ping' is set off in the FBI's system that this person has been stopped, but usually the local police will not themselves be notified."[3]

"America's challenge is to act and perform and share information as a single police department," Los Angeles County Sheriff Lee Baca told me in 2007. But the federal government was getting even less coherent on the issue than it was before. "You just don't know who's in charge anymore or why something is decided," he said, which leaves large urban areas to do more and more for themselves, and to try to pull smaller jurisdictions into their networks. Baca's is the largest sheriff's department in the country, with sixteen thousand officers. But "eighty percent of the police departments of America are twenty-five people or less," he said. "The small communities, all they would require is one computer hookup to the larger system." As it was, they didn't have a prayer. "I think the FBI is truly trying to make intel available," said Ed Davis, the chief of the Lowell, Massachusetts, police department, with three hundred and fifty officers. "However, we have found . . . we're pretty far down the rung when it comes to discussion of terrorist threats. The information is so heavily vetted that it becomes of little value. It is about what you get in a press release."[4]

One of Baca's big worries in East L.A. and Los Angeles County is the growth of extremely violent and extremely well organized gangs from Central America like Mara Salvatrucha, also known as MS-13. The José Padilla case suggested the potential for gangs or, more likely, gang members to be sucked into the vortex of jihad as converts to Islam. Several of the core plotters of the Madrid bombing had been petty criminals and drug dealers. But how are you going to track any of these guys as they move freely across the United States unless you can nail them when they screw up in some minor way? What's needed is something like Jack Maple's version of quality of life policing on a national scale: "Catch the crooks when the crooks are off-duty." Pick them up for speeding or credit card fraud, check the database, and bingo, there's your arrest. Baca said he'd been talking to the chief of police in the little town of Powell, Ohio (population 12,000, with a force of about twenty-five). If a gang member or terrorist suspect were to show up in Powell, the local chief wouldn't have the funds he needs to hook up into one of these fusion centers in another part of the country. Baca was thinking of bringing him into the Los Angeles web "just as an experiment."

"We want to share all the information that's not classified," said Baca. Protecting sources and methods of the CIA and FBI was all to the good, but a hell of a lot of the material gathered about potential terrorists really didn't require secret or top-secret treatment. It was just about criminals. "Like any other heist or murder, it involves weapons, conspiracy, planning, transportation, communications systems," said Baca. "You have to demystify the idea that terrorists are operating at a higher level. They are not."

When Kelly and I sat down to talk about all this in early 2007, I asked him how *he* saw the role of local police in the global war on terror.

"Well, I think the involvement of local police is a necessity, just by sheer numbers," he said. "We have, at most, twelve thousand FBI agents. I think they're *trying* to get to that number. That's the agency that has the primary responsibility for counterterrorism in this country and they just don't have enough troops on the ground. So local law enforcement is a tremendous force multiplier. And they are the ones that are going to have the contacts, going to have the information. And whether or not you can mine that information—whether or not you can get to it, analyze it, distribute it in a way it should be distributed—is still an ongoing challenge. But it just makes sense that local law enforcement should be involved in the fight, because how else can you get necessary information that's going to help you defend the country?"

I wondered aloud if cops in other parts of the United States really were well equipped to deal with the subtleties of fighting terrorists who planned crimes on a scale never seen before.

"You know," said Kelly, "I'm not certain that it is that much different than investigating conventional crime if you add a certain training element to it, a certain awareness." Cops could be taught the signatures, the key events in the development of a terrorist cell, "certain indicators that may present some small piece of the puzzle," said Kelly. "And I think that's happening. It's not happening in a consistent, coherent way across the country. But there is an effort to train local law enforcement. There is an effort certainly to *involve* local law enforcement. And we're doing it here, not only internal to our department, but we're doing it with other departments because we're concerned about the region, also. We can't just think the five boroughs of New York City. We know that in the first World Trade Center bombing, the plot was hatched and the bomb was built essentially in New Jersey. So we've got to think in those terms. We are doing that here."

In 2006 the NYPD put in place what it called "Operation Sentry" to bring together twenty-five police executives from within a hundred-and-fifty-mile radius of New York City: cities and towns in Connecticut, upstate New York, Pennsylvania, and New Jersey. "We've agreed to conduct training exercises for them," said Kelly. "We want to train them so they can go back, be eyes and ears to protect the city. I mean, it's self-interest what we're doing. There's no question about it. But local law enforcement can be a very valuable tool in identifying homegrown threats."

Some training could be funded or run through Homeland Security.

"They have relationships with certain colleges and universities," said Kelly. "We do some of the training for them. But I think the bottom line is that it's not enough."

Do you think there will be a greater appreciation of the role of local police as it's understood the military approach to fighting terrorism—the invade-and-occupy approach—is not the best way to go?

Kelly said he hadn't seen that sort of appreciation from Washington, at least not yet. "I've seen, as far as Homeland Security money is concerned now, pork-barrel politics. There's a lot of money out there. But I have not seen money spent for training at the level that I think it should be."

Again and again, the question of who in local law enforcement got what from the federal government came down to matters of politics or old-boy connections. As Bratton said out in L.A., when it came to working with the FBI, "the level of cooperation seems to vary greatly depending on the personalities of individual Bureau and police chiefs. Too often, the FBI cuts itself off from local police manpower, expertise, and intelligence. More than six thousand state and local police now have federal security clearances, but the historical lack of trust is still an issue. For example, many police chiefs complain of calls they get from their JTTF alerting them to a potential threat, but when they ask for the detailed information needed to launch an investigation, they are told by the Bureau: 'We can't tell you,' or 'You don't need to know.' "

And when the personal and professional chemistry turns bitter, fighting terrorism quickly gives way to fighting among the law enforcement agencies, which is what happened in New Jersey.

In 2005, Leslie G. Wiser, often cited as the agent who broke the Aldrich Ames case at the CIA, took over as special agent-in-charge of the Newark FBI field office, and his relations with his former colleagues Caspersen and Curran started to get ugly. The existence of their aggressive little operation rankled the Feds for the same reason Kelly's did. The New Jersey State Police hierarchy didn't have much use for them, either. As one friend of Caspersen's put it, "the State Police and the

FBI didn't like his operation because it wasn't theirs. They said, 'We're gonna stamp out this cockroach.' "

Governor McGreevey, who had supported Caspersen and Curran, made their rivals' job a great deal easier by appointing a handsome young Israeli, Golan Cipel, as his nominal homeland security advisor (nominal because Cipel, a foreigner, couldn't get a security clearance from the FBI and so couldn't be read into any of the important traffic). In 2004, under threat of a sexual harassment suit from Cipel, McGreevey resigned his office and declared that, yes, even though he was married to an attractive blonde, he was sincerely gay.

With McGreevey gone, Caspersen and Curran had no protection at the upper levels of the New Jersey government when, in 2005, questions were raised about whether they were conducting "racial profiling" against Arabs and Muslims. The evidence presented was based on raw intelligence fed back to Caspersen, and the effect of the accusations was to destroy the New Jersey Office of Counter-Terrorism as it had been run by the retired FBI veterans. When the new governor, Jon Corzine, took office in 2006, Curran and Caspersen were on their way out. And by the end of the year, they had new jobs.

David Cohen hired them both, putting Caspersen in as his effective number three, and Curran in charge of overseas intelligence gathering.

APATHY

Rising Threats and Waning Patience

In the election-year summer of 2004, the intel division saw terrorist threats gather like the swirling clouds of yet another enormous storm headed toward New York City. The Republican National Convention was due to be held in Madison Square Garden at the end of August, and reports kept coming in that Al Qaeda and anarchists, homegrown terrorists and random crazies were preparing attacks. The president and thousands of Republican delegates would be in the city, along with hundreds of thousands of peaceful protesters. The Republican leadership had picked New York for the convention precisely because it was the site of Ground Zero, precisely because it would remind the public of the self-described "war President's" leadership, and to defy whatever group threatened U.S. security. The decision was made before the invasion of Iraq, which had gone well, and the occupation, which had not. Now, the mobilization against the war and the president promised to be enormous. And Bush was still in the tough-guy "bring 'em on" mode that he affected when he defied Iraqi insurgents to come after American troops in the summer of 2003.[1]

That's politics. But the real challenge was for policing. The NYPD, working with the Secret Service, and other federal, state, and city agencies had to try to avert a new disaster on American soil. And the thunderheads of chaos just kept gathering, and tightening, and moving across the radar screen toward Manhattan.

The horrific carnage in Israel in 2002 and the coordinated attacks in Casablanca in 2003 had shown the terrorist potential of pedestrians with well disguised explosives, especially when they got on public transport. The Madrid bombers set out to change the course of Spain's elections in March 2004, and they had. There was every reason to think radicals inspired by the same messages might try the same sort of attack on New York's trains. Just a month before the Madrid atrocity, a suicide bomber had blown himself up in the Moscow subway, killing forty people (the NYPD detective in Tel Aviv was sent to the scene to gather operational details). In 2003 the Saudis had arrested a *jihadi* whose computer contained plans for an inventive device, known as the *mubtakkar,* meant to release cyanide gas in the New York subway.[2] Meanwhile, the cat-and-mouse game with the Iranian surveillance teams continued.

Kelly's officers had done a lot to secure the city and would do much more, and still they were nervous. Looking back, an NYPD report on the events of August–September 2004 would describe the eighteen months from the announcement that the convention would be held in New York City to the day it ended as a time of enormous peril: "By any measure, this was the most intense eighteen-month threat period of the post–September 11, 2000 era."[3]

But there was another dangerous factor the official pronouncements did not, and in a sense, dared not talk about. And that was the growth of apathy among the general public, and sometimes alongside it anger at the government. Almost three years had passed since 9/11. People were tired of being scared, and especially tired of having their leaders frighten them. On New York streets, the American flags put up after the atrocity still flew from car antennas and hung from windows and awnings, but they were tattered and faded now. The first anniversary of the increasingly bloody occupation of Iraq had just passed with no end in sight, and scores of American soldiers were being killed every month: more than five hundred were dead, which seemed like a lot back then.

In the spring of 2004, pictures had come out of Iraqi men stripped, bound, sexually humiliated, and in at least one case beaten to death by American soldiers at Abu Ghraib prison outside of Baghdad. Suddenly Americans found it harder to see themselves as the good guys. Whatever enthusiasm the public had felt for this Global War on Terror was gone, and that started to affect the way they reacted to safety measures at home. Many people suspected the system devised by Homeland Security to alert the public to increased threats was more closely tied to the Bush administration's political needs than to real dangers. As orange alerts flashed on and off, public irritation grew. The storm might be just over the horizon, but folks just didn't want to board up their houses anymore. They just didn't see it. More and more, they just didn't want to believe it. But, still, the danger was out there.

Inside the NYPD, the last six weeks leading up to the convention felt like a countdown to disaster. KSM's "second wave" attacks had been stopped and the CIA, after waterboarding him, had him safely warehoused in a secret prison. But some of the information KSM coughed up pointed to Al Qaeda operatives still at large who might be in the United States. Attorney General John Ashcroft issued a list of plotters thought to be roaming the country—maybe. In fact, the roster was little more than the names of known English speakers among the Al Qaeda Most Wanted: the female neuroscientist Aafia Siddiqui, who had disappeared with her children in Pakistan in March 2003 as the KSM network was rolled up all around her; Amer el-Maati, a brain-damaged rug salesman and former mujahideen from Toronto; the Tanzanian Ahmed Khalfan Ghailani, sometimes known as "Foopie," who had helped mount the 1998 attacks on American embassies in Africa; Fazul Abdullah Mohammed, another one of the men who plotted the Africa bombings; Adam Gadahn, an American convert to Islam whose grandparents were Jewish and whose parents raised him as a homeschooled evangelical Christian; Abderraouf Jdey, also known as Faruq al-Tunisi, the Canadian passport holder who had bailed out of KSM's plot to fly planes into West Coast targets; and one Adnan Shukrijumah, a young multilingual and multicultural Saudi identified by KSM as the man he thought would lead attacks—someday.

But Ashcroft's list left out the name of the most worrisome figure on the intelligence radar that summer: Dhiren Barot, a young Briton from a Hindu family (thus he was sometimes known as Esa al-Britani or Issa al-Hindi) who had converted to Islam and fought in Kashmir in the mid-1990s before hooking up with Bin Laden's networks. Even before KSM had choked out his name, Barot wasn't exactly anonymous. As Al-Hindi, he had written a widely circulated manifesto called "The Army of Madinah in Kashmir," advocating "stealthy modern-day war stratagems" including "germ warfare."[4]

According to an intelligence document obtained by *Newsweek* that summer, KSM had sent Al-Hindi to the United States in 2000 as part of an advance team to case targets in New York. Al-Hindi continued living in Britain, kept under surveillance, on and off, by the British authorities. He could thus keep networking with other *jihadis,* unwittingly helping to build up the counterterrorism intelligence files of the British and of the American agencies with which they cooperated, including the NYPD.

But in that long, tense summer of 2004, friendly intelligence services picked up talk that Al Qaeda operatives were gathering in the mountainous hinterlands around the Pakistani–Afghan frontier to plan a new offensive against the United States. And as the chatter intensified, so did the search for a way to penetrate the plot—whatever it might be. The CIA and Islamabad's security forces stepped up their own offensive, nabbing one of the Africa bombers, "Foopie" Ghailani, in the city of Gujrat in central Pakistan. He was not, as it turned out, anywhere near the United States. Much more importantly, they grabbed a twenty-five-year-old computer engineer named Mohammed Naeem Noor Khan, who served as a kind of Web-based switchboard operator for Al Qaeda's secret global communications networks. He quickly agreed to cooperate, but in secret. If there was a big plot about to move from planning to action, he was now the double agent best positioned to stop it.

On Noor Khan's laptop were photographs and detailed surveillance reports about five financial institutions in the United States: the New York Stock Exchange and the Citigroup building in Manhattan; the Prudential Financial building in Newark, and the World Bank and International Monetary Fund in D.C. The pictures and reports appeared to be from Dhiren Barot aka Al-Hindi, from his reconnaissance trips back in 2000 and early 2001. And even if they were three or four years old, they provided a detailed blueprint for terrorist operations. Meanwhile Al-Hindi, at that precise moment in late July 2004, seemed to have slipped out of sight in London.[5]

"Many people who join this group will die, be wounded or jailed," proclaimed one Internet chat site. "Some of you may be forced to shoot some constitutional rights usurpers who are 'just doing their job' and some of them will have families." That is, some of you will kill cops. Another website, waxing lyrical at the prospect of carnage in New York, seemed to draw on Dadaism and Jacques Derrida for inspiration: "In our actions we must be strategic, ruthless, efficient, as well as chaotic," the site told sympathizers. "Like a string of tornadoes and quakes, we will manifest brutal attacks against key targets, physically deconstructing the aesthetic of our oppression. We will erect barricades of fire and reclaim space as carnival. Our rage as well as joy will be present on every street corner."

The radical fringe of the global opposition to globalization was planning to hit New York City with a vengeance during the Republican convention. And if the goals often sounded quixotic, they were dangerous nonetheless. Since 1999, when "the Battle of Seattle" pushed a city to the brink of collapse and forced the breakup of talks by the World Trade Organization, fires had indeed burned, people had been badly injured, and at least one had died. By 2001, minuscule groups of anarchists were on a triumphant spree, "summit hopping," as they called it, going from one violent high to the next, with the names of cities hosting hitherto mundane economic conferences suddenly making headlines around the world: Prague, Nice, Québec, Porto Alegre, Göteborg.[6] The events became increasingly about the cops and the crazies, with little or no space left for peaceful demonstrators to get their message out. Each confrontation had to be more violent, more spectacular to make headlines, so the rampages kept picking up pace. And then, in July 2001 leaders from the seven most industrialized countries and Russia came together in Genoa, Italy. This was a big one. Security was supposed to be very tough. The protesters, both peaceful and violent, were to be kept far out of sight of the new American president, George W. Bush, and the other heads of state meeting in the splendor of an ancient palace at the center of what was designated "the Red Zone." To protect it, mounted cops in riot armor positioned themselves for charges from behind towering fences.

The protesters generally, and the radicals especially, saw all this as a challenge. Among the crowds were small cells using the tactics known as black blocs to confuse the police and avoid arrest. Dressed entirely in black (or, in some cases, entirely in white) and often wearing masks, they could strip off their monochrome disguises and look more or less normal in street clothes as soon as they left the scene. When arrests were made, many of these protestors carried no ID and lied about who they were.

The streets around Genoa's Red Zone quickly degenerated into a maze of burning barricades and close-quarter confrontations. Dumpsters were pressed into service as makeshift tanks, pushed by demonstrators toward phalanxes of carabinieri. Shopping carts stolen from supermarkets, first employed to carry bottles of water for thirsty demonstrators, now ferried paving stones to the battle lines. My journalist colleagues and I watched as cars were tipped over and set on fire, shop windows smashed; the smoke mingled with clouds of teargas. Demonstrators donned swimming goggles and painters' masks against the swirling fumes and wrapped their bodies in foam rubber, cardboard, and packing tape before charging to the front. Water bottles, now filled with gasoline, became Molotov cocktails.[7]

Far from the besieged sanctuary of the Red Zone, a couple of cops in a patrol car suddenly found themselves cut off from the rest of their force. As the crowd closed in on them, a young protester named Carlo Giuliani raised a stolen fire extinguisher to smash in the car window. One of the terrified cops pulled his Beretta nine-millimeter pistol and shot Giuliani in the head.

The smash-and-burn rampage during the Genoa summit racked up about forty-five million dollars' worth of damage and vastly overshadowed whatever good was accomplished by activists like Bono and Bob Geldof, who were trying to get billions of dollars of debt relief for developing countries. The Italian cops, meanwhile, took their revenge. In the hours before dawn the day following the riots, they poured through the hallways and rooms of a school being used as a dormitory by some of the protesters, beating many of them senseless before dragging them off to jail. Later investigations would show the Italian cops had planted two Molotov cocktails in the building as "evidence" to justify their actions. Out of ninety-three people arrested at the school, seventy-two had been injured.[8] All eventually were released without charges.

The Al Qaeda attacks on New York and Washington seven weeks after the Italian bloodshed made Genoa and Seattle look less like battlegrounds than playgrounds. The 9/11 aftershocks drained the anarchists of zeal. For more than a year they failed to make headlines and, indeed, retreated from the field. But in 2003, with anger about the war in Iraq helping to swell their ranks once more, "direct action" groups started to resurface with a vengeance.

Their tactics were designed, as before, to skirt the edges of violence and lawlessness, to shut down cities rather than blow them up, to injure, insult, and incite the cops. The NYPD Intelligence division pulled together a long list of typical projectiles used against police lines: "rocks, paving stones, bottles, batteries, ball bearings, nuts and bolts, billiard and golf balls, hockey pucks, nail-filled potatoes, live CS canisters, frozen water balloons, all of which could be catapulted with wrist rockets, slingshots, large rubber bands, paintball guns, or lacrosse sticks." Often the protesters threw Molotov cocktails or bags full of excrement. They carried grappling hooks, sledgehammers, and crowbars to bring down security fences. They had devices called "sleeping dragons" they could use to hook into one another to form "inseparable human chains," or bicycle D-locks they could use to shackle themselves together, or to immovable objects. They filled Super Soaker squirt guns with noxious chemicals; they used oil, marbles, and ball bearings spread on roads to bring down police mounted on horses. Some had obtained infrared transmitters that could change traffic signals from six hundred yards away.

In San Francisco in March 2003, direct action groups managed to shut down more than forty key intersections around the city, then re-grouped and tried to take the Oakland Bay Bridge at rush hour. At a meeting of the World Trade Organization in Cancún, Mexico, protest-ers battled with police near the eight-foot-high security fence that cut them off from the delegates. Some of the radicals attacked the Mexican cops with iron bars and stones. In the middle of the melee, a South Korean farmer, part of a highly disciplined protest group, climbed the fence and committed suicide by plunging a knife into his chest. Two months later, extremists among the twenty thousand people protesting a free trade conference in Miami fought pitched battles with police that ended in two hundred and fifty arrests.

The black blocs were back and they would be coming to New York.

In early 2003, soon after the Republicans announced their national con-vention plans, Cohen set up a special RNC unit charged with gather-ing information on any groups that might use violence to disrupt the convention or to shut down the city. But how would you distinguish guerrilla theater from guerrilla warfare among those who designed their strategy and tactics precisely to obscure the difference?

You couldn't set up static defenses and wait to get hit in street battles like the ones that rocked Seattle and Genoa. You had to go out and find the groups, conduct surveillance, and penetrate them. Their Internet sites and chat rooms helped you narrow the field, but could be mislead-ing. The site telling sympathizers they might have to kill cops with fami-lies contained "no significant intelligence," a report from the RNC unit noted in late December 2003, a month after the group first appeared on the Web. "It remains unclear if the subscribers are supporters or merely curious."[9]

Kelly and Cohen decided they would have to push beyond what many Americans and New Yorkers had come to think of as acceptable boundaries for police investigations of political groups. A U.S. Supreme Court ruling and the Patriot Act had removed some of the hurdles, but the NYPD, partly as a result of its abuses in the 1960s and 1970s, faced particular guidelines. They grew out of a lawsuit, *Handschu v. Special Service Division,* brought against the undercover unit of the NYPD in the name of a young activist named Barbara Handschu in 1971. After years in the courts, the guidelines were formalized in 1985. Use of undercover cops to look at any group with a political or religious coloring required review by two senior police officials and a mayoral appointee, had to be renewed regularly, and could be challenged by people who thought they were the object of such an investigation.[10]

Kelly, the veteran cop, knew all about *Handschu*. "It agreed to restrict investigations of religious or political entities, greatly restrict them," said Kelly. "Investigations can only be conducted by one small unit in the Intelligence division. There was a *Handschu* board that monitors those investigations and the information could not be shared. So in 2002 when I came back here, I moved to modify that."

A year and a day after the 9/11 attacks, David Cohen argued in an affidavit submitted to United States District Court Judge Charles S. Haight Jr. that "given the range of activities that may be engaged in by the members of a sleeper cell in the long period of preparation for an act of terror, the entire resources of the NYPD must be available to conduct investigations into political activity and intelligence-related issues." Five months later, on February 2003, Haight agreed. New York's cops could essentially adopt post-9/11 federal guidelines as their own.[11]

With the legal avenue now open, Cohen dispatched his detectives to California, Connecticut, Florida, Georgia, Illinois, Massachusetts, Michigan, Montréal, New Hampshire, New Mexico, Oregon, Tennessee, Texas, and Washington, D.C., to hang out with the loosely organized anarchists, direct action provocateurs, libertarian clowns, conscientious protesters, and potential killers setting their sights on Madison Square Garden. He also tasked his men in Canada, Europe, and Israel to find out as much as they could. And they came up with some disturbing, if far from definitive, reports. Two of the most prominent figures organizing direct action confrontations at summits in Europe, Latin America, and the United States had traveled separately to Israel, where each had gotten involved with Palestinian activists. Whether their purpose was to teach direct action to some Palestinians, to learn techniques for heightened violence from others, or just to have a look-see, the Israelis had deported one and put the other on a watch list.[12]

Nothing was clear except the nightmare. An attack like the suicide bombings in Jerusalem or the train bombings in Madrid would be hor-rific in any case, but if one came amid the confusion of anarchist-caused chaos, whether coordinated or not, the disaster would be much worse. And for almost two years, Cohen had been watching a plot take shape in Brooklyn that might conceivably make that happen.

Kamil Pasha was a kid from Bangladesh. He'd spent most of his twenty-three years in the States, since he was seven years old, but that hadn't made him any less a Muslim. Maybe it had made him more of one, because it made him think about what Islam really meant. Anyway, that was the kind of thing the twenty-three-year-old could say when he moved into a neighborhood full of Muslims in Bay Ridge in the fall of 2002. He looked and talked and pretty much thought like a lot of other people there. He prayed like them. He believed like them. And they found it easy to believe in him as an innocuous neighbor. He was an easy fit.

Kamil Pasha was a cop, in fact, and the name was false, even if the faith was not. He had graduated from John Jay College of Criminal Justice, where so many ambitious members of the force had taken degrees, and he was about halfway through the police academy in October of 2002 when Cohen spotted him and pulled him out for an assignment with the Special Services Unit, the undercover operatives of the Intelligence division. He would live in Bay Ridge, get to know people, and be, as he said later, a kind of walking surveillance camera, never pushing for information, never trying to lead a conversation. The job was to "observe, be the ears and eyes" of the NYPD inside this community. But his contact with the police department was kept to an absolute minimum. There was no dropping by the precinct house of the Six-Eight. His contact was a veteran undercover detective sergeant in Cohen's shop. At first, they communicated only through e-mail.[13]

The terrorism hotline run by the police had gotten some calls about a young man named Shahawar Matin Siraj working at Islamic Books and Tapes, a shop next to the Islamic Society mosque on Brooklyn's Fifth Avenue. Was he just mouthing off about wanting revenge for what was happening to Muslims in other parts of the world, or was there something more to it? Siraj's family were Ismailis, the followers of the Aga Khan normally known for their hard work and moderation, and rarely if ever associated with violent jihad in modern times.[14] But Siraj was slow witted and hot tempered. Maybe there was something there.

About three weeks after Kamil Pasha moved to Bay Ridge, he started hanging out at the mosque and the bookstore and getting to know Siraj. They were roughly the same age, and like a lot of young men in the neighborhood, Pasha said he was looking for a job. Siraj said maybe his uncle, who owned the store, could help out. They kept talking, kept praying, and Siraj started to think of Pasha as a friend. He had never had very many of those.

In school in Pakistan, Siraj had struggled to keep up with other students. His IQ was a very low seventy-eight, but that was not the only problem. The Ismailis are regarded as heretical by strictly religious Sunnis and Shiites, and Siraj was mocked by his teachers, and sometimes beaten up by other kids, who called him an "Aga Khana." They made fun of him for not being able to read or understand the Qur'an. So Siraj found escape in video games until finally at the age of seventeen he left Pakistan to join family in the United States.

At Islamic Books and Tapes, poring over the tracts that lined the shelves or listening to tapes and watching videos, arguing with customers, praying in the mosque, Siraj tried to teach himself how to be a good Muslim like those Muslims who had tormented him for so long.

The ranks of *jihadis* in the West are full of self-taught fanatics who, with an extremely tenuous grasp of theology, history, tradition, or even the fundamental texts of the faith, convince themselves they've somehow got a direct channel to Allah and His will and, especially, His anger. And that was the path Siraj was on when Pasha first met him.

Were there suicide bombers in Israel? Good, Siraj would say. He would do the same thing if anyone treated his family badly. The United States had to feel the pain it inflicted on the rest of the world—which was why Osama bin Laden was such "a talented brother and a great planner." Siraj told Pasha he hoped Bin Laden was planning "something big for America." As the Bush administration led the United States to war in Iraq, the news on television bolstered Siraj's anger. While

American coverage was all about victory, what Siraj could read and see from Muslim sources was all about victims. Kamil Pasha listened to the would-be warrior, and watched, and wrote up seventy-two contacts with him over the course of many months.

In the fall of 2003 the young Pakistani got a new friend, an older man whom he would come to call "brother" and who sometimes called him "son." Osama Eldawoody had trained in Egypt as a nuclear engineer, but after he came to the United States in the mid-1980s he never was able to find a job that used those skills. He drove a taxi, worked in the restaurant business, sold real estate in New Jersey. All that was easy to share with Siraj, along with the righteous anger. And all of it was true. But there was more to Eldawoody's story. He also was a paid agent, a "confidential informant" of the Intelligence division's Terrorist Interdiction Unit.

In the months after 9/11, Eldawoody often found himself under surveillance or receiving visits from the Feds and the NYPD at his house in Staten Island. "Why all this discrimination?" he demanded at one point in October 2002. He had shown he was willing to work with authorities before: he wore a wire and helped bust a corrupt building inspector in New Jersey. Maybe he could be of use to the NYPD now on more important cases. It took a while to seal the deal, but many months later, in July 2003, Cohen's people signed up Eldawoody and sent him to Bay Ridge to check out the young wannabe firebrand working at Islamic Books and Tapes.

In the mosque, Eldawoody was conspicuous for the passion of his beliefs. Often his prayers moved him to tears. If a stranger—a non-Muslim—appeared at the door, Eldawoody complained. It was after he became a regular at prayers, his face familiar to everyone, that he started visiting the bookstore. Siraj liked him. Probably he was impressed by his education, and clearly he liked the time and attention this fifty-year-old man devoted to him. Siraj lived in Queens, and Eldawoody often gave him a ride home. They talked for hours about the world, about Islam, about conspiracies against Muslims, and more and more about jihad.

And there was one more friend, but he was in many ways an even sadder case than Siraj. James Elshafay was still a teenager, and a very troubled one. His mother was Irish-Catholic; his father was an Egyptian Muslim who moved out when he was two years old. Elshafay, like Siraj, was a terrible student. He was also schizophrenic. Three times he tried to pass ninth grade and failed. When he was twelve, his father had told him to embrace Islam, but he did so without much sense of conviction, much less militancy. Big, ugly, awkward, and unstable, he didn't fit in anywhere as he grew up on Staten Island. And then, when he was sixteen, 9/11 happened. Suddenly people he'd known all his life were out carrying placards attacking Arabs. Whatever the signs said, he read them as "Kill Arabs" and "Kill Arab Babies," and got into a fight. Confused, wanting to prove himself, Elshafay tried to enlist in the army and, with more discipline than he'd ever shown before, he managed to pass the required test to get a high school diploma. But the army wouldn't have him because of his psychiatric problems.

In 2002, when he was seventeen, Elshafay had gone to Egypt to spend some time with his father's family and came back to the States much more interested in learning about Islam than ever before. He went to the mosque in Bay Ridge, and to the bookstore in the fall of 2002. Siraj was there watching a tape that purported to show the 9/11 attacks were really a plot by the United States government to justify a crusade against Arabs and Muslims. It was the first time they met, but Siraj would teach Elshafay a lot about the Islam he'd discovered. And about American conspiracies. And about the Jews and their plots to rule the world.[15]

In the late spring of 2004, just months before the Republican convention, the publication of photographs showing American men and women soldiers humiliating Arabs at Abu Ghraib confirmed for Siraj everything that he believed about the evil of American actions. Now when he talked to his mentor, Eldawoody, or to the kid that he mentored, Elshafay, he talked about moving from bull sessions to real bombings, if only they could find the explosives. The informer Eldawoody said he knew someone upstate with a group he called "the Brotherhood" who might be able to help. Elshafay started talking about spectacular plans—hitting the bridges that linked New York and New Jersey to Staten Island—

including the enormous Verrazano Bridge as it comes in over Fort Wadsworth. But Siraj favored subway stations. He'd dressed like a bum to check some of them out, he said. Subway stations, transportation hubs, that was the kind of target you wanted. The sage Eldawoody agreed. That would be real jihad. He would talk to the Brotherhood. What he did, in fact, was to start wearing a wire.

Kamil Pasha, on Cohen's orders, had slowly pulled back from the case. Sometimes he'd cross paths with Siraj and even Eldawoody at the bookstore, but the cops wanted to keep Pasha's undercover work undercover if they could, which meant keeping him and his testimony out of court. "What we did was the reverse of the way it's usually done," Kelly explained later. "Usually you have a CI who makes the first contact, and the CI introduces a cop, because the cop is able to give better testimony and it's usually less dangerous for him. But here we had the cop, the undercover, basically turning it over to the CI." There were other reasons, too: questions of personality, and perhaps personal authority. "Eldawoody had a kind of avuncular style that I think just kind of blended with this kid," said Kelly. "And he had a relationship with the mosque, and it was just a more comfortable fit." And then, there was a question of discretion in the legal tangle created by *Handschu* and the NYPD's challenge to its old guidelines. "This is New York City," said Kelly. "Running a program like this is sensitive." As lawyers would point out later, Pasha had started visiting the mosque and the bookstore before the *Handschu* guidelines were changed.

So Siraj and his friends Elshafay and Eldawoody continued making plans. And by July 2004, they had almost settled on a target: the Herald Square subway station at Thirty-fourth Street. The Manhattan Mall above the station might be destroyed, too, if the bombs were powerful enough. The detonations, death, and destruction would be right at the foot of the Empire State Building and only two blocks from Madison Square Garden, the site of the Republican convention, which was now only weeks away.

ANGER

Conventions and Causes

So many plots, so little time.

Where was Dhiren Barot? Where was this guy who had conducted such detailed surveillance of Wall Street and the Citigroup building? He had been in London in July 2004. The Al Qaeda computer-geek-turned-double-agent Muhammad Naeem Noor Khan was in touch with him via e-mail. If the British and American intelligence services could get him back squarely in their sights, they might be able to let him run for a while longer. He operated as if he were Bin Laden's main man in the UK, and maybe he was. He knew his way around lower Manhattan as well as he did Lahore or the East End and he had contacts with people in operational and sleeper cells. As long as you could watch him in action, you could trace his contacts and you could lay the groundwork to roll up those operations. The Brits knew this. So did the CIA and the FBI and the NYPD.

But apparently the message didn't get through to some people in Washington. From the time the White House had seen the rundown on Noor Khan's revelations and the content of his laptop on the morning of July 30, reelection imperatives had been trumping national security concerns and, for that matter, common sense.

On August 1, the head of Homeland Security, Tom Ridge, told Kelly in a videoconference call that he was planning to go public with some of the basic information from Noor Khan's computer: the names of the targets. "Ridge was rolling with that 'the president has to level with the American people' kind of crap," as one of the commissioner's close associates told *Newsweek* a few days later. Kelly didn't think that naming targets would make the city any safer. The FBI's Pat D'Amuro had shared the outlines of the threat with him the same night the White House heard about it, and the NYPD had alerted the relevant corporate security personnel to make sure they were aware of the heightened risks. Kelly also sent some of the ESU men with their helmets, body armor, and M-4s to the target sites, showing anyone who was watching that in New York City terrorists would be prey as well as predators. Some of the Feds might claim that was a tip-off to the terrorists, but it wasn't much different from the usual random deployments of surges and Hercules teams. The tip-off had come in Washington, where the White House had given Noor Khan's name and some details of his laptop's contents to several reporters.[1]

The pattern for the Bush administration's behavior was well established. Whether on a waterboard or a keyboard, a source somewhere in the world would reveal some dire-sounding threat to the United States that might, or might not, have some operational plausibility. Washington officials would start to cover their asses in case something bad went down. The leaks would become a torrent. And so it was, just as soon as the White House learned of the intelligence on Noor Khan. Homeland Security announced an orange alert, and the next day *The New York Times* published a story saying Noor Khan had been captured and was cooperating.[2] An unnamed senior official in the Pakistani government provided details. Barot and his accomplices were now warned that the authorities were on to them.

This leak was so problematic for New York City's security that New York Senator Charles Schumer pointedly sent identical letters to Condoleezza Rice, who was then Bush's National Security advisor, and Frances Townsend, the president's Homeland Security advisor, demanding that they investigate the leaks (which may have originated in their own offices or, indeed, with them). "Mr. Khan had been providing invaluable information to our allies, because he continued to maintain contact with al-Qaeda operatives even after his capture by our allies," Schumer said. "According to several media reports, British and Pakistani intelligence officials are furious that the administration unmasked Noor Khan and named other captured terrorist suspects." Indeed, they were. But if Schumer ever got an answer, it never was made public.[3]

So, where *was* Barot? When Scotland Yard caught up with him on August 3, he was getting his hair cut at the Golden Touch barber shop in Willesden, North West London. Fortunately, he surrendered without a fight. But then the question became, what did he know? Finding that out was going to be a very long, very slow process.

A week before the Republican National Convention was set to begin, the Egyptian nuclear engineer Osama Eldawoody had come back to Islamic Books and Tapes in Bay Ridge with good news for the plotters there. He'd talked to his buddies with "the Brotherhood" upstate, he said. They would provide the explosives. So now it was up to young Siraj and Elshafay to figure out precisely how and when they wanted to plant the bombs. The two lifetime losers had never seen the explosives and never would, since both the Brotherhood and the bombs were Eldawoody's seductive fictions, but their own ideas started to make them nervous. As the prospect of a real attack grew near, they grew more cautious, as shown in their discussion with Eldawoody in his car, which was recorded secretly on video.

Avuncular old Eldawoody told them that (the nonexistent) Brother Nazeem upstate was "very, very happy, very impressed" with their plans, but maybe the idea of blowing up the Verrazano Bridge "is a little bit complicated," Eldawoody said gently. "We are not that big, that strong, it's too heavy for us," he quoted the upstate guy as saying. There would be a time for such things, but "it needs a nuclear bomb, not a regular bomb," and since those were not readily available around Bay Ridge or Staten Island or even upstate, "that will be later," he said. On the other hand, "Thirty-fourth Street is on."

"Hmm," said Siraj in the backseat, not exactly ecstatic now that he was going to have to move from talk to action. "Tell him that we are very careful about people's lives. Have you told him this?"

The Egyptian-American CI's answer was carefully noncommittal. "We've spoken of many things."

"I don't want to be the one who drops it and have people die," said Siraj.

Eldawoody assured him that mythical Brother Nazeem understood this. "No suiciding, no killing."

"No killing, only economy problems," said the young Pakistani with the seventy-eight IQ. "I'm going to work as a planner."

The Egyptian detected more than a shadow of a doubt. He couldn't let Siraj back out of the plot, but he couldn't be seen on video to be pushing him—to be entrapping him. "Are you okay with it?"

"I have to, you know, ask my mother's permission," said Siraj.

His mother's permission? This was all starting to unravel. Eldawoody started pushing a little harder. "Okay, here is the point. Are you willing to do jihad?"

Siraj said again he'd think about being a planner for the mysterious Brotherhood. He'd had big ideas about bringing the American economy to its knees, but now, well, "Dropping the bomb? I'm not sure. I have to think about it. Give me some time to feel comfortable with it."

So Eldawoody laid a guilt trip on him about the reaction of the Brotherhood. "Okay, I'll tell them that, because they were depending on you the most at Thirty-fourth Street station." And anyway there would be *two* people placing the bomb in a garbage can, he said. Siraj wouldn't be alone. But . . . "whatever makes you comfortable."

"I already gave the brothers the idea. They liked it, right? But the thing is, I will not be the person who puts it in the garbage can," said Siraj. "Because if somebody dies, then the blame will come on me." Apparently it had just occurred to this zealous autodidact that God might punish murderers. "Allah doesn't see those situations as accidents."

"So you are out of jihad?"

"Planning is also jihad, brother."

Now the schizophrenic Elshafay, who had just spent several days in a mental institution at the beginning of the month, decided it was time for him to speak. "Am I going to do Thirty-fourth Street?"

"Yes," said Eldawoody.

"Can they maybe get someone who is more trained to do this?"

Siraj liked that idea and backed up his young buddy. "We're new. We don't even know what we are doing. We only know that I made the plan and we are working on the plan."

"If I'm going to do Thirty-fourth Street, I want to go there a few more times," said Elshafay, his feet starting to turn ice cold. "I want to check it out a little more. And if they can get someone better qualified than me to do it, then I think they should, because I'm not really experienced in this and might not know what to do. Is that okay?"

Eldawoody spoke for the transcript that only he knew would be made from this conversation. "Okay. Whatever you feel. Whatever."

"I'll do it," said the young schizophrenic.

"The time to check out the station is in the morning from three o'clock to five o'clock," said Siraj, as if he thought he was in charge here. "When the train stops, how many people get out? Find out which car is empty, so people have a chance to survive, you know. That way, it will be nice."

Nice.

"I have an idea," said Elshafay. "If I go in to do it, I'll dress like a Jew. I'll have the bomb on me so it looks like a belly. I'll take it out and put it in the garbage can. I'll tuck in my shirt and walk out the Thirty-fourth Street entrance."

"Don't put it in the belly," said Siraj.

"But I'm going to dress like a Jew," said the half-Irish-Catholic, half-Egyptian nineteen-year-old. "That way no one will check me."

"Jews do carry bags. See what bags they carry. What kinds of things they carry. Maybe it could be a Macy's bag."

"They'll never check a Jew, 'cause they know Jews aren't the ones doing it," said Elshafay.

"Okay," said the informant Eldawoody, moving right along. "Are you going to be with him, Matin?" he asked Siraj.

"Yeah, I can be with him."

"No," said Elshafay. "It's better if I just go in myself. Walk down there, inshallah, and everything will go the way Allah planned it. But I gotta get Jewish garb."

"The ponytails, too?" Siraj wanted to know.

"Yeah, those curls too. I gotta have 'em." (The revolution, it would seem, had become a costume party.) "Is there any way they can make the bomb look like something different?"

"I don't know," said the CI. "But I don't think so."

"Could they make it look like a clock?"

"A clock?"

"'Cause if they make it look like something different and I get checked, they just won't see that it's a bomb. They don't have X-rays there in the subway."

"I know that."

"So, yeah, definitely. If they can get the bomb to look like something different, I'll get dressed up like a Jew and go put the bomb there."

"So, Matin, what's your part?" asked the informer. "Your part is out? You don't want nothing?"

"With the Thirty-fourth thing?"

"Yeah, Thirty-fourth?"

Siraj suddenly changed the subject, asking this older man he thought was his friend as well as his coconspirator why he'd started smoking again. "You cannot let that thing control you," he said.

"Smoking is not good," the older man agreed, "but did I say that smoking is good?"

"It hurts the lungs," Elshafay chimed in.

"But I don't inhale the smoke."

"Then you can get tongue cancer."

"Tongue?"

"Tongue cancer."

"If I am dying, I am not going to die from cigarettes. I would die from other things." There came a pause worthy of *Waiting for Godot*.

"I miss Egypt," said young Elshafay.

"I do, too," said Eldawoody. "I really do."[4]

Three days after that conversation, and two days before the start of the Republican convention, on August 27, 2004, the NYPD arrested Siraj and Elshafay. Kelly wasn't taking any chances: "These guys went out, they drew maps of the police stations in Staten Island, in Fort Wadsworth, they go to the Forty-second Street subway station, they go to Herald Square subway station," Kelly told me after the trial. Siraj, in other sessions with the informant, had first said he wanted to dress like a Puerto Rican to blend in and kill Jews. "Then he doesn't want to kill people. And then he wants to kill people. We didn't know if this guy was going to show up with an AK-47 or something, so we grabbed him. And David Cohen and the Intelligence division ran this case. It was tried in the federal court, but local police agency did this. And we learned a lot from it."

Both the young Muslims were charged with plotting terrorist acts. Elshafay quickly agreed to cooperate. Siraj pleaded innocent. At trial, Siraj's lawyer, Martin Stolar, would claim entrapment. Siraj, he said, was "a pliable young man, not the brightest bulb in the chandelier," and he seemed to have a good case. But at the very end of the trial the prosecutors called the undercover officer, Kamil Pasha, as a rebuttal witness. In a day on the stand, the young cop born in Bangladesh described the hatred and anger and longing for violent revenge he'd heard from Siraj long before the confidential informant Eldawoody ever came on the scene. Siraj was stunned as he listened in the courtroom. So was his defense team. The jury handed down a guilty verdict and in late 2006, Judge Nina Gershon sentenced Siraj to thirty years in prison.

Kelly and Cohen took a lot of criticism about the Herald Square case, since the press rarely failed to point out how ineffectual the conspirators had been and how much money the confidential informant Eldawoody had been paid. (The total was $100,000 for his services and his relocation, after which he complained publicly he'd been short-changed.) There had been no bomb. Probably there never would have been.

But the example of the El-Nosair group back in the early 1990s suggested just how dangerous such motley conspirators could become, even when some were morons. El-Nosair's inept gang had been infiltrated and mentored by another Egyptian CI working for the FBI. But he'd been dropped by the Feds because they thought he was costing too much and not delivering enough prosecutable terrorism. The guy the conspirators found to replace him was Ramzi Yousef, and less than six months later they set off their bomb in the World Trade Center parking lot.

The Herald Square case also served other purposes for the NYPD. It illustrated the threat of "homegrown terrorism" among self-taught Muslim radicals. "There were no international linkages at all," said Cohen. "But motivated by what you can pick up on the Web, they get comfortable with the global jihad. They're wanting to participate in it, and able to meet people, independent of going to any camp."

The arrests and trial also were a none-too-veiled message to home-grown *jihadis:* they could not trust anyone; even in a group of two or three, one of them might be an informer. Indeed, he might even be a cop. If a police organization can sow mistrust, it can reap disunity. As conspirators bicker and fall out, their plots fall apart. More informers can be culled. And all that helps build security.

In other words, the cops were doing just what the lawyers who had fought the battles for the *Handschu* guidelines had feared (Siraj's lead attorney, Martin Stolar, had been one of those). The NYPD was performing just the way direct action groups and black bloc crazies said it would. And by the NYPD's lights, that was just fine.

But in late August 2004, these intelligence and counterintelligence stratagems weren't going to be enough. As Siraj and Elshafay spent their first nights in jail, thousands of Republican delegates were arriving in town, and so were hundreds of thousands of demonstrators, and the NYPD was reviewing plans for mass arrests.

On the first day of the convention, Sunday, August 29, the march against Bush and the Iraq War pulled together by the group United for Peace and Justice drew enormous crowds. Usually organizers inflate numbers and the police play them down, but this time the low-ball figure of five hundred thousand came from UFPJ, while the NYPD claimed there were eight hundred thousand. It was the biggest protest march any convention, and possibly New York City, had ever seen.

Wave upon wave, hour after hour, crowds that included veterans and the wounded, celebrities and politicians, Michael Moore and Jesse

Jackson, Rosie Perez and Marisa Tomei, walked and partied past Madison Square Garden to the end of the official route at Union Square. Then thousands just kept on heading north to the Great Lawn in Central Park, where they'd been refused a permit by the mayor's office. Cops were all over the place. Still, the marchers protested and partied on. The arrests that did take place that day were at a separate protest in Times Square. Altogether, 255 people were picked up, mostly for "administrative code violations," "disorderly conduct," and "reckless endangerment."[5]

The next day, August 30, was much quieter: only a dozen arrests for minor infractions. But everybody knew what was coming. The anarchists and direct action demonstrators, the crazies and the street comics were girding for the day designated by someone on the Internet, it was never clear exactly who, as "A-31" or "The Day of Chaos": Tuesday, August 31, 2004.

This was when all the months of intelligence gathering and planning were going to pay off for the NYPD, or not. This was the moment when the demonstrators would cross the line for sure, and the cops might, too, if they lost control: the Chicago '68 moment; the Genoa 2001 moment; the moment when direct action could provoke an unequal and excessive reaction that would put the day in the history books.

That did not happen.

"All of our activities were legal and were subject in advance to *Handschu* review," Deputy Commissioner for Public Information Paul Browne said afterward. "We didn't interfere with lawful demonstrators, but tracked the few who planned vandalism and worse. In a few instances, we kept track of individuals who planned to come to New York for the RNC and who had resorted to extreme violence in the past. For example, we kept track of convicted terrorist Richard Picariello. He had a history of resorting to bombings to express dissent. He was sentenced to prison in 1978 for his role in blowing up a plane at Logan International Airport, two National Guard trucks at the Dorchester Armory, and the Essex Superior Courthouse in Newburyport to protest alleged U.S. imperialism and oppression. He fled to Canada, returned, and bombed a power plant in Maine. Despite his public assertions to the contrary, Picariello came to New York for the RNC." He was watched, not arrested.

When the cops made their move, the groups they had singled out as high risk were taken by surprise—and handcuffed with plastic straps and taken away. Ahead of the relatively small clots of problematic demonstrators moving through the streets were plainclothes officers, sometimes identifiable, sometimes not. Behind were uniformed police. More cops would arrive on scooters, motorcycles, or mountain bikes. "We were trying to dramatize the effects of Bush's preemptive foreign policy and we ended up being preempted by the New York City police in a policy of preemptive arrests," Matt Daloisio, an activist from the New York *Catholic Worker,* told the left-wing news service Democracy Now! Daloisio was part of a group that had started its protest at Ground Zero. "About three minutes into our walk, we were stopped by a line of police, surrounded by police on bicycles, and then we were wrapped in an orange fence and told we were under arrest. It was a large net they cast. We had a Republican delegate in with us and members of the media. In within two hours, there were over two hundred and fifty people arrested."[6]

In fact, there were many more. On August 31, the NYPD picked up 1,188 people. The total during the days leading up to and just after the convention was 1,827. The plans for such large-scale arrests had been put in place months before and, although the police denied it, part of the design obviously was to keep people out of circulation for the duration of the convention once they were detained, even if they claimed to be (and in some cases were) innocent bystanders.

A key police decision was to make arrests instead of, in effect, writing tickets. The danger that hard-core terrorists disguising their identities might be among the protesters was one reason given, and not without justification. Terrorists had countless aliases, and as if to reinforce the department's fears, three members of a radical Islamic group were picked up in the lobby of one of the hotels where Republican delegates were staying. Hard-core anarchists and direct action protesters, meanwhile, made a shtick out of giving false names and addresses. "Because of the comingling of the threat," said an NYPD after-action report, "it was essential that those who were actually involved in breaking the law be arrested rather than simply given summonses, allowed to move on, and permitted to break the law again." Each person picked up would be photographed and fingerprinted and the fingerprints processed before he or she was released.

To accommodate all the people it expected to round up, the NYPD had rented Pier 57, one of the cavernous, semiderelict structures left over from the days when oceangoing ships steamed up the Hudson to dock on the edge of Chelsea. It was close to the action, so police vans and buses could empty their prisoners quickly, and there was lots of room. Portable toilets and fencing were brought in. But the place, previously used as a garage for city buses, was a mess. Instead of being processed and released after an hour or two, hundreds found themselves confined there for a day, two days, and in a few cases even longer. Some of those who sat or slept on the oily floor complained of rashes and many said they feared asbestos contamination. In police documents, Pier 57 was called a "Post-Arrest Staging Site," or a "triage center." But many of those who wound up in the place, and some of the press, took to calling it "Guantánamo on the Hudson."[7]

Kelly and his people were, and remain, unrepentant.

"I never saw NYPD do a better job than during that RNC," said Sheehan. "Those cops that protected the city during those days were absolutely magnificent. Number one, they protected the right of the protesters to march in massive numbers in New York City and protest against the Bush administration in a peaceful way, but in a huge way, loud and huge. It was a tremendous burden on NYPD to police that thing and I think it went tremendously well. And I think there might have been some complaints by some of the protesters, but for the hundreds of thousands of protesters there—and I saw their interactions with police—it was extraordinarily positive. And then on the other side you had the Bush administration and the Republican Party, a protection of their ability to have a convention in the city and not to be disrupted, and to be protected against terrorist threats or other people that were actively planning to really cause havoc on that convention. We protected it. It went off without a hitch. It went very, very well. The Republican committee members had the same smiles that the protesters had interacting with the cops on the street. I couldn't have been prouder."

What about the many hundreds held at Pier 57? "I watched most of those people get arrested," said Sheehan. "And these were people, most of them, who wanted to get arrested. They knew they were block-ing traffic. They were causing disruption. They were prepared to be ar-rested. And they got brought away. Now you can criticize, maybe, the processing was too slow. Some people have said that. I know that we just did our very, very best to expedite that and to handle it the best we could."

Sheehan said he went down to the pier the morning after the arrests and saw a police sergeant pushing a cart full of Froot Loops for the prisoners. "Froot Loops!" The cops "weren't trying to abuse anybody's rights or tramp on anybody's liberties," said Sheehan. "It's unfortunate when you see some twenty-two-year-old girl on her bike and she gets ar-rested and then she is in detention for a long time. Nobody wants that. They're trying to move the process forward. But it's a legal process and you got hundreds of people there that you got to move through the sys-tem. And it takes some time. Maybe we can do it better next time, but overall I thought it was a phenomenally good job."

The convention had come and gone, but terrorism had not come. The black blocs had failed. The police had been provoked repeatedly. The only serious injury had been to a cop dragged off his scooter and beaten by someone in the crowd. Direct action demonstrators had thrown what turned out to be fake shit ("faux feces," in the words of Paul Browne). But still, the cops had remained restrained. And that same week the U.S. Open was held in Queens, and the Mets and the Yankees played at home. There was even a marathon. Away from the convention site, business and pleasure and policing went on more or less as usual in the big city. *The New York Times* called the event a turning point: "It ap-pears the New York Police Department may have successfully redefined the post-Seattle era, by showing that protest tactics designed to create chaos and attract the world's attention can be effectively countered with intense planning and a well-disciplined use of force."[8]

But black blocs could adapt. Al Qaeda–inspired terrorists certainly would. And the Dhiren Barot case blown by Washington still rankled. The more that authorities in Britain and the United States learned about Barot's networks, the more dots they saw that they needed to connect, but could not. After the computer guy Noor Khan's cover was blown, the Brits had been forced to pick up thirteen suspected Al Qaeda operatives and fixers to keep them from disappearing altogether. But there wasn't enough evidence to hold many of them. The cops also discovered that Barot had conjured plots targeting the London Underground. (*Newsweek* reported in November 2004 that the FBI legatts in the UK had quietly stopped taking the tube.)[9] It was only much later that investigators saw possible links between Barot and a young British Muslim living near Leeds named Mohammed Sidique Khan. And it was later still that they came to understand how vital the Pakistan connection was to "domestic" terror in Britain. But by then it was too late.

The London Bombings—2005

Installation art is not what Mike Sheehan had in mind when he had the Van—or the Leeds Van, as it's sometimes called—put together in the parking lot of the CT division out in Brooklyn. But just as art surprises and provokes, this place has a strangely disturbing effect on a visitor. Time and space seem compressed, as if you'd really stepped into a grungy, ground-floor flat in a collection of low-rise apartments on a suburban side street in the working-class north of England.

The neighbors must have known something odd was cooking at 18 Alexandra Grove. The plants outside the bathroom window were withering from strange fumes. To get to a nearby bus stop, kids in the neighborhood often took a path that went right by the apartment, and probably they smelled something noxious, something not to be expected. But they didn't talk about it to anyone, or at least not to anyone who cared enough to do anything about it. Meanwhile, the black hair of the young men who came and went at odd hours had started to grow perceptibly lighter. When members of their families asked them what was happening, they said they'd just been doing a lot of swimming to keep in shape.

Of course, what they were really doing was mixing the explosives they would use on July 7, 2005, to stage three near-simultaneous suicide attacks on the London Underground and one, about an hour later, on a double-decker bus. They killed fifty-six people including themselves, horrified the British public, and stunned the British government, which had somehow come to believe that terrorists with Muslim backgrounds might come and go in the UK, they might live there, they might even have been born there, but they didn't explode there.

Kelly and Cohen were close with Scotland Yard. They had their man Ira Greenberg there picking up on what the Brits knew, and maybe contracting some of their blind spots, too.

For more than a year before the July 7 bombings, a picture of something frightening had been taking shape, something out of control and contagious, but hard to diagnose precisely. Would-be terrorists among the British Muslim community, many of them British citizens, were increasingly active and increasingly mobile. In April 2003, two of them had gone to Israel to take advantage of the fact that they were Brits and Asians, not Palestinians or Arabs, and could therefore go places Hamas or the Al Aqsa Brigades could not. On the night of April 30, twenty-two-year-old Asif Hanif, a tall man known around his home town of Hounslow as a gentle giant, a "teddy bear," blew himself up in front of a pub called Mike's Place on the Tel Aviv seafront.[1] The bomb killed three other people and wounded more than fifty. His traveling companion, Omar Khan Sharif from Derby, failed to detonate the explosives he was carrying, dumped the bag, and ran. His body washed up on the Tel Aviv beach almost two weeks later.

"This was not the first time that the State of Israel has been the target of foreign terrorists bearing British passports," said a statement from the Israeli Foreign Ministry.[2] Something sinister was going on. But the British authorities were still surprisingly complacent. "By and large, in 2003 the UK was a net exporter of terrorism," said Peter Clarke, head of the counterterrorism branch of London's Metropolitan Police.[3]

Just how wide the jihadis had cast their web and how deeply it had sunk into the currents of British society began to be apparent after the arrest in New York City, among the parking lots near the corner of

Hillside Avenue and 166th Street in Queens, of a twenty-nine-year-old American citizen named Mohammed Junaid Babar. He had been born in Pakistan, but came to the States with his parents when he was only two, and he'd spent most of his life in the five boroughs. But at the time of his arrest in April 2004, he was more famous as a holy warrior than perhaps he realized.

In 2001 in the immediate aftermath of 9/11, Babar had left the United States and gone to Pakistan to join the jihad against the Americans then descending on Taliban forces and Al Qaeda in Afghanistan. Babar identified with a group called Al-Muhajiroun, centered in London but with a presence in New York City. (Hanif and Sharif were reported, after their deaths, to have had Al-Muhajiroun connections, as well, but the group denied it.)

For reasons best known to Babar, in those first intense weeks in Pakistan in 2001 he decided to give a series of extraordinary interviews to television correspondent Jon Gilbert, which CNN promptly broadcast around the world. Babar was a nerd with a pudgy face, a wispy beard, and thick glasses. He talked about jihad and war and murder with a pronounced, nasal New York accent. "There is no negotiation with Americans," he declared. "I will kill every American that I see in Afghanistan, and every American I see in Pakistan." But the weirdness of the interviews didn't end there. His mother, it turned out, had worked in the World Trade Center. On that horrible Tuesday morning, she had struggled down the smoke-filled stairwells slick with water, emerging into the light just in time to survive, but she never fully recovered from the trauma of what she'd been through. And still, Babar said he was going to fight to defend the people who had planned that atrocity. He talked about the racism he'd encountered growing up in Queens, where he claimed he was not only the only Muslim but the only dark-skinned person in his school. He said his grandfather had taught him that his first loyalty should always be to his faith, not his country. But like any American, he seemed to think he deserved his fifteen minutes of prime time. He could speak for the cause. "There's more sides to the story than just the one the Western media is portraying," he insisted. "They use any excuse to attack Islam."[4]

After his stint on television, the mujahid *from Queens worked at a*

*training camp in Pakistan, where he came in contact with other zeal-
ots born or brought up in the West. But he also got married to a local
woman and became a father. Like so many of these guys, it was hard for
outsiders to reconcile the image of the family man with all the talk of
martyrdom, and perhaps it was for him, too.*

*Babar told Gilbert he would never go back to the United States, no
way, no how. Yet after reportedly attending an Al Qaeda "summit"
in Pakistan in March 2004, Babar showed up in New York City once
again toward the end of that same month. He took classes to become a
cabbie, but couldn't quite get his license. There seemed to be "administrative issues." And then the Feds, who had been waiting and watching
since his star turn on CNN, picked him up in Queens.*

*They took Babar to the Embassy Suites Hotel in Manhattan, room
538, just one long block from Ground Zero, and they gave him a choice:
he could either spend his life in jail or turn state's evidence. He took the
Feds' deal and pleaded guilty on five counts of providing material support to terrorists.[5] He also spilled his guts about all he had seen and
everyone he knew in Pakistan, and agreed to do the same on the witness
stand in London.*

*The British domestic intelligence service, MI5, had focused in on
a group of young men, most of whom had Pakistani backgrounds,
who managed to buy thirteen hundreds pounds of ammonium nitrate fertilizer and were planning to blow up a shopping mall . . . or
nightclubs . . . or Britain's gas distribution system—MI5 recorded endless bull sessions about what target they meant to hit. At the height of
this investigation in February and March 2004, before Babar had even
been picked up, the British authorities had invested 34,000 man-hours
of intelligence and police work in what they called "Operation Crevice."[6] Now Babar could testify, and eventually did, about spending time
with the group's leader, Omar Khyam, in a jihadi training camp. Khyam
reportedly was in touch with Abdel Hadi al-Iraqi, one of Osama bin
Laden's top lieutenants. The whole case fit together neatly, and in 2007,
after a trial in London lasting more than a year, Khyam and four of his
cronies were sentenced to life in prison.*

*But by then, long after the 2005 bombings, the story of the investi-
gation had changed. What fascinated and horrified the public was not*

the alleged plots of the Crevice conspirators, but the extent to which the British cops had focused on the wrong people.

Babar had told the Feds and the Brits that while he was at a training camp in Pakistan in 2003 he had met a young British Pakistani called "Ibrahim" who seemed to be smart, serious, committed, and dangerous. The surveillance work on Operation Crevice had generated extensive files of photographs of the would-be fertilizer bombers meeting scores of acquaintances, sympathizers, and, perhaps, conspirators in other plots. But MI5 didn't have time to track down all their names and connections. Some of those pictures were passed along to Babar, but he did not identify any of them as Ibrahim. Only after July 7, 2005, when the passport photograph of Mohammed Sidique Khan was broadcast around the world, did Babar put that name to the face.

The morning that the bombers set out for London on their mission of mass murder is chronicled in images from Britain's ubiquitous closed-circuit television cameras. In the predawn dark, just before four in the morning, we're looking at the main street near 18 Alexandra Grove in Leeds. Here is a tiny car with three men crammed inside: Sidique Khan, his buddy Shehzad Tanweer—who had gone to the Pakistani training camp with him in late 2004 and been photographed, as well, by MI5 during the Operation Crevice surveillance—and their young friend, eighteen-year-old Hasib Hussain. In the next series of pictures, it's almost an hour later and the three men have stopped for gas on the highway to London. Tanweer buys some snacks and haggles with the cashier over the change. Almost another hour passes and they pull into Luton station about thirty miles outside the British capital. The fourth man, a convert to Islam named Jermaine Lindsay, is already there waiting for them. They transfer some items between cars, leaving smaller bombs and a nine-millimeter pistol behind.

All four enter the station together. At 7:21 the CCTV cameras pick them up standing on the platform waiting for the commuter train that will take them into Kings Cross, a transport hub in the heart of London. All are carrying backpacks with an estimated five to twelve pounds of explosives inside. CCTV catches them again an hour later, now inside *the Kings Cross station. They are hugging one another and appear, in the words of the British police report, "happy, even euphoric."[7] Khan boards an underground train on the Circle Line headed west. When his bomb goes off, he and six other people are killed, one hundred and sixty-three are injured. Tanweer gets on the same line headed east. His bomb kills him and seven others; one hundred and seventy-one are injured. Lindsay gets on the Piccadilly Line headed south. He seems to have been standing when his backpack exploded. In his carriage twenty-six people die along with him, and three hundred and forty are injured. It is just 8:50 in the morning.*

Five minutes later the fourth bomber, Hussain, appears on closed-circuit cameras leaving Kings Cross and trying to call the other bombers on his cell phone. No answer. He ducks back into a W.H. Smith magazine shop and buys a nine-volt battery. He goes to a McDonald's outside the station, then leaves ten minutes later. He boards one bus, then transfers to another, and climbs to the upper deck. At 9:47 his bomb goes off, killing fourteen people including himself and injuring more than one hundred and ten.[8]

The Madrid bombings the year before had been a wake-up call at One Police Plaza, but London was a seismic shift for the NYPD, with aftershocks felt for years. The attacks might have been on the far side of the Atlantic, but they were all too close to home: the subway, the Pakistani community, the fact that these were British citizens who could come to the United States without visas, and that they had no criminal records, nothing that would put them on a watch list. That two of them had been photographed and even recorded in connection with Operation Crevice, that Babar had information about them and Dhiren Barot (Issa al-Hindi) may have been the operational connection between them and Al Qaeda Central in the wilds of Pakistan—all that was not known or even suspected until later, and that shook up New York still more.

Kelly's first reaction was to get his guys on the ground. NYPD Detective Greenberg already had a desk at New Scotland Yard, but Kelly also dispatched cops with more technical expertise to get as many op-

erational details as possible. The patrols in New York's transit system were stepped up, as usual, for deterrence as well as for enforcement. But there was a question whether to go further. Maybe it was time to start searching bags and backpacks. New Yorkers wouldn't like it. There would be legal issues. Kelly waited. And then, exactly two weeks after the 7/7 attacks, four more would-be bombers tried to bring new carnage to the Underground. Mercifully, they had botched the recipe on the homemade explosives. The bombs just fizzled. But you couldn't count on luck like that.

"That was on the twenty-first of July 2005, when the second round of attempted bombings took place," Kelly told me afterward. "I called a meeting here, and I said I want to put in a search system in the subway. I talked to Andrew Schaffer, general counsel here, and said, 'I want you to take a look at it, a look at the structures that are in place that have passed constitutional muster.'" Kelly had in mind the precedent of random stops on the street to check for people driving while intoxicated, that sort of thing. "So we came back an hour later, and he says this is what we have to have: it has to be random. Profiling is a concern for us." Profiling was something you never wanted to be accused of, much less nailed for in court. On the other hand, you were going to stop a lot of little old ladies and look in their purses. And sure enough, two weeks after that second bombing, which is to say two weeks after the search policy went into effect, the New York Civil Liberties Union sued Kelly and the city.

"Since the subway search policy was put into effect on July 21, 2005," read the brief, "police officers have searched the purses, handbags, briefcases, and backpacks of thousands and perhaps tens of thousands of people, all without suspicion of wrongdoing." This violated the Fourth Amendment protection against unreasonable search and seizure, the NYCLU maintained, and, it wasn't even going to be effective, the civil liberties lawyers insisted: "The NYPD is not conducting searches at most subway entrances at any given time, is giving advance notice about searches at those entrances where searches are being conducted, is allowing people selected for search to walk away, and is not basing the searches on any suspicious activity of individuals," the brief contended. "Consequently, as common sense would suggest, the

NYPD's subway search program is virtually certain neither to catch any person trying to carry explosives into the subway system nor to deter such an effort."[9]

Perhaps. Yet most people complied. The photographs that had leaked of the gruesome scenes in London's Underground stayed in the mind of any straphanger in Brooklyn. And, possibly to drive home that point, on the same day the suit was filed, Kelly called a meeting of private security officers and police representatives from other jurisdictions so he and Sheehan could brief them in detail about what had been learned from the London investigations. Although Paul Browne would later insist that all the points raised by Kelly were from open sources, the British press treated many of them as news. Browne also said the briefing had been cleared by the Metropolitan Police, but later retracted that statement and said he regretted it.[10]

The chemicals used to make the bombs were hydrogen peroxide (hair bleach) and citric acid, according to the NYPD's information. "Initially it was thought that perhaps the materials were high-end military explosives that were smuggled, but it turns out not to be the case," said Kelly. "It's more like these terrorists went to a hardware store or some beauty supply store." (You can see Kelly thinking about Operation Nexus, the business outreach program.) What they cooked up was something called HMDT, or hexamethylene triperoxide diamine. The stuff degraded and destabilized when it got warm, so keeping it on ice was imperative. "In the flophouse where this was built in Leeds, they had commercial-grade refrigerators to keep the materials cool," Sheehan told the security officers and cops. That kind of anomaly would be something to look for in the future, "an indicator of a problem," he said (and it was just the kind of detail lovingly reproduced in the Leeds Van in Brooklyn). The explosives had been taken to Luton in picnic coolers. The triggers for the bombs, as in Madrid, were mobile phones set to go off at a specific time, in this case 8:50 a.m. Sheehan also said the NYPD worried about unspecified indications that the July 7 bombers were connected to broader "organizations" and might have other cells operating in the United States.[11]

* * *

For months, well into 2006, British authorities continued to maintain that Sidique Khan and his fellow bombers were independent operators conducting an act of "indiscriminate terror." They might be inspired by Al Qaeda, but they had little or no direction from it. This was despite what Babar was telling them about meeting "Ibrahim" in the Pakistan training camp and, perhaps more to the point, despite the fact that the increasingly professional media arm of Al Qaeda, Al-Sahab (the Cloud), had produced a video that included "martyrdom" tapes recorded in Pakistan by Sidique Khan and Tanweer. In the same video, Ayman al-Zawahiri claimed Al Qaeda had direct responsibility for the attack.

More and more evidence suggested Sidique Khan was not just an inspired leader—he was an active Al Qaeda recruiter, trolling for would-be mujahideen in Britain's Muslim communities. In July 2006, a BBC television documentary even linked him to the two British suicide bombers who attacked on the Tel Aviv seafront in 2003. Indeed, Khan himself visited Israel just a month before that incident, possibly to reconnoiter. When the Tel Aviv bombers made their trip, they followed the same route through Jordan into Israel that Sidique Khan had taken.[12]

By early 2007, Cohen had rethought his analysis of the way Al Qaeda and its minions operated. The threat, he said, was "trifurcated": "There's the 9/11 Al Qaeda purist attack that would emanate from Al Qaeda Central," he said. "They have operatives still that are of the same capabilities and skills as Mohammed Atta, for example. And they're trying to resurrect that capability." Al Qaeda Central was still looking for "the big bang," said Cohen, and it might or might not succeed.

"The second stage is what I would call the franchising out. So you have a lot of organizations and individuals that will design, plan, and structure a plot largely on their own, but with, at a minimum, a dotted line connection back to Al Qaeda." This was the case with Sidique Khan, said Cohen. And this sort of "homegrown terrorism" was especially dangerous because it could start local and go global. "The homegrown threat could be individuals coming here to New York City from the UK, not necessarily just born and raised here. When I talk about the homegrown threat, it could emanate from almost anywhere." And fi-

nally, there were the little groups like the guys in the Herald Square case: "No international linkages at all, but motivated by what you pick up on the Web . . . I think that's a real and a growing threat," he said. "So it's evolved into a three-headed monster."

For groups like the London bombers and the Herald Square plotters, he said, the way the NYPD was gathering intelligence was "of enormous import. . . . They are more likely to be identified and derailed and detoured by activity that we will uncover as a result of our trip-wire operation than the CIA will be able to do with its focus overseas." Once you have the NYPD handling domestic intelligence and the CIA working internationally, "the combination of the two will enable us to clap with both hands rather than one," said Cohen. "When we're referred to as the gold standard, I think that's the part that people are referring to."

THE
PRECARIOUS
BALANCE

BAD NUMBERS

The Battle for Morale

In 2004, just as so much else was going right for the NYPD—the success of the Republican convention security operations, the arrest of the boys in the Herald Square plot, the intelligence flowing in from Babar, the growing respect showed by Washington, and continued declines in crime—Kelly started losing cops. The problem was not criminals and terrorists, but attrition and arbitration. Or, to put it another way, money.

Even with a budget of some $3.8 billion a year, the police force found itself constantly scrounging for funds. Sometimes they came from the federal government, sometimes from businesses and private donors contributing to the Police Foundation, which kicked in $500,000 a year for the living expenses of the ten liaison officers Kelly assigned overseas. The city just didn't have any more to give.[1]

"Generally speaking, police personnel are the most expensive in local government," said Kelly. "So, very few police departments are overstaffed. Most of them are understaffed." But in New York City, you had the added burden of the constant terrorist threat, and the need to answer that with special training, special strategies, special units. The challenge was always to do more with less. And sometimes that worked very well. The intelligence division actually had a smaller staff in 2007 than it did when Cohen arrived in 2002, down from six hundred and fifty to six hundred and twenty-five. And in 2002, the division had had a reputation as a glorified escort service for VIPs. Now it was one of the most effective counterterrorist operations in the world.

But Kelly throughout his career had been a firm believer in the power of numbers—having enough cops to put on the dots. He had seen the disastrous impact on public safety and the quality of life in New York City when there was a dramatic decline in the police ranks during the 1970s, and the huge improvements when the numbers went back up in the 1990s. "It's not brain surgery," as he liked to say. And now his department was shrinking dangerously by the day.

In October 2000, there had been 40,800—almost 41,000—uniformed members of the service. By 2006 the "authorized" number had dropped to 37,800, but that was a peak achieved twice a year for only a few weeks after new classes graduated from the academy. Between two and three thousand cops retired every year. According to Paul Browne, the NYPD had been running about four thousand cops below the 2000 staffing levels the whole time Kelly had been commissioner. And now the academy was getting fewer and fewer recruits.

In 2004, after negotiations with the police union stalled, the new contract had gone to arbitration. The resulting judgment would save money for continued salaries and benefits to veteran officers by cutting the wages of cadets. The union and Kelly agreed. "They decided to eat their young," as one sergeant put it. A cadet would earn the equivalent of $25,000 a year during his six months at the academy, and that was before federal, state, and local taxes in one of the most expensive cities in the country. No recruit with a family could even dream of supporting it on that kind of money, and those who were single often had to live at home with their parents. At those prices, you could also forget about attracting talented young men and women from other parts of the country. (Cohen was bringing in his top analysts as civilian employees.) The bright lights and big city, and even the Hollywood-worthy rep of the NYPD, weren't going to make up for starvation wages.

"It's absolutely a disgrace!" said Kelly when I sat down with him in

January 2007. "There's no question about it. I've just talked to a group of executives this morning and I asked them this question: Who are you hiring in this most expensive city in America for $25,000? Certainly not the most critical employees in your organization. Yet that's what police officers are. You can't hire a receptionist in New York City for less than $30,000. Here we're expecting people to have at least sixty college credits and to be vetted: to look at their medical situation, to give them physical exams, to have in-depth background investigations, in-depth psychological testing—and pay them $25,000. It is bizarre. And that has to change."

No subject we talked about prompted so much passion from the commissioner. "People say, 'Ah, well, listen, the people who want to be cops are going to be cops anyway!' Well, that's a percentage. But that's only a percentage. It's a portion. As I say, people have to exist, have to live. Where the hell are you going to live? So we see people leaving. We had an attrition of fifteen percent in this last class. We normally have about seven percent, and that's for all causes: they fail out, they drop out, they go to a job with higher pay. This was *fifteen* percent."[2]

If corruption was not growing inside the NYPD, it certainly persisted. Kelly had a reputation for cracking down on bad cops that went back to his days cleaning up the 106th Precinct after the torture scandal there in 1985. When he was commissioner the first time around in 1993, he gave his head of Internal Affairs the first pick of every sergeant or lieutenant seeking a supervisory assignment in a detective unit. "Since then," Jack Maple wrote in a rare nod to Kelly, "the best, brightest and hungriest crook-catchers in the department have been compelled to complete a two-year tour of duty in Internal Affairs before they get where they want to be."[3]

Yet during Kelly's second tour as commissioner, stories broke one after another about cops gone bad. Mostly the allegations were the same old tales: cops working as muscle for drug gangs, ripping off drug gangs, sometimes running drug gangs. They were like the plot elements for generations of film noir police movies. In more than one case, narcotics cops were caught pocketing some or all of the drugs they captured on busts. A thirteen-year veteran of the force was charged with running a marijuana ring raking in two million dollars a month.

Police corruption numbers don't show up on CompStat and the NYPD won't release many details about the investigations that the Internal Affairs Bureau conducts, so trends are hard to spot. But in October 2007, the *New York Post*'s veteran police reporter and columnist Murray Weiss got a hold of the IAB's annual report for 2006, and the numbers it showed were disturbing. Arrests of cops were up 25 percent, from ninety-one to one hundred and fourteen. The number of cops caught using drugs jumped from eight incidents to nineteen. Fraud allegations involving insurance, credit card, and welfare swindles jumped 85 percent. "The number of cops stripped of their guns and badges and placed on modified duty jumped fifty-five percent," Weiss reported.[4]

The largest single group of Internal Affairs cases—34 percent of the 1,057 corruption investigations launched in 2006—involved theft. Most of it was relatively petty, but some of it was downright bizarre. An officer in the Sixtieth Precinct (Coney Island) was accused of answering 911 calls for people who apparently had died of natural causes, taking their credit cards, and using them to buy gas for his car at Home Depots in New York and New Jersey (sometimes cops, as well as criminals, are not the brightest bulbs in the chandeliers, it would seem).

Even when such cases made headlines, the public outcry was minimal. The city felt safe, most officers seemed to be doing their jobs. It wasn't like the 1960s when the city seemed to be going to hell, and people identified corruption as one of the causes. None of the corruption cases had the potential to undermine the counterterrorist operations by fundamentally undermining confidence in the police force. But the shooting of Sean Bell was something different.

Late the night of November 24 and early the morning of November 25, 2006, four undercover detectives showed up at the Kalua Cabaret near the railroad tracks in Jamaica, Queens. They were part of a special unit set up to look at clubs with reputations not only for drugs and prostitution, but as places so rough that city inspectors backed away. Several young men were partying there. One of their group, Sean Bell, was due to get married later in the day to the woman he'd lived with for several years and who already was the mother of his two children. This was his send-off, and it went on late. As Bell and his friends finally headed out into the street, they bumped into a Haitian immigrant named Fabio Coicou, who'd just parked his SUV. Bell thought Coicou said something about them being drunk, which he had, under his breath. Shouting started, Bell bumped Coicou chest to chest, then Coicou put his hands in his pockets, "giving the impression that he had a gun," according to the court ruling handed down later in the case. One member of Bell's party threatened to take it away. Another one, Joseph Guzman, said he'd go get his own. And the undercover cops, catching snatches of conversation, thought they saw some big trouble in the making. They followed Bell and his friends around the corner to Liverpool Street.

Detective Gescard Isnora, a baby-faced man of color, approached Bell's Nissan Altima as Bell got into the driver's seat and his friend Guzman got into the passenger seat. Isnora may have had his badge out, Bell might have seen it, or might not. Isnora did have a gun. Suddenly the Altima surged out of the parking place, knocked Isnora aside, and ran head-on into an unmarked police van that had just turned onto Liverpool. Probably Bell was drunk and more than a little scared. Those streets near the tracks feel like the end of the earth. All the talk about guns was bullshit. He didn't have a gun and neither did Guzman or their buddy, Trent Benefield, in the backseat. Bell threw the Altima into reverse and up onto the sidewalk, hit a gate, and jumped forward again, smashing into the police van another time. Officer Isnora saw Guzman twist around in the passenger seat and "move his body as if he were reaching for a weapon." Isnora shouted "gun" and started shooting.[5]

Detective Michael Oliver, a white guy who had been on the force twelve years and had never before fired his weapon, testified later that he thought he was going to die. "I saw Detective Isnora, with his arms out, and his gun in his hands, yelling, 'He's got a gun! He's got a gun!' " Oliver said. "I yelled, 'Police! Don't move!' And I still see a passenger appearing to be raising a gun, so I started firing my weapon."

There was all the noise, all that threat, all that adrenaline and testos-
terone mixing the way it does when there's shooting going on. When it
was all over, just minutes later, Oliver would tell another cop he didn't
even remember pulling the trigger. But he had. And again and again and
again until all sixteen bullets had sprayed out of it. Then he dropped
that empty clip and rammed in another one and just kept shooting. Two
other cops on the scene were firing, too. In seconds, they'd pumped fifty
rounds out of their nines, gravely wounding Guzman and Benefield and
killing Sean Bell.

Fifty bullets. That figure became a focus for outrage, an incantation
to conjure all the ghosts, revive all the suspicions about trigger-happy,
completely unaccountable cops. Fifty bullets that killed an unarmed
bridegroom on his wedding day.

"You are trained to keep shooting until you eliminate the threat,"
Oliver told the court.[6]

For Kelly, the problem was one of public trust. This kind of violence
was not endemic. Kelly himself had argued against letting cops carry
nine-millimeters with fifteen-round clips when he was commissioner in
the early 1990s. There were obvious echoes of the Amadou Diallo case
that had helped pave the way for Howard Safir's demise as commissioner. Kelly would have to follow careful procedures focusing on an
investigation, a grand jury, a trial for the officers. Then he'd have to
contain the immediate aftermath, whatever the verdict might be, without demoralizing his force or inflaming an angry community. No cop in
Kelly's position was ever going to forget the long history of hell breaking loose in New York, in Los Angeles, and many other places across
the country whenever cops were accused, then acquitted, of abusing or
killing innocent black people.

Months passed, then more than a year, and finally the verdict came
down: "not guilty" on all counts. Kelly had blanketed the streets with
regular cops, plainclothes cops, and around the Queens courthouse he
put cops with "NYPD Community Affairs" emblazoned on their jack-
ets. "They formed a human flag, flying the colors of the New York Police Department," wrote Jim Dwyer of *The New York Times*.[7] Anger

rose, but no riots erupted. The crisis on the streets passed. Still, the erosion of confidence provoked by the Bell case would take a long time to go away. It was the kind of incident that might start people wondering about limits, and whether any existed for the NYPD. It was the kind of case that could have all sorts of hidden consequences.

LONERS AND COPYCATS

The Contract on Kelly

The voice was by turns mumbling and inaudible, then just clear enough to be horrifying as I listened to the digital recording on a computer in police headquarters. I pressed the earphones tighter with both hands. You could hear the clatter and the chatter in the visitors' room at the Rikers Island jail. "The subject," as the police transcript called him, was trying to put out a contract on Commissioner Ray Kelly. He wanted him beheaded. And he wanted more. He wanted One Police Plaza bombed. "I want people to feel my wrath and my rage," said the man. "I want to be . . . like I'm a terrorist. I want them to feel like I am a motherfucking terrorist, ya know?"

The plot never got past the talking stage, and probably never would have. It was another one of those. The accused was David Brown Jr., a forty-seven-year-old, four-hundred-pound repeat offender in a wheelchair with a rap sheet that included ten convictions, three of them on felony counts, the most recent for attempted murder. He was not entirely helpless, it would seem, but his lawyer, Justine Olderman, claimed he was mentally ill and, at least as far as this alleged plot was concerned, harmless. Brown had no ties to any terrorist organization—and nobody claimed that he did. When he was arraigned in March 2007 for trying to get Kelly killed he was charged with nonviolent criminal solicitation of a felony.

Brown wasn't trying "to do jihad," didn't want to redress the grievances of Palestine, didn't care about reviving the caliphate. Whatever Abu Mus'ab al-Zarqawi thought he was fighting for when he hacked through his captives' necks in Iraq, that didn't matter to Brown. But the image did. He wanted to take revenge for the killing of Sean Bell, even though he didn't know him. This was all about making people feel your motherfucking anger and your rage. No Islam involved, and no mystery, either. "Widespread information creates copycats," said Deputy Commissioner Paul Browne.

But "copycat" is a benign sounding word, and what copycats do is not. Loners can pick up on the techniques of disciplined terrorist organizations and be just as effective at killing people, maybe more so. When Timothy McVeigh blew up the Murrah Federal Building in Oklahoma City in 1995, murdering one hundred and sixty-eight, he used a truck bomb similar to the one cobbled together by Ramzi Yousef's team that attacked the World Trade Center in 1993 and killed six.

Loners are hard to track. Once inspired, they don't need to inspire anyone else. Their weakness—their inability to relate to other people, much less to lead them—is also their strength. There's nobody to rat them out. Once they decide to act, all they need to do is carry enough ammo for their assault rifle, or get the mix and the wiring right on the explosives. Joel Hinrichs headed for the big game at the University of Oklahoma in 2005 carrying a backpack worthy of the Madrid train bombers, full of his own home-brewed TATP. If he hadn't blown off his head, he could have taken a lot of people with him. "You can all kiss my ass," he wrote.

The killing power and the staying power of the individual are not to be underestimated. The "Mad Bomber" George Metesky went on blowing up places and maiming people in New York City for sixteen years during the 1940s and 1950s. "Unabomber" Theodore Kaczynski mailed his first exploding package in 1978, his last in 1995. The Zodiac Killer in the San Francisco area never was caught.

The "Alphabet Bomber" Muharem Kurbegovich, who terrorized

Los Angeles in 1974 (and who sends me a demented letter now and then from state prisons in California) firebombed the houses of a judge and two police commissioners, burned down an apartment building, and bombed the Pan Am terminal of Los Angeles International Airport, killing three people and injuring eight. He was a talented Yugoslav aerospace engineer who had immigrated from Sarajevo in 1967 (we would call him a Bosnian Muslim today) and he became a one-man chemical weapons factory. A quarter century before Osama bin Laden's training camps taught holy warriors how to generate poisonous cyanide gas near the air-conditioning intakes of high-rise buildings, Kurbegovich bought twenty-five pounds of potassium cyanide and nitric acid to do just that. He hid it so effectively in his Los Angeles apartment that the police didn't find the chemical stockpile until he told them about it, more than two years after his arrest. He was also well on his way to producing a supply of sarin nerve gas. Kurbegovich, Jeffrey Simon at the Monterey Institute wrote in 1999, was "a terrorist ahead of his time."[1] It's doubtful he'll ever get out of prison. (He has "whiled away the hours mailing death threats against U.S. presidents and other U.S. and foreign officials," noted a deportation order in 1985.)[2] But, inevitably, there will be other individuals who can do what Kurbegovich or Kaczynski, Metesky or Hinrichs did. In February 2003, with little elaboration, the FBI warned its field offices to be on the lookout for "lone extremists" who "represent an ongoing terrorist threat in the United States."[3]

"What the deal is [is] that I need the police commissioner killed immediately," reads the transcript of Brown's conversation at Rikers Island. "You see, every second of every day that he's alive burns my soul."

The undercover policeman, posing as a member of a criminal family able to carry out contract murders, wants to know who is going to pay. Brown claims "my financial backers support me . . . up to a million dollars that I could get from them." But the main backer, says Brown, is "so low-key that he does not want to get involved," adding, "I don't even have any money in my account right now."

In fact, Brown, as heard on the recording, is trying to buy murder and mayhem on credit: "They"—whoever "they" are—"said that when

I get out on the street, everything will be taken care of, no matter what the price is." The cop with the hidden microphone plays along, as one might imagine, with a fair degree of skepticism.

"Do you have access to explosives?" Brown asks him.

"To who?"

"Explosives."

"Explosives? . . . What is it you want to do?"

"One Police Plaza. . . . I want that blown up."

"You're talking about some serious number two. You understand what I'm saying? . . . I don't know if my people want to fuck with that."

The dialogue is similar when Brown comes back around to Kelly, blaming him for being too soft on the cops who shot Sean Bell.

"I want his head chopped off," says Brown.

"Um-hmm," says the man Brown thinks is a gangster. "You can't do something like that in the street. You know what I'm saying?"

They haggle over prices. Brown wants to pay $15,000 for Kelly's beheading, and $50,000 for the bombing of police headquarters. The undercover cop insists $150,000—"some serious fucking money"—is a more suitable price.

Brown was a loser if ever there was one, disconnected from any network, and indeed from reality. Even Siraj and Elshafay plotting the Herald Square bombing looked competent by comparison. But ignorance, as they say, is no excuse, and from a public security perspective, no assurance. The NYPD's analysts concluded after years of study that a lot of would-be terrorists were losers ("Al Qaeda is simply not very good," as Mike Sheehan would say). But you couldn't count on that if you were going to keep people safe in New York City. It was too easy for like-minded loners and losers to get together and get radicalized. And when they did, even the dumb ones could be dangerous as hell.

CLUSTERS

Homegrown Terrorism and National Resources

On the cramped but sunny terrace behind a hole-in-the-wall restaurant on Atlantic Avenue, one of Cohen's bright young analysts was burning with excitement—and curiosity—about a forthcoming report from the NYPD. Under the title *Radicalization in the West: The Homegrown Threat*,[1] the ninety-page booklet was meant to distill everything learned over the previous five years about the way "clusters" or "groups of guys" or "bunches of guys" (the jargon kept changing) came together, convinced themselves to be terrorists, and then moved from bluster to bombs. I had gotten a draft copy from a friend and was surprised to learn that the analyst sitting in front of me had not seen it. *Radicalization* was just about to be published, but it hadn't been shown to any of the stellar young academics in Cohen's shop. So all that my lunch guest, one of the best and brightest, could say was, "I can't go into details."

Presented as analysis for public consumption, the report was highly political: an expression of what the NYPD thought it did right—intelligence-led policing—while the GWOT had gone wrong overseas and the Feds kept floundering in the States. It was saying: Look at us, we know how the bad guys think, we know how to spot them, and we make prevention a reality, not just a slogan. It was also saying—and this was critical—we do not profile individuals, we look at groups, and you civil libertarians, and for that matter the FBI, need to know that is legal, and constitutional, and necessary. As one of Cohen's people said, "It was a shot across Washington's bow."

The driving force behind *Radicalization* was Larry Sanchez, the sky-diving CIA veteran sent to New York City by George Tenet in 2002. He had played a vital role funneling intelligence from KSM's lips to David Cohen's ear, and over time Sanchez had developed his own small coterie of analysts at the NYPD. They weren't dazzlers like the young, world-class scholars Cohen had made the core of the main analytical section, but they were steady. They weren't going to be moving on. Sanchez's guys were middle-aged and firmly in the civil service, and they had other virtues. One, for instance, was said to be close to Israel's security services, especially the domestic one, the Shin Bet. Sanchez tended to admire Israel's operations. "He sometimes whispers in Cohen's ear, 'Look at what can be done in dusty villages on the West Bank . . . ,' " a colleague of Sanchez's told me. But Cohen, as ever, remained skeptical about the wonders of Israel's actual intelligence-gathering techniques.

Two other members of the Sanchez team, Mitchell D. Silber and Arvin Bhatt, did most of the research and analysis on *Radicalization,* with Sanchez editing and amending along the way. One of the outside consultants was Marc Sageman, a psychiatrist and former CIA case officer whose book *Understanding Terror Networks* and other works described a fundamentally decentralized Al Qaeda in which the dynamics of small groups were more important than Bin Laden's efforts at command and control. The NYPD study looked at eleven specific cases of terrorist groups in Europe and the United States said to be inspired but apparently not directed by Al Qaeda.[2] They ranged from the savagely successful bombers in Madrid and London to a luckless group of regretful and ineffectual former would-be mujahideen busted upstate in Lackawanna in 2002.[3] The conclusion: In the six years since 9/11, the threat to the West that had taken shape was not from abroad but from within, and most of the plotters were what the report called "unremarkable" people with unremarkable jobs and educations. "Direct command and control by al-Qaeda has been the exception, rather than the rule," Silber and Bhatt concluded. Radicalization of young Muslims took place not in spite of a Western environment, but in many cases because of it. Communities that felt like Muslim ghettoes, isolated from the Western world and the Western values around them, were especially vulnerable to extremism.

Much had been written already about the way the Internet served as "a driver and enabler for the process of radicalization" (the new Afghanistan, as Kelly liked to say). But Silber and Bhatt fit the Internet incitement into a much bigger picture of what seemed clear and observable stages in the making of a homegrown terrorist.

The first was called "pre-radicalization." Some characteristics of "pedigree, lifestyle, religion, social status, neighborhood, and education" are common to members of these groups "just prior to the start of their journey" toward violent jihad. They're not poor. "Middle-class families and students appear to provide the most fertile ground for the seeds of radicalization." They are mostly male Muslims under the age of thirty-five and local residents or citizens of Western liberal democracies. Some of "the most vulnerable" were born to other faiths and recently converted to Islam. They were of varied ethnic backgrounds—and almost all were "clean skins" in police parlance; they had no records. The bottom line: At this stage they were effectively impossible to identify.

The second rung on the ladder was "self-identification." This was where the winnowing began; the terrorists-to-be started to practice what the report called *salafi* Islam, which emphasized a "pure" faith harking back to the early days of conquest and empire in the caliphate of the seventh century. In fact the ideology they embraced was even narrower than that. It was the version often ascribed to Al Qaeda but espoused by other radical groups, as well, which twisted the revelations, words, and deeds of the Prophet Mohammed to the service of focused anti-Western rage. A political or personal crisis could provoke this phase. So would association with small clusters of other angry young men (and occasionally angry young women).

Then came "indoctrination." Goaded by the "group think" of fellow believers and fed by a constant diet of Internet propaganda, the terrorist candidate would come to believe that his faith demanded action.

Most likely there would be what the report called a "spiritual sanctioner" who literally blessed the idea of violent jihad with his teachings and opinions. There would also be a sort of "incubator"—whether a mosque or bookstore, student group or other small organization—where contacts could be made and fanaticism reinforced by the group's approval.

Finally there was "jihadization." Members of the group would call themselves holy warriors, seeing violent jihad as a personal duty and planning their attacks. Typically, they didn't want to waste any time. While the earlier evolution from unremarkable guy to would-be mass murderer might take years, "this jihadization component can be a very rapid process," said the NYPD report, "taking only a few months, or even weeks to run its course." At its center would be an "operational leader" like Mohammed Sidique Khan, who commanded the July 7, 2005, bombings in London, or like Mohammed Atta, on September 11, 2001—both of whom seemed quite unremarkable just months before the attacks, or so the NYPD report contended.

Such consistent patterns provided "a tool for predictability," according to Silber and Bhatt. But as the report described the process of radicalization that turned men to monsters, it raised questions it did not answer about when and where and how to stop that process. The strong implication was that wherever the cops saw signs of radicalism, they should send in the spies. "Intelligence [is] the critical tool in helping to thwart an attack or even prevent the planning of future plots," the report concluded.[4] But in practical terms, how would you do that in New York City?

Around the cubicles of the intel division's warehouse offices, the basic techniques were well known. "We've arrested people for sitting on two seats in the subway," one of the senior operatives told me. In effect, once a group is seen to be taking shape, the cops use many techniques to disrupt it, sowing fear and mutual suspicion among its members. If one is picked up for a silly offense, like straddling two places in the subway, and taken into the station, not only is he likely to be intimidated, but his buddies may think he's going to sell them out under interrogation. In effect, the intel detectives are using Jack Maple's old principle of catching the crooks for minor infractions when they're not paying attention.

"We disrupt, we divert, and we've noticed monitoring these groups over time that they don't go back," said the operative.

Sanchez tended to talk about these kinds of actions as if they were a grand experiment. He sometimes referred to the city's 700,000 Muslims as if they were just so much agar in a petri dish, and the test of *Radicalization* reflected that sort of thinking. It asserted, with little evidence, that "the City's Muslim communities have been permeated by extremists who have [sown] and continue to sow the seeds of radicalization." They ranged from "university students, engineers, business owners, teachers, lawyers, cab drivers to construction workers." The universe of potential radicals was enormous—and yet, for all that, only two New York City cases were cited by the report. One was Herald Square, where the supposedly vital roles of "spiritual sanctioner" and "operational leader" were both played by the police informant Eldawoody (the report never mentioned him by name). The other New York case was the U.S.–UK nexus involving two men associated with the disbanded Al-Muhajiroun organization. One of those, Mohammed Junaid Babar, had become a government witness in the Operation Crevice cases and a key source of intelligence on British networks that, in fact, had some direction from Al Qaeda Central. The report leaves out those details, too.

Some of the wording in *Radicalization* was so problematic that the day after the NYPD published it, Deputy Commissioner for Counter Terrorism Richard Falkenrath tried to dial back on the language during an appearance on National Public Radio's *Brian Lehrer Show*.

"When they make a statement like 'the city's Muslim communities have been permeated by extremists,' that sounds like a red flag going up," said interviewer Errol Louis of the *New York Daily News*. "I mean, is that true?"

"I think the word 'permeated' makes it sound like it's pervasive," said Falkenrath, "when really it was just around a few individuals. More widely, it's not the case. New York City's Muslim populations and the country's Muslim populations are very moderate and law abiding. This is aberrational behavior that we're focusing on."[5]

One of the ironies of the study was that the behavior it described was the kind of thing you'd notice only if you were a part of the Muslim community. With that in mind, the report might have been circulated as an internal NYPD document, or it might have been shared quietly in consultation with Muslim community leaders. Instead, Kelly presented it at a press conference under the auspices of NYPD Shield, an organization that mainly pulls together corporate security managers and consultants. Predictably, activists in New York's Muslim communities flipped. Then right-wing pundits got into the game, attacking the activists for attacking the NYPD report. "For Islamists in America, charges of 'profiling' and 'inappropriate' methods are the preferred reply to critical discussions of almost all significant matter," wrote *The Weekly Standard*.[6]

The real problem with the report, as some inside the department warned when they had seen it, was that it misled the public about the extent of the homegrown threat and risked misleading the cops themselves. Such cells could be dangerous, sure, but none of those discovered in the United States were even close to operational. In eight of the cases looked at, no bombs ever went off, or were acquired or cobbled together. If, as Sheehan had said, Al Qaeda central just wasn't all that competent, homegrown Al Qaeda was even worse. In Europe, the Madrid atrocity seemed to fit all the criteria Silber and Bhatt set down: a homegrown Internet-inspired group of guys using their own resources with no apparent direct link to Bin Laden, but there were persistent reports of closer connections to Al Qaeda operatives. The 9/11 terrorists worked in very close coordination with Al Qaeda Central, no question about that, and two of the London bombers in 2005 had extensive training in Pakistani camps. *Radicalization* did not begin to describe the complicated overlapping relationships between New York and "Londonistan." When you looked at a character like Babar, raised in Queens, speaking English with a thick New York accent, and organizing an Al Qaeda safe house in Pakistan, you had to ask yourself just what home the terrorism was supposed to have grown in. The same held true for Assem Hammoud, the playboy college professor in Lebanon who was arrested in Beirut in 2006 for allegedly masterminding (in chat room diatribes) a suicide attack on the PATH trains. Mark Mershon of the FBI's New York field office called this plot "the real deal" by "a group of Al Qaeda followers who have targeted the Hudson River tubes that connect New Jersey with lower Manhattan." Mershon told a news conference "we've identified a number of the players around the globe, some of whom are in custody of foreign services. The real story here is the symphony of cooperation and coordination not just in the New York–New Jersey metropolitan area, but, frankly, around the world with a number of intelligence and investigative services. It's beyond textbook; it's, in fact, storybook." But you could hardly call that homegrown, and Silber and Bhatt didn't mention it at all. They also left out the August 2006 "aircraft plot," the alleged conspiracy in Britain that led to dozens of arrests and the ban on passengers carrying drinks onto planes that endures to this day. The would-be terrorists had been planning to mix liquid chemicals on board ten airliners crossing the Atlantic and blow them up in midair, a truly scary plot. Were they acting on their own or under direction? The report didn't say anything about them.

In the summer of 2007, as the NYPD got ready to publish *Radicalization in the West,* stories of terrorist conspiracies kept popping up on the crawl that moved across the bottom of the screen on headline news programs. The tabloids splashed them for a day or two, then they sank out of sight. Some fit *Radicalization*'s paradigms and some did not.

One was the plot by four ethnic Albanians from former Yugoslavia who teamed up with a Palestinian-Jordanian cab driver and a Turkish pizza deliveryman to attack Fort Dix in New Jersey. The conspiracy had all the elements of quixotic fantasy and stupid thuggery that are "homegrown" trademarks. These guys were losers from the get-go. Three of the Albanians were brothers constantly in trouble with their neighbors for raising chickens and sheep in their suburban yard. The group was discovered and then infiltrated after members took a videotape of themselves shooting guns, training, and shouting "Allah akbar" to Circuit City to be converted to a DVD; the clerk there called the cops, who called the FBI, who in turn brought in paid informants. Then the conspirators moved to buy weapons from undercover cops: AK-47s and M16 assault rifles, M60 machine guns, rocket-propelled grenades, handguns, plastic explosives, and nitroglycerin. At that point, the Feds arrested them in May 2007.[7]

The evening of August 4, 2007, on a lonely stretch of South Carolina highway near the little town of Goose Creek, a couple of young Arabs got stopped for speeding by the local sheriff's deputies. In the trunk of the car the boys had "a drill, four sections of PVC pipe, which were later determined to contain a mixture of kitty litter, potassium nitrate, and a sugar substance, a package containing twenty feet of safety fuse cord, a five-gallon gasoline container, which was three quarters full of gasoline, and a box of .22-caliber bullets," according to court documents.[8] And then there were the videos picked up with the guys, which showed how to convert the circuits for radio-controlled toys into remote-control triggers for bombs. No need to blow yourself up, says the voice on the video, a brother "can use the explosion tools from distance and preserve his life, God willing, the blessed and exalted, for the real battles."[9]

But the biggest terrorist splash that summer was the alleged plot to attack the jet fuel pipeline and storage tanks at John F. Kennedy International Airport, and that was hardly homegrown at all. In fact, it grew out of a botched FBI effort to track down major players in Al Qaeda believed to be operating out of Guyana and Trinidad and Tobago. Yes, there was one angry, sixty-three-year-old Guyana-born American named Russell Defreitas who used to work at JFK and now wanted to destroy it. But the only other guy in his "group" was an FBI informant. He was trying to set up connections with radical Islamists in the Caribbean, perhaps even the infamous Adnan Shukrijumah, a Saudi with a Guyanese passport who once was KSM's protégé. Over a period of months, Defreitas and the informant virtually commuted to Guyana, but as they tried to arrange meetings with prominent Islamists, suspicions about them grew. Key players dropped out of the plot. Then Defreitas was detained by United States Customs and Border Patrol on one of his returns from Guyana in February 2007. The officers took his phonebook and copied it, after which Defreitas told the informer that he was "extremely suspicious that the United States government knew about their plans." By May, it was clear that the big fish had looked at the bait and swum away. So in June the FBI announced the arrest of Defreitas as if he were a terrorist mastermind.[10]

Basic assumptions about the weakness of Al Qaeda's structure and the strength of its ideas, which were taken as conventional wisdom in

2006 by much of the intelligence community, and which were key to *Radicalization in the West,* had started to look questionable by the time the paper actually was published in August 2007. A National Intelligence Estimate released the month before concluded that Al Qaeda had reconstituted itself in the wild tribal areas of western Pakistan, near the Afghan border, and was plotting new attacks.[11] Nothing homegrown about that. At the same time, there was mounting evidence that fierce doctrinal disputes inside the terrorist ranks deeply undermined the *"jihadi-salafi"* ideology that Silber and Bhatt had described as "proliferating in Western democracies at a logarithmic rate."

The three-headed monster Cohen had described for me earlier in the year made more sense and put the emphasis in the right places: Al Qaeda Central was still trying to pull off a new 9/11 with highly trained and well-funded operatives; then there were more loosely affiliated and self-motivated groups that nonetheless had "dotted lines" leading back to AQC, like the London bombers in July 2005; and finally you had the truly homegrown (and much less effective) bunches of guys like plotters discovered in Miami, Toronto, and Bay Ridge.

Two months after *Radicalization in the West* was published, Larry Sanchez was on Capitol Hill with Mitch Silber testifying before a sympathetic Senate Committee on Homeland Security and Governmental Affairs. Wearing a yellow tie (what used to be called a "power tie"), his biceps visibly bulging beneath his gray business suit, Sanchez put a very particular and unabashedly paternalistic spin on the role of the NYPD. "Rather than just protecting New York City citizens from terrorists," said Sanchez, "the New York Police Department believes part of its mission is to protect New York City citizens from turning into terrorists."[12] In other words, the police would save Muslims from themselves.

To stop radicalization, said Sanchez, "the key to it was first to understand it." Patterns of behavior that "most people would say would be non-criminal, would be innocuous"—that might be regarded as "protected by the First and Fourth Amendment rights"—might really be "potential precursors of terrorism." In this view, constitutional protections might not be protecting people from themselves.

Committee Chairman Joseph Lieberman nodded approvingly.

"You know," said Sanchez, "New York City of course has created its own methods to be able to understand them better, to be able to identify them and to be able to make judgment calls if these are things that we need to worry about. I—in a more—in a closed forum, I could go into a lot more detail, Senators."

"Understood," said Lieberman.

As Sanchez explained the motives behind *Radicalization,* he suggested that an important one was to inform the police in other cities who just might not be doing their jobs terrorism-wise. "We are hoping we have a handle on things that are incubating in the streets of Queens, but what we don't have confidence in is things that are incubating in the United States in another city." In places where crime rates were high, the local cops might not be too concerned with terrorism, especially if they thought New York would be the ultimate target, "so it makes it difficult to be able to create some kind of comprehensive approach to this in the United States." (Privately, Sanchez had grown increasingly worried abut Paterson, New Jersey, and Buffalo, New York, where large Muslim communities had been turning inward, much like those in Britain that proved so dangerous as terrorist incubators.)

Senator Susan Collins, a Republican from Maine, asked deferentially about the reaction to the report from the FBI and the Department of Homeland Security. Sanchez used the language of survival. The relationship with the Feds had gotten better, he said, "stronger and a lot closer," but "I'll be honest and tell you when we, the NYPD, got into this business, it was horrible. There were a lot of turf issues, as one might expect. There was a lot of hostility. But I guess the size of our department kept us alive, and our commitment that we're not going to go away kept us alive.

"One of the problems that the Feds have—" Sanchez stopped himself. "Part of our mission is to protect New York City citizens from becoming terrorists," he repeated. "The federal government doesn't have that mission." The Feds have more constitutional constraints. "They're going to have a heck of a lot harder time," said Sanchez, when the actions observed might not reach "a standard of criminality that you need if your prime objective is you're going to lock them up."

What Sanchez was looking for a way to say was that old-time law enforcement was about arresting people after they committed a crime. The NYPD was committed to stopping the crime of terrorism from happening. To that end, the threat of prosecution and jail is much more useful than the fact of it. If need be, you can nail a guy for sitting on two seats. You identify a potential informer and you put it to him that he has a choice of incarceration or cooperation, and there's a good chance he'll choose the latter. What a study like *Radicalization* could help you do was not only identify where trouble might develop, but at what stages you could best infiltrate your undercover officers—not only to disrupt plots but to recruit new informers.

Sanchez was surprisingly frank about why the NYPD rushed *Radicalization* into print. "It was important for us to get this out quickly, because, you know, every day we're fighting the war of civil liberties. . . . And we couldn't be too politically correct on all this" if the NYPD was going to "continue to be very aggressive" disrupting plots in New York City.

Sanchez also hinted at the payoff for the Feds—obsessed as they were not only with political correctness but with security clearances. They could get information from the NYPD's networks of detectives, spies, and informers that they could never get from their own. "The beauty of it is that the people who have the clearances can guide those that may not have clearances, that are doing the work," Sanchez told the Senate. "You can always protect sources and methods and still guide direction and operations, and I think we have found the way to actually make that work."

And there was more. But this Sanchez did not say at the hearing. While New York City was protecting its Muslims from themselves, it could also be a vital center for what the CIA used to call "national resources." Bay Ridge, say, or parts of Queens would become windows on the world.

"I really can't talk about this," said one of Cohen's NYPD colleagues. "This is a place I cannot go."

"But that's just what Cohen used to do, working the home front in the 1980s," I said. "That was the job that made him at the Agency. And the police force has all the coercive power that the CIA never had. For that matter, that the FBI never had."

The guy smiled. "You've got all the tools of the NYPD, forty thousand people at your disposal," he said. "You take the arrest records and go break them down by nationality, ethnicity, religion." You find the Yemeni or the Somali, the Palestinian or the Iranian who is vulnerable, and you use that vulnerability to recruit him to spy on his community, or, indeed, his country. "And then there's the diplomatic corps," said my friend: all those consuls and ambassadors to the United Nations and their guards and drivers and cooks. "That would be a real trove. But of course we're just talking theoretically here."

Another senior intelligence officer in Cohen's shop, while careful not to reveal sources and methods, summed up the NYPD's relations with the CIA and other spy networks like this: "I've never seen a police department develop into a full partner of the intelligence community. But this one has. I think we have *worldwide* capability. We have the ability to reach out and *collect* worldwide—if we want to." And that may well be what is required to keep a city safe.

THE FRENCH CONNECTION

Confronting Chaos

France's leading freemason is an old friend of Ray Kelly and a close associate of French President Nicolas Sarkozy. In fact, it's a pretty tight circle. When Sarkozy was still the French minister of the Interior in 2006, *le top cop,* he awarded Commissioner Kelly the Légion d'Honneur at a grand ceremony in the French consulate on Fifth Avenue. But Alain Bauer, the freemason, is the man who sees Kelly and Cohen the most, because Bauer is also one of France's best-known criminologists. And his core business is chaos. Or, rather, early-warning analysis to keep chaos at bay. A rotund bon vivant with a large bald head and a little mustache, Bauer has something of Agatha Christie's Hercule Poirot about him, even if his very French analysis, in translation, is sometimes a little hard to follow. A full page of *Radicalization in the West* is written by Bauer as an "Outside Expert's View," and some of it is in such French-style academese it's well-nigh incomprehensible. "We need to be able to move out of the culture of reaction, retrospect, and compilation," Bauer declares.[1]

But the criminologist's core point is taken very seriously chez Kelly. Too many policymakers, he suggests, are longing for the clear-cut confrontations of the past—the crusade against Hitler and Tojo, the long, tense standoff with the Soviet Union. This was the signal mistake of the Bush administration when it tried to turn the fight against Al Qaeda's alliance of *jihadis* into a confrontation with the Evil Empire(s) of Iraq, Iran, and North Korea.

Bauer likes to point out that for centuries, whether cold or hot, "world" or regional, the basic notion of what constituted war was not in question. *States* waged wars. *Uniformed armies* waged wars. And even in civil conflicts the combatants held on to those legitimizing principles: thus in the 1860s and long afterward, Southerners insisted on calling the Civil War the "War Between the States," and Latin American guerrillas still wear uniforms, however ragtag they might be.

But the conflicts that exist today no longer really fit those paradigms of formality. "Previously clear distinctions—between attack and defense, the state and civil society, the public and private sectors, civilians and the military, war and peace, police and the army, legality and illegality—are being blurred," Bauer wrote in a book called simply *World Chaos,* which he coauthored with fellow criminologist Xavier Raufer in 2006. "New forms of confrontation have emerged in which the determining factor is no longer nation or ideology but race, tribe, greed, or religious fanaticism." Little clans developed transnational interests. The ease of travel, commerce, and mass communications allows what Bauer calls "chaotic wars" to spread and the groups fighting them to evolve more like metastasizing cancers than hierarchical organizations. "The adversary is increasingly a sort of hybrid, part common criminal and part political," say the authors. "A warlord, a tribal leader, or a fanatical fundamentalist might head a militia or terrorist network funded by extortion rackets and trafficking in human beings, arms, drugs, protected species, and toxic waste." As such, "for the foreseeable future, warfare, the ultimate form of conflict, will have a criminal dimension."[2]

As Al Qaeda was crushed, then regrouped, was attacked, then recovered, the key to its resilience lay in its enormous flexibility and its extremely loose structure. If Al Qaeda were the kind of organization where individuals in a clear chain of command were key to its operations, it would have been out of action long ago. As an example, Bauer suggests imagining what would happen to a large multinational corporation like General Motors, for instance, or for that matter the CIA, if five or six thousand of their international executives and staff suddenly were killed or imprisoned. Imagine that at the same time they had their offices closed down, their records pillaged, their bank accounts and financial resources confiscated. There would be nothing left. But all of that happened to the conglomeration of criminals, terrorists, thugs, and ideologues known as Al Qaeda, and it kept going.

Cynical about the real-world ways of today's law enforcement agencies, Bauer thinks there's too much emphasis on what amounts to the fake sharing of information. The results are little more than unwieldy and outdated watch lists and spreadsheets full of irrelevant statistics. The challenge, he likes to say, is to convince the cops, the Feds, and the spooks that they are fighting against the same enemies—the forces of chaos, if you will—and to make them understand that if those enemies cooperate informally, quickly, and easily, the government institutions that are up against them have to learn to do the same thing.

The FBI legatt in Paris was not convinced. If the NYPD wanted to send one of its cops to France, then that hapless cop was going to be treated as the embassy's enemy. But for Kelly as much as Cohen, this was a critical assignment. The French had some of the most effective counterterror investigators and operatives in the world, and Kelly had gotten to know many of them personally. So the man picked for the job in 2006 was John Rainbold, a seasoned detective who'd already done a tour in Montréal and spoke fluent French. The idea, as with other cops stationed overseas, was to have him work out of police headquarters. He'd have a desk in the French cops' intel division on the Île de la Cité, not in the U.S. embassy on Place de la Concorde or one of its annexes, where most American law enforcement types were relegated by the State Department, somewhere on the far side of the boutiques on the Faubourg Saint-Honoré.

The legatt told his contacts at the Interior Ministry that this was a bad idea. The NYPD was full of loose cannons. Look at what had happened after the London bombings. The NYPD cops at Scotland Yard had passed on important operational information to Kelly—the composition of the explosives, the cell phone triggers—and he'd gone public with it.

None of this was true, the New York cops insisted, but all of it was damaging. Weeks passed without the requisite approvals. Then months. And then Bauer intervened. Kelly's friend Sarkozy made it happen. By early 2007, Rainbold was at his desk on the Île de la Cité. And the legatt was still inside the embassy, fuming.

RINGS OF STEEL

Defending Ground Zero

Nights were still cold in April of 2008, and Michael Fleming, a sometime addict who'd drifted into New York from Ohio and had been sleeping rough, was looking for some cardboard to keep the chill of the concrete out of his bones. The backing on two big sets of architectural drawings rolled up and stuffed in a trash can at the corner of West Houston and Sullivan looked like it might do the trick. But then Fleming read the cover page: "World Trade Center—Tower One," and the warning that said "Secure Document—Confidential." He flipped through the drawings. Fleming liked to cobble together bits of art and craft, "construct things out of recycled items I find on the streets," and peddle them at Union Square. If these were plans for the old Trade Center, they'd be great to use for that purpose. But they weren't; they were for the new one, the Freedom Tower going up at Ground Zero, which will be, as soon as it is finished, and maybe even before, the target every terrorist in the world is going to want to hit. Dated October 2007, the drawings were identical sets of schematics that showed the building's concrete core and its exact thickness, the location of air ducts, elevators, the electrical systems, and support columns. That is to say, the plans were just the sort of thing you needed to know if you wanted to try to bring the building down or poison everybody inside.

Fleming, perhaps figuring his fifteen minutes had come, decided to call the *New York Post,* which sent a reporter and a videocam to the scene. "It's better that I found them than Osama bin Laden found them," said Fleming, who just figured, "do the right thing and the right thing will come around."[1]

When the story broke, I sent a link to Michael Sheehan, who was still in the Middle East. "Yikes, what dopes!" he wrote back. "But sadly, not surprised."

Sheehan, when he was head of the Counter Terrorism Bureau from 2003 to 2006, had made himself the man that architects—and city planners and property developers and the Port Authority and the governor, for that matter—loved to hate. Part of the CT bureau's function was to dictate defenses for the city's infrastructure and its landmarks. But in keeping with Kelly's efforts to protect and deter without intimidating or stagnating, Sheehan tried to avoid throwing up bollards, those concrete obstacles supposed to stop trucks and cars on suicide missions, or otherwise hardening targets that probably weren't targets at all. "If NYPD encouraged or allowed New York City to become an armed camp of barriers, walls, and closed streets it could undermine people's confidence about living, working, and investing in this great city—and still there'd be no guarantee that security had improved," Sheehan wrote after he'd left the NYPD.[2]

But in 2004 when Sheehan looked at the gorgeous plans by architect Daniel Libeskind for the soaring Freedom Tower, which had been approved by just about all the parties involved except the police, he started worrying not only about that building, but about all of lower Manhattan. It would be "economically devastated by a third attack against the World Trade Center," he said. And from the look of the Libeskind design, that was just about inevitable. It was simply too vulnerable to truck bombs for any terrorist to pass up.

"The Freedom Tower was projected to be a glass structure that stood only twenty-five feet from West Street, a major six-lane highway that connects Brooklyn to lower Manhattan via the Brooklyn Battery Tunnel," said Sheehan. Twenty-five feet—that's considerably less than the distance from the service line to the net on a tennis court. It's the distance dictated in some jurisdictions for smokers to stay away from outdoor diners. "Hundreds of massive trucks would rumble by the building daily, and it would be impossible to inspect them for improvised bombs."

Yes, Libeskind had designed a strong core that would keep the tower from "pancaking" in a matter of seconds the way the original Trade Center towers had done, but a truck bomb would still kill a lot of people, and in the end the tower would have to be taken down again, which would deliver, in slow motion, another stunning victory for the bad guys. "Lower Manhattan and perhaps all of New York City couldn't stand another blow to its financial heart," Sheehan thought. "People and businesses would simply move elsewhere."

So Sheehan raised hell. Kelly backed him, and so eventually did Bloomberg. A meeting was convened with Trade Center developer Larry Silverstein, who was the Libeskind design's main sponsor and strongest promoter. Sheehan brought experts from the RAND Corporation, from engineering faculties, and from the CIA. All agreed the tower was a disaster in the making, and a perfect gift to every lunatic who could pack fertilizer into a Ryder truck. Finally, in May 2005, Governor George Pataki presided over a press conference with all the major players, and Silverstein publicly surrendered. "We have read the recommendations of the police department and accept them in full," he said. "The Freedom Tower as we formerly knew it no longer exists. It will be completely redesigned."

That job was undertaken by Skidmore, Owings & Merrill, which conjured a tower that could stand up to an enormous truck bomb blast. "They also incorporated hugely expensive design features to ensure the safety of the building's inhabitants in a way that no other building in the world did," Sheehan concluded.[3]

Those were the plans that Mike Fleming found in the trash at the corner of West Houston and Sullivan.

Yikes, indeed.

*   *   *

In 2006, New York City announced a three-year, nine-figure plan called the Lower Manhattan Security Initiative to protect the core of the financial district. It was more than a little influenced by systems in place for the city of London, which has Europe's closest equivalent to the Wall Street area, and which boasts a so-called "ring of steel" to preserve its security. The basic principle, in fact, is more a ring of electronic eyeballs, those closed-circuit television cameras that are pretty much everywhere you look in Britain, covering the London financial district like swarms of flies on the wall. But Kelly wanted to go way beyond anything the Brits had done. "It's really a ring of celluloid in London, not a ring of steel," he said.

Central to the program is the cooperation, practically the incorporation into the NYPD, of the private security forces working for the banks and trading houses and other institutions in the area. As planned, the public sector will put up one thousand closed-circuit television (CCTV) cameras, and the private sector will put up two thousand. So within the 1.7 square miles covered by the initiative you'll have, as Kelly put it, "three thousand cameras melded together." Big Brother may not be watching you, but plenty of other people will be. And that's just the beginning. The police intend to have computerized license-plate readers all over the place: thirty-six will be moved around constantly, another eighty will be in fixed locations, and not only around Wall Street and Ground Zero. "They'll be in all the bridges and tunnel crossings coming into Manhattan," said Kelly, and they will be linked to radiation detection equipment funded by the Department of Homeland Security's "Securing the Cities" program.

The record of public/private CCTV policing in Britain, for all the billions spent on the technology, has not done much to stop crime and terror before the fact or win cases afterward. According to New Scotland Yard's Detective Chief Inspector Mick Neville, who's in charge of the Visual Images, Identifications, and Detections Office (Viido), only about 3 percent of the muggings in London have been solved using CCTV pictures. "CCTV was originally seen as a preventative measure," Neville told a security conference in May 2008. It was assumed you'd see those electronic eyes on you, or maybe just feel them, and you'd think twice about knocking the little old lady over the head, or, for that matter, carrying those exploding backpacks into the subway. But this proved to be one of those common-sense assumptions that didn't really fit the way criminals and terrorists think or act. "Billions of pounds have been spent on it, but no thought has gone into how the police are going to use the images and how they will be used in court. It's been an utter fiasco," said Neville. Deterrence? "There's no fear of CCTV," said Neville. "Why don't people fear it?" Because, he said, they think "the cameras are not working."[4]

As for license plate detection, it's hardly foolproof. Computer scanners may read a thousand plate numbers a minute and match them instantaneously to a database of cars reported stolen or otherwise suspect. But the scanners tend to read *only* the numbers, not the states, so the false positives flash by as quickly as sparks flying up a chimney. The biggest practical problem with the electronic eyes, however, is a human one. Somebody has to look at the screen or review all that tape, says Neville, and ultimately that's more work than most cops want to do.

Kelly's enthusiasm for the project is undiminished. An aficionado of consumer technologies (for years he's worked out in the morning listening to podcasts of the news, and he now reads his *New York Times* on an Amazon Kindle), the commissioner is confident that he'll have not only the manpower but the mathematics in place to make the whole thing work.

The Lower Manhattan Security Initiative was designed from the ground up, as the Freedom Tower ought to have been, to thwart attacks by what Kelly now refers to in military jargon as a "vehicle-borne explosive device," or a truck bomb. A control room at 55 Broadway is set to coordinate the movements and assignments of what Kelly calls "a cadre of six hundred police officers" in lower Manhattan and at all the island's bridges and tunnels. The private security forces are expected to be watching the cameras, checking on anything or anyone suspicious. And beyond that, says Kelly, "we are looking to use predictive software." Computers will analyze movement—or nonmovement. "The most basic example would be where a car goes around the block three times," says Kelly. "Based on some sort of algorithm, that sets off an alarm. A package remains at a location for a certain period of time. That generates another type of alarm where we can have a response if needed, either by public or private sector means. The software has come a long way and will continue to advance in that area."

What won't be advancing, however, is the normal traffic pattern around the sixteen-acre World Trade Center site. Most private cars are to be banned; all delivery vehicles will be screened. And at a moment of crisis, huge barriers will allow the cops to block off streets with the push of a button at the command center. Subways, buses, and PATH trains will still come and go on normal schedules, but Ground Zero and its environs will become, in effect, an enormous pedestrian mall watched over by those omnipresent, perhaps omniscient cameras. When Donna Lieberman of the NYCLU talks about "blanket surveillance of millions of law-abiding New Yorkers," she's only stating the facts.[5]

Kelly insists the program is not only legal, it's inevitable if business in this part of town is going to thrive the way it did before 9/11. "It's just common sense," he said. "In order for it to be commercially viable it has to be safe, because you have to be able to rent it." Anybody who works near Ground Zero will know what happened at the site, and wonder if it can happen again. The measures put in place are a promise to the occupants that, in Kelly's words, this "will be the safest business district in America."

The cost, Kelly estimated in August 2008, would be about $106 million, some of which would come from federal funds and some from city capital funds. On top of that will be the personnel costs, as cops are detailed to patrol, respond, and man entry points. "It's a major ongoing expense that will be borne by the city," said Kelly, "but frankly I see no alternative."

With all this technological glitz, the fortune spent on those telescopic eyes in the sky, those lenses on every street corner, those dots and maps and databases and algorithms, there is a risk of self-delusion for law enforcement. Certainly the federal government fell into the trap, for many years, of believing that electronic intelligence and signals intelligence—technical means—were the way to fight terrorism. And in a limited space like the few acres of the financial district, that might be true. But the most effective preventive measures over the long term, and for the length and breadth of the city, as Alain Bauer likes to tell Kelly and Cohen, preaching to the choir, is "human intelligence, human intelligence, human intelligence." And often the key to that is treating humans intelligently.

URBAN LEGENDS

Of Eccentrics and Immigrants

Because I'd been following the careers of terrorists for a couple of decades, I had been following the career of defense lawyer Ronald Kuby.
He had worked with and for the incendiary, infamous William Kunstler,
whose theatrical defense of the Chicago Seven way back when boomers
were young seemed so passionate and so smart. Kuby and Kunstler always championed the legal underdog, which often meant defending terrorists caught dead to rights. They had taken on the case, for instance,
of Yu Kikumura, the Japanese Red Army operative subcontracted by
Qadhafi to terrorize New York. Although Kuby had once joined the
Jewish Defense League when he was a kid, he and Kunstler wound up
defending Rabbi Meir Kahane's killer, Sayed el-Nosair, and, amazingly,
beat the murder rap in his first trial. They also represented Sheikh Omar
Abdel-Rahman, the blind cleric from Egypt who served as the spiritual
sanctioner for many terrorists in his home country and a handful here.

I would have recognized Kuby, in fact, anywhere. With his now-
graying ponytail braided and dangling to the middle of his back, he was
a made-for-media eccentric who had cohosted a radio talk show with
the self-promoting crime fighter and "Guardian Angel" Curtis Sliwa.

But I'd never actually met Kuby until one afternoon in June 2007 when I went to his office down on West Twenty-third Street.

The place was clean and polished and funky all at once. I thought of all the friends I had in the 1970s who came from wealthy families and had great educations and decided to become carpenters. This was their kind of place. And here was Kuby, who'd half forgotten the appointment, but was laid-back and ready to talk.

The alleged plot by Guyanese-American loser Russell Defreitas to blow up JFK Airport was all over the papers just then, so we started with that.

"If Mr. Defreitas is an example of America's challenge, I think we've pretty much won," said Kuby.

I had just read the federal government's complaint and asked him what he thought of the role played by "The Source," a former drug dealer described in the document as the key informant in the case. The Feds, Kuby said, "took the snitch and gave him the sort of standard deal: you don't get an A for effort, you get a sentence reduction for results. So what do you do if you're him? You find Mr. Defreitas, who has been thinking about this attack for maybe ten years? And without doing anything about it?"

There were bigger objectives, I suggested. Kuby looked at me quizzically, more casually amused than truly interested. So I changed the subject. "Tell me about Yu Kikumura," I said.

"Kikumura's back in Japan after serving twenty-two years minus 'good time,' " said Kuby.

And did the Feds ever learn more about what he planned to do?

"They never came up with a target for him," said Kuby. "They came up with a map, creased around an army recruiting station."

I thought of how frustrated spooks are when they get into this sort of conversation. They know, or they think they know, so much about a case. But so little of it can be proved. No wonder the intel division expended very little effort—or less than that—taking suspects to court.

One of the most high-profile conspirators Kuby and Kunstler defended together was Omar Abdel-Rahman, who from beneath his little turban and behind his blank eyes encouraged a loose-knit bunch of guys to try to blow up the Holland Tunnel and the United Nations, among other targets. It was supposedly a follow-on plot after the Trade Center bombing in 1993. Kuby called it "Son of Trade Center." A key figure in the case was an Egyptian informant (one of the many, it would seem) named Emad Salem. He was the guy who penetrated the group around El-Nosair while working for the FBI, then pulled out when they FBI didn't want to pay him anymore, which forced the gang of fools to find Ramzi Yousef ("the Zelig of terrorism," as Kuby called him), who really did show them how to cook up a bomb and blow up a skyscraper. After the Trade Center blast in 1993, the Feds saw the error of their ways, rehired Salem, and ran him in on the clique around Omar Abdel-Rahman. "Clearly it was Emad Salem who was the deus ex machina of that group," said Kuby. "Had these guys been left to their own devices, nothing would have happened."

Pleasantly but persistently, Kuby remained in defense mode until I asked him about the 1997 suicide bomb plot in Brooklyn and Gazi Abu Mezer, whom he did not represent. "That one in Brooklyn was real," said Kuby.

"Yeah. And we got real lucky on it," I said.

"You could make the argument that luck played a part in all them," said Kuby.

"So," I said, "what do you do to make sure you stay lucky?"

Kuby leaned back in his chair and then forward, and I started to sense what listeners to his radio show had noted, that he'd changed some after 9/11, become less reflexive in his defense of everyone and anyone accused of plotting horrific crimes against the people of the United States and, most often, his hometown of New York.

"How *do* you stop terrorists?" I asked.

"The fact that they might get caught is not a deterrent, so you do it in other ways," he said. New York is full of people holed up in their rooms typing angry, inflammatory, explosive language into their computers and onto the Internet or scrawling words of inchoate rage across pages of paper, and then in the margins and on the back, and sending them off to enemies who have never seen or heard of them. There are countless groups of guys fulminating endlessly. And then—nothing. "Why don't these people explode more often?" said Kuby. "Because New York is one of the few places where they can be what they are. They can be batshit crazy. They can be mole people sending out their letters. And they know, deep down, they know that anywhere else they'd be arrested just for showing up." Kuby smiled. "I mean, Sheikh Omar *loved* it here."

New York City was not like Israel, where a whole population of Palestinians pretty much shared the same hatred of a common enemy. There was little or no social backing for suicide bombers in this city, while in Gaza and the West Bank the networks were extensive and popular acquiescence assured. In Brooklyn, would-be terrorists looking for support "are likely to find someone who says 'no' and turns them in," Kuby said. He chuckled thinking about poor, terrified, but brave Abdel Rahman Mosabbah pleading with the LIRR cops in his nonexistent English, *"Bomba! Bomba!"* "Most of these plots have been disrupted by human intelligence, people just dropping the dime," said Kuby.

"I think there's a lot to be said for creating a stable, functioning democracy," he continued. That's a lot more than most people can expect in their home countries, where life can be a cycle of endless intimidation and inescapable indoctrinations. "Here, you know, you get tired of the madrassah and you want to go out and have a beer."

"But can you count on that kind of freedom to keep you safe in a world of crazies? You look at what the police are doing. Kelly and his people are good. But you look at the threat and the consequences—at Ground Zero—and you wonder if it's really enough," I suggested.

"It works often enough that it argues for keeping the city the way it is," said Kuby. The use of intelligence work and the emphasis on police training under Kelly had tried to take that into account, Kuby suggested without, clearly, wanting to sound too enthusiastic. "Look, what's the process by which a talker becomes a doer, a yakker becomes a bomber? They get radicalized by an issue that is a totally legitimate issue. The kind of thing that motivates people is invading a country, or stories of American soldiers raping a fourteen-year-old girl, or Abu Ghraib. And when people feel they have no other means of expression, that's when they explode. But fortunately, New York is still a really good place to have arguments. It's still a good place to get a permit to walk down the street and hand out poorly spelled leaflets."

Kuby considered his last point for a second. "I think there's been an overemphasis on policing demonstrations." Then he considered further.

"But Giuliani and Bratton would cancel these things outright. Kelly has them infiltrated and surveiled."

"Sometimes that's the best way to catch terrorists," I said.

"I guess it sort of depends who you're infiltrating," said Kuby.

I was still thinking about Kuby's notion of the social contract between New York and a population that might not really fit in anywhere else when I had breakfast a few weeks later with Jeremy Travis, the president of John Jay College of Criminal Justice. He'd been a deputy commissioner of the NYPD, and from that experience he had a feeling for the limits of tolerance in the city and the impact of policing. But Travis said he'd also been following the work of one of John Jay's professors, James Lynch, who was studying the question of why crime rates continue to decline in some cities and not in others, even when policing strategies, staffing, and techniques are similar. "He's working on the hypothesis that immigration is the key," said Travis. The more first-generation immigrants, the more secure a big urban environment in the United States becomes.

Then, in November 2007, *Congressional Quarterly* published its annual Safest City Award and I looked at the top ten with populations over five hundred thousand. Four were in Texas: Fort Worth, San Antonio, Austin, and the border town of El Paso, which was listed as the second-safest big city in the country. Two were in California: San José and San Diego, which, again, was right across the line from Mexico. The safest city of all was Honolulu, with its very diverse population, while New York City ranked fourth.[1] Not bad for a place with a population of 8.5 million, some 40 percent of whom were not born in the United States of America.

I called Lynch. "Almost everyone who has examined this issue and is not an ideologue has come to the same conclusion," he said. "In the United States, immigrants engage in common law crime at rates lower than the native population." And it's not just that newly arrived immigrants are less likely to be part of an urban nightmare, it's that they bring their own positive dreams. Robert J. Sampson, chairman of the Sociology Department at Harvard University, talks of a growing consensus that "immigration revitalizes cities around the country." Instead of becoming empty urban wastelands, marginal neighborhoods fill up with new immigrants who want to build their futures, and wind up building the economy.

That was essentially why when Rudy Giuliani was the much-heralded law-and-order mayor of New York City he was more than happy to embrace immigrants who had entered or stayed in the United States illegally. Indeed, he made New York a safe haven for them. "If you come here and work hard and you happen to be in an undocumented status," said Mr. Zero Tolerance, "you're one of the people we want in this city."[2] That was also why in 2007, then-Governor Eliot Spitzer proposed issuing driver's licenses to illegal immigrants. If first-generation immigrants are helping to make cities more secure, then doesn't it make sense to have as much information about them as possible? Or is it smarter to make them live as far outside the law as possible? Spitzer, long before his other peccadilloes were discovered, found himself pilloried by his opponents for a proposal that would seem to be common sense. But, of course, it wasn't commonly seen that way.

Most Americans think newly arrived foreigners are essentially, even intrinsically, dangerous. A recent study showed 75 percent of Americans think "more immigrants cause higher crime rates."[3] Full stop. A single sensational incident involving illegal aliens, like the execution-style murder of three students in Newark, New Jersey, in the summer of 2007, seems to confirm the fears of people already nervous about all the newcomers. And that feeling is especially strong in less urbanized parts of the country, which is why immigration was a big issue, and badly understood, when presidential candidates were campaigning in Iowa, New Hampshire, and South Carolina. (Certainly in South Carolina, where I spend part of each year, laborers from Mexico have changed the whole tenor of daily life.) Yet if ever there was an issue where conventional wisdom was misleading, it was the dangers posed by large numbers of foreigners coming to American shores.

"I would say, if you want to be safe, move to an immigrant city," Sampson told me on the phone from Harvard. Nationwide, over the previous fifteen years we had seen the largest wave of immigration, in absolute numbers, both legal and illegal, ever to cross the frontiers of the United States. Foreigners fresh off the boat or plane or climbing out of cars and trucks and buses represented almost 13 percent of the U.S. population, which was almost as high even in percentage terms as during the late nineteenth century, when Jacob Riis was chronicling the wonders and horrors of urban immigrant life. According to a 2007 report from the nonprofit Immigration Policy Center, the estimated undocumented population had doubled to 12 million since 1994. Yet the violent crime rate nationwide declined more than 34 percent during the same period, while crimes against property dropped more than 26 percent.[4] If there is a single huge caveat, it's that the second generation and the third, as they become more American, often become more troubled and troubling. Among them, crime often rises. The overall challenge for society is not to keep immigrants out, but to keep their dreams alive for their children and grandchildren.

And terrorism? Americans remember that terrorism flew in from abroad on September 11, 2001. If they look at analyses like those in *Radicalization in the West,* or thumbnail sketches in news reports, they might easily conclude that immigrant society is "permeated" with dark-skinned young men named Mohammed and Ahmed conspiring, cooking up explosives, and just waiting for the chance to strike. But that certainly is not the case. Some individuals and small groups may be dangerous, but they are very few and mostly very ineffective. As Falkenrath said, they are aberrations.

Indeed, one of the critical signs that a group of guys might get dangerous—one of the key trip wires Cohen and his people are looking for—is the moment they stop going to the mosque and start to withdraw into their own little world, because self-taught radicals know the society they live in, the immigrant-American society, including the Muslim-immigrant-American society, won't tolerate their violent ideas. And in the end, it was precisely the way Kelly and Cohen drew on New York's diversity for linguists and undercover officers and detectives—and the faith and trust they put in them—that allowed the NYPD to create one of the most effective counterterrorist operations anywhere in the world.

NEW YEAR'S EVE

The Countdown

As I get ready to leave my apartment on the Upper East Side and head down to police headquarters, Matt Lauer and Ann Curry are telling me on the television that Benazir Bhutto has been attacked while running for election as prime minister of Pakistan. A bomb. Gunshots. This is the second time in a matter of weeks. The picture isn't clear, but we know she is injured. Maybe worse. It's 8:30 a.m and now there's breaking news as I'm headed out the door. Bhutto is dead. I'm trying to think what this means for the New York City Police Department. There are so many Pakistanis in this town. Do they stay cool? Mourn quietly? Blame . . . somebody here? I'll have to call one of the lawyers for Matin Siraj, the Herald Square kid. She's from Pakistan originally and she knows Bhutto's husband well. He's been living in New York.

What a city this is. Only in New York can you see this many angles at once. And play them. And still get blindsided.

Christmas is just a few days past and it's wet and cold on Seventy-seventh Street. The free morning newspapers that somebody hands you as you head down the slick-gritty stairs into the subway don't have anything about Bhutto yet. No time for that. They're all about the cops' incredible year. *AM New York* banners "Safe to the Core: Murders in Big Apple Hit Record Low"; *Metro* headlines "Murders May Hit New Low in City Crime Drop." Since reasonably accurate record keeping began in 1963, there have never been fewer people killed by criminals. It looks like the total will be under five hundred. That's a hell of a contrast to the annus horribilis 1990 when 2,245 died. Reading through the regular papers on the Number 6 line headed downtown, I see the *Times* is cautious: "City Is Doubling Police Program to Reduce Crime: As Violence Declines, a Focus on Areas That Remain Troubled." The police blotter column in the *New York Post* reports a young man robbed in Chelsea and another corpse found with stab wounds.

On the thirteenth floor at One Police Plaza, Paul Browne hasn't come down from the morning meeting yet. The televisions suspended above the public information officers' cubicles are all Bhutto all the time. Now there's a report about former Mayor Giuliani running for the Republican presidential nomination. He's issued a statement denouncing terrorists behind the Bhutto killing and underscored the risk for the American public. The TV reporter notes that Giuliani is pretty quick off the mark. The White House has yet to comment. One of the cops, half listening, raises an eyebrow.

The nine o'clock is over. Kelly, Cohen, and Falkenrath were all there, but there was no scramble. Deployments for this kind of event run almost "on automatic pilot," says Cohen. The cops know already there are five Pakistani-owned banks in the city, three of them in the Wall Street area. Extra officers are sent to keep an eye on them. The same is done for the Pakistan Airlines offices, the consulate on Sixty-fifth Street, and the residences of the consul general and the United Nations ambassador. The police also know that there are more than a hundred thousand Pakistanis who've immigrated to the city, mostly over the last fifteen years, and they're concentrated in three precincts: the One-One-Five just south of La Guardia Airport, the One-Oh-Five, on the far eastern edge of Queens, and the Seven-Oh in the middle of Brooklyn. The patrol officers in those precincts got special briefings prepared by the intel division: what's happened, what it means, what it might mean in New York—weeping, rage, possible score settling. Cohen's attitude is that patrol cops aren't going to absorb heavy doses of information about a situation like Pakistan unless they feel they need to know it right now. This is one of those mornings. "It's a question of when you inject it," he says.

As Browne and I are talking, we're heading for Madison Square Garden, where the police academy is holding its graduation exercise. There the floor's been covered and more than nine hundred chairs set up for the recruits. The top cops are on the stage: on the left, the chiefs in uniform. Kelly and Bloomberg are in suits, but they sit with the men in blue. On the right, all suits: Cohen is in the front row, Falkenrath is seated behind him. Frank Sinatra's "New York, New York" blasts out of the loudspeakers as the recruits file in—men, women, tall and short, burly and petite, white and black and many shades of brown.

I'm talking to the other reporters and photographers standing around and quickly realize I am as fascinated as they are jaded. "We've all had our little 'situations' with these guys," says a woman photographer. "Because we are the visible face of the press. You print guys can step in and out." Her point: She takes a lot of shit, and sometimes some rough stuff, trying to get her pictures. The NYPD doesn't love the press when it's not toeing the line.

A police baritone sings the National Anthem. The police chaplain, a rabbi, gives the invocation. Bloomberg speaks, rattling off statistics to be proud of: the crime rate down 26 percent in six years, the murder rate the lowest on record, and this graduating class from all over the map. "One out of every five of today's graduates was born overseas, in fifty-two different countries." A lot have come to the police from the military, including the class valedictorian, Karolina Wierzchowska, who immigrated from Poland, joined the army, then the police, and aced all her exams.

"The truth is, each one of you took a different path to reach this point," says Bloomberg. "In your previous lives, you've driven taxis . . . waited tables . . . taught schoolchildren . . . and one of you even had a career as a dancer—in this job, it helps to be quick on your feet!" He gets the expected laugh.

After Bloomberg speaks, each branch of the military is named, the veterans now serving as recruits stand and a strain is played from their respective hymns. The Marine Hymn sounds, and now Kelly is on his feet, too. When the speeches are over, the recruits stand with their hands behind their backs. Their fingers work quietly but furiously, pulling the white gloves off and holding them clinched. The announcement comes that they're now officers in the NYPD. Blue and white confetti pours down from the ceiling. The gloves are thrown in the air. The families come for embraces.

All 914 rookies are headed into the field, into the toughest neighborhoods in the city. Cops on dots. But even before that, they'll be headed to Times Square on New Year's Eve.

After the graduation there's a lunch with the brass at Carmine's in the theater district. Kelly and Cohen and Browne and a bunch of chiefs are there. Somebody's ordering pasta with porcini for everybody. The place is noisy as hell and I'm trying to hear Cohen over the racket. "You think Bin Laden's still got another big one in him?" I shout. "That motherfucker wants to do it before he dies!" Cohen shouts back. Nobody wants to look tense. Everybody knows New Yorkers are in no mood for unwarranted warnings and emergencies. "You can't really expect an entire city of eight million to stay in a state of quasi-heightened alert," says Browne. Apathy has become ingrained. "People have such short attention spans," he says. "That's to be expected. The police department certainly expects it." But the clock's ticking toward midnight on Monday, December 31, three and a half days away, so it's time to get back to work. "We've got a New Year's Eve ball hanging over our heads," says Cohen.

Lunch is over, everybody's headed in separate directions. I'm going out to the Counter Terrorism division in Brooklyn, and I hear Browne talking to Cohen: "Are you going to be at Ground Zero on Monday night?" Then Browne hears himself. "Bite my tongue—at Times Square?"

The CT division has got all its gear ready for New Year' Eve, including the "radiation suite" that goes in a roof rack on top of an unmarked SUV. They've got detectors for neutrons, alpha, beta, and gamma radiation. In addition to officers sent to the Department of Energy and other agencies for training, they've got outside consultants steeped in the minutiae of chemical, radiological, and biological threats. They'll be working with the FBI and DOE guys, too, and relying on their own contacts with the local communities in addition to whatever the intel division is producing. "We need buy-in from community leaders," says Detective David Kao. "We have to create this huge radar network to detect the smallest ripple in the water." Today the cops even have an accidental inside track on the Pakistan situation. One of the CT division's men was in-country when Bhutto got blown up. He was going to his sister's wedding.

But the officers at the CT division see the public apathy, too. It's been a long time since 9/11. "There's always some return to normalcy," says one. "I don't want the little old lady raising children to worry about terror. I want the professionals to worry about terrorism."

"What about loners?" I ask. Big events like New Year's Eve are perfect targets for the friendless lunatic, including one smart enough to brew some anthrax or cook up a dirty bomb. You can't penetrate his group. He doesn't have one. How do you stop him?

"How you stop that," said the cop, "is by tracking the material they use to make the bomb. We can't read people's minds, but they need the stuff to build the bomb." And then there's deterrence, "Homeland Security theater," says one of the cops, which is one of the big reasons nine thousand police will be out in the streets the night the ball drops.

"It's the old omnipresence," says Kao. "Like we're everywhere."

It's getting late at One Police Plaza but Chief John Colgan and Chief Vincent Giordano are still working full tilt, sorting out the endless details of deployments for New Year's Eve. Giordano's got a noticeable twitch near one eye, and it's not surprising. There's so much to keep track of. Some of it you see, like the thousands of cops in the streets. And a lot you don't, like the shooters among the skyscrapers. "We want to put things in place to prevent and deter operations that might be in the planning stage," says Giordano. "We also want to deter future operations, to the point where somebody looking at this may say, 'We don't want to do that city in the future.'"

Colgan sits back and listens. Giordano twitches, and seems to be taking the emotional burden on himself. "I tell my family you have to lead your life, go to work, go to school, go play—but you have to be aware. If you see something that doesn't look right, tell somebody."

I ask if I'll be seeing them both in Times Square.

"As a cop," says Colgan, "if you're in the New York City Police Department, that *is* where you *want* to be."

The next morning I'm in Cohen's office early and he's drinking coffee out of his CIA cup. It seems like he's got a lot of time for me, like he's confident that his machine is running smoothly. "We're an organization now," says Cohen, "not just a gaggle of guys chasing things around. Six years ago we were a gaggle. Not now. And right now one of my big objectives is to make sure all of this continues on. I don't think any of us come here to make the city safe only for the time we're here.

"We now know what we know," says Cohen. "Before, we'd have to find the book that had it." I look at his coffee cup. "We have made our bones with a very traditional low-technology intelligence program where the emphasis is on human talent and accountability. Ninety-eight percent of what we do is humint." The practical is always stressed over the theoretical. "We are not in the 'must be going on' business. We are in the what *is* going on business."

But as I listen to Cohen, I'm wondering how any of this can really function without him and Kelly on the scene. For starters, who could throw weight around in Washington the way they do? Who could recruit talent the way they do? And as times change, if terrorism still continues to decline, who could command the resources that they do? I wonder, too, if I would trust anybody else to have the kind of power that Kelly and Cohen have accumulated, and at times, I wonder how much even they can be trusted.

At one point Cohen talks about all the information that's out there that really never has been processed yet. Look at KSM's confessions at Guantánamo. "I mean, he confessed to everything. Who knows what's real and what's imagined and what's deflected?" Then there was Dhiren

Barot aka Al-Hindi: "There are large volumes of material that we still have yet to go through."

I mention that Kelly had told me at a dinner a few nights before that even the contents of Ramzi Yousef's computer had never been fully decrypted. "Yeah, and we don't know what's in there," said Cohen. "Just this week I was trying to drive home to the NSA that we need to go back through those and see if there's technologies that will get us into things that we couldn't get into two years ago."

And then there are prisoners, high-value detainees. As Cohen saw it, they were a problem a little like the computers. You had to go back to them. "Let's re-debrief prisoners," he said. "We didn't ask questions about radicalization before. We were asking about operations. We need to ask, 'What did you do when you were twelve years old?' "

There's just so damn much to know.

I ask him what he can tell me about Bhutto's killing. In his outer office the television news is running and rerunning pictures of what seems to be a man with a gun firing at her as she stands up through the sunroof of her SUV, and then the explosion.

"We all concluded that we didn't fully understand what happened in terms of the assassination or what the trickle effects of that will be." Any idea who did it? "We just don't know. We know it's not good."

Cohen asks himself the next question. "How important is Pakistan to New York City? There are few countries that are more important for us than Pakistan. . . . We've tried to tease out the meaning of it in the Pakistani community here. There are a lot of family ties. But the challenge that Pakistan poses for us is that it has reportedly sixty nuclear weapons—and ten thousand madrassahs. To me, that brackets the concern."

On the morning of December 31, 2007, I went to the ceremony at One Police Plaza where a plaque was dedicated to the three officers severely wounded by the bombs of Puerto Rican terrorists twenty-five years before, then spent the day walking around lower Manhattan looking at other bits of history. I strolled across the Brooklyn Bridge, which I had never actually done before, and wondered if Iyman Faris—or KSM—

might really have found some way to bring it down. I imagined, too, what the scene must have been like when a crazed Jordanian started shooting up a van full of yeshiva students driving across it in 1994. I went over to Wall Street to look at the shrapnel scars in the stone wall of the J.P. Morgan building and then walked from there to St. Paul's Chapel and the churchyard behind, where ancient tombstones frame the emptiness across the street at Ground Zero.

And then I took the subway to Forty-second Street, "the Deuce," as veteran cops call it. I wanted to check it out before it really shut down and the only way I could move was with a police escort. Everything was peaceful. Orderly. Vincent Giordano's nervous attention to details allowed everybody else to be calm. Or, at least, relatively calm.

In police headquarters I watched the last rays of the sun fade through cameras perched high over the city, from Sixth Avenue to the Brooklyn Bridge, from Times Square to Macy's, the images transmitted back to the screens on the walls of the command center. Below them, scores of representatives from every city, state, and federal agency that might be needed to meet a threat or an emergency drank tepid coffee by the gallon—and waited.

A few yards away in another corner of the building, only a handful of detectives remained in the sepulchral light of the Real Time Crime Center. Most of the staff were in the mobile version of the same room set up closer to Times Square, in case it became the new Ground Zero. From there they could connect information from the spot interrogations to global databases, if that was necessary, pulling up everything from arrest records to water bills, anything that would shed light on identity, background, and connections.

Out in the night, I caught up with the CT division's David Kao and his weapons-of-mass-destruction-detecting SUV. Electronics were piled around the front console: one Toughbook laptop reading license plates by the thousand, another Toughbook showing radiation levels and comparing them to carefully compiled records of the background radioactivity that is always present. But when the doors were closed and the interior lights dimmed behind the smoked windows, all of that was invisible. "I look like a soccer mom driving around with this," said Kao. "People think I'm going camping."

Crowds on foot poured into Times Square through layer upon layer of security, but rarely took notice of the makeshift fortress erected around them. Massive blocks of concrete weighing thousands of pounds partially blocked every street, with police cruisers positioned across the gaps between them. If need be, the police vehicles could be pulled back to open the way. But if someone wanted to ram a car into the crowd, or a truck bomb, he wasn't likely to get by. The next line of the defense was visible but discreet farther down each block: officers from the Emergency Service Unit in full battle gear with assault rifles ready to open fire. And then, another set of concrete blocks and another patrol car gate to get through.

As people reached the square they were herded to fenced-in corrals by the hundreds. There was standing room only, and until the ball dropped at midnight, there would be no chance to leave. There were hours left to go. A few Japanese tourists told a reporter they were wearing diapers. But there was no way to let people wander around in here without clogging the carefully planned paths between the corrals meant to let emergency personnel move quickly and freely. I understood all that, of course, but as I moved with the police—I could not keep myself from doing this—I kept thinking of animals in pens waiting for the slaughter.

A little farther down Broadway, I hooked up again with Giordano, who was watching his officers every bit as closely as Elaine Kaufman watched her waiters. Colgan was there, too, and he was right, this was clearly the place to be for law enforcement types, including a lot of FBI agents whose crisp suits and ties and cloth coats always set them apart, even from the best-dressed detectives. Giordano introduced me to one that I thought might be a Fed, but then, maybe not: Chief James R. Waters, the ranking NYPD detective on the Joint Terrorism Task Force. We exchanged the usual pleasantries.

"A whole lot of people, a whole lot going on," I said noncommittally, shouting over the slow-building crescendo of New Year's Eve noise.

"But of course," said Waters, shouting back, "we've got quite a crowd that's gonna show up tonight. The weather is beautiful, and New

York is the center of the universe—and we do remain in the crosshairs of Al Qaeda."

"Sure," I said. "But how's things on the JTTF? Are frictions between the NYPD and the Feds really resolved?"

"With the Big Dog? The FBI? The Major Partner, as I refer to it?"

That would be about right, I said, and he reports things are fine on the JTTF, even if "no marriage is perfect."

"And what about between the FBI and the intel division?" I asked him. And Waters smiled. "Some people describe it as friction, I consider it deconfliction."

"Some people say you guys on the JTTF have gone over to the dark side," I shouted. "Have you?"

"Absolutely not," said Waters. "We're one thousand percent blue."

As the hour approaches, I am with two ESU marksmen positioned high above the square. They're middle-aged, affable, the kind of guys you'd like to take bass fishing with you. Their high-powered rifles are left discreetly inside their unzipped cases for the moment. Their main tools just now are three-thousand-dollar binoculars and one-million-candlepower handheld lights. One of them points to a building a few hundred yards across the square, to the darkened windows of apartments where, it seems, nobody is home. "I could tell you what's going on in that room," he says, focusing the beam on a window. "That's the kitchen right there." If anyone inside looks suspicious, a call goes in to the Real Time Crime Center, which comes back quickly with the name of the occupant. The cops will deploy quickly to check out the situation. If something more than suspicious is going on, then one of the men with me above the square will "get on the rifle" while the other spots for him.

There are teams like this positioned well out of sight all around the area, many of them on rooftops. The helicopters high above us, silent and invisible as well, are watching to see if anyone else is on those roofs or terraces. On a cold night like this, the heat signature of a man lying in wait will show up on the chopper's screens even after he has moved on.

I ask the guys with me how long they've been snipers. One of them looks at me laconically. "The bad guy would be 'the sniper,' " he says, "so *we* are the countersnipers." He does not answer the rest of the question.

For the final countdown, I met up with Police Sergeant Joe Gallagher, who worked with Paul Browne. There was nothing to do now, really, but work our way to the center of the square and wait for the ball to drop, and for whatever else might happen. I looked up at where I knew the snipers were. I looked around at the three defense perimeters. And the guys wearing radiation detector backpacks. And the rookies in their new uniforms and all the tourists in their funny red hats handed out by Pontiac. Men, women, children, Americans, Europeans, Latins, Asians: hundreds of thousands of them all together on this clear, cold night. What an irresistible target all this was for the homicidal maniac, the suicide bomber, the crazed loners and malignant clusters, cornered Shiite fanatics and the multiple varieties of Al Qaeda, whether Core, or connected by the dots, or making it all up while they went along. What a target this place would be for the "martyrs" who had flown into the World Trade Center six years before, or the one who blew up Benazir Bhutto and killed uncounted bystanders only a few days ago. Karachi was not so far from Queens anymore, and Queens was just across the bridge.

How could you possibly defend against all the madness that existed in the world, so much of it focused on this place, these people? What would you do to stop it? What *wouldn't* you do? I had come to think of Kelly and Cohen and Sheehan and Falkenrath—I will admit this—as heroes who had somehow found the right balance. But would it work tonight? I sure as hell hoped so. And could it go on working for months and years and decades to come? Because the threat was not going to go away, even if the public fears did.

I looked at Joe. No need to shout out a conversation like this just here, just now, in the middle of the Deuce with the ball about to drop. Joe was dressed sharp, as usual, and I told him I liked his tie and jacket, which I did. But I noticed something was missing. Where was the gas mask that all cops were supposed to have right at hand tonight?

"Listen," Joe told me, "if you're in the hot zone, you just straighten your tie—and you sit down, and you die with dignity." I wasn't sure if this was fatalism or a vote of confidence in his organization. Maybe a lot of both.

The last minutes ticked by. The crowd shouted the last seconds. But only confetti exploded on the scene. That was all that happened in Times Square on New Year's Eve 2007. The NYPD had done its job.

EPILOGUE

The conference room where Ray Kelly holds morning meetings with the heads of counterterrorism and intelligence—the room where they made up the playbook, as Cohen likes to say—was empty on an August afternoon in 2008. The long table was bare, the speaker phones silent. There were no windows, but there was a vision of the outside world—on wall-size video screens showing CCTV images from different corners of the city.

The place had something of a war-room air about it, but the war seemed, at that moment, to be in abeyance. The playbook was working for now, but the future was fraught with peril, and while the NYPD had done so much so well to meet the threats of the last seven years, might cops themselves become a danger? They had done what they thought they needed to do to get the power they had to have to stop terrorist attacks. "Grabbing it and pushing it and shoving it," as Kelly said, they had been able to create an unprecedented space for themselves in the world of intelligence as well as law enforcement.

How far would they go to protect the lives of millions of people all around them whose homes and jobs, whose schools and whose houses of worship were part of the number one terrorist target in the world? There were times when they were so damn close to the edge of legality. Maybe Kelly and his team could be trusted to walk that line in a reasonable way. Maybe. But it's all too easy to picture the abuse of power that might have come under some of Kelly's immediate predecessors. Already a city-state in many respects, could New York become a police state? I wanted Kelly to address this head on.

"I think there are enough built-in governmental controls and trip-wires," said the commissioner, citing the presence of five district attorneys and two U.S. attorneys in the city, the boards against corruption, the boards against abuse, the relentless attentions of the media. But he reflects. "You know," Kelly added, "it's uncharted water to some extent. We understand that."

Sam Rascoff, the red-haired wunderkind who headed the intel division's analytical operation from 2006 to 2008, sees the approach forged by Kelly, Cohen, and their teams as a model that is much more useful, in fact, for the Federal government than it is for most local police. The former clerk for U.S. Supreme Court Justice David Souter notes that all the major legal battles against counterterror operations have centered on the detention of suspects at home and abroad, whether at an old pier in New York, or, much more egregiously, at Guantánamo, Bagram, and Abu Ghraib. But it makes no more sense for the Feds to focus on detaining people as the primary tool for fighting terrorists than it does for the NYPD. The aim should be to gather information and intelligence, identify risks, and then manage those risks by intervening selectively to protect against the threat. Sometimes that means detaining a suspect, but use of information and intimidation to disrupt potential plots may be even more effective. Sometimes all that's required is to make a target harder to hit, or to put on a show that makes it seem so. These are the lessons the NYPD learned.

Rascoff, who teaches at New York University, thinks the goal should be to lead the federal government places it would not normally venture. He draws an analogy with California Governor Arnold Schwarzenegger pushing environmental policies that go way beyond federal guidelines, but, because of California's size and its clout, may force Washington to keep up. While the president and Congress have failed to develop a coherent and constitutional model for domestic intelligence gathering, the NYPD has provided its own.

"With local law enforcement," Kelly points out, "you have more flexibility in recruiting confidential informants, and obviously in arresting people. The whole package is in one agency." As the walls between the Feds' prosecution mindset and the prevention mentality of the NYPD's intel division have been chipped away, new FBI guidelines have been promulgated and will continue to be adapted. Rascoff believes that eventually they will weaken what's known as "the criminal standard" for federal investigators, allowing agents more leeway watching, infiltrating, and recruiting among members of incipient terrorist cells who have, in fact, broken no laws, but may be headed in that direction.

All this will have to be examined and debated at the national level. Such tactics would have to be regulated. The waters would have to be charted. But it makes more sense for the federal government to be using the NYPD's tactics elsewhere in the country than for local cops to try to emulate them. There is no need for most municipalities to do what the NYPD does to stop terrorists, not least because they're not as big a target for the bad guys. The intel division's collection methods that pushed the edge of the legal envelope and created a product envied at the national and international level, the extraordinary web of back-channel ties to the intelligence community, the liaisons with other police forces and indeed other governments as far away as Abu Dhabi and Singapore—no other local force in the United States could command those kinds of resources and, arguably, none ought to. Even the technical means used by the NYPD are likely to be beyond the grasp of other state and local police. Few other cities could or would or should acquire the array of devices that watch the five boroughs from the sky, from the streets, on the surface of the rivers and from under the water in the harbor to keep the town and its people safe, or at least safer, from nuclear and chemical attack.

In fact, it's likely the New York police themselves will have to dial back on their costly programs. Their success has weakened their reason for being. "Every day we go without an attack the public becomes more complacent," Kelly says. When the nation's economic crisis has people terrified about losing their jobs, the threat posed by terrorists seems less important. The financial crunch also hits police funding directly. New

York City's government, including the cops, largely lives off tax revenues generated by the financial services industry that began to collapse in the summer of 2008. "The next administration will be under tremendous pressure as far as the budget is concerned," Kelly warns, adding that the impact of the economic crisis "is going to last, in my judgment, for several years. So there will be pressure, either direct or indirect, to change what we're doing."

All the while, the world is changing, too, and not for the better. The overseas campaigns of the GWOT have created more terrorists than they eliminated. The Taliban are resurgent in Afghanistan; Al Qaeda has regrouped in Pakistan. Americans desperate to declare victory and get out of Iraq have decided to call it a win if they can escape the Mesopotamian mire with anything short of complete defeat. The Middle East is far from peace, as far as ever, with Iran's influence growing amid the wreckage of Washington's policies. The risk increases every day that Israel will start a war with the mullahs that the United States may have to finish. Any one of those distant conflicts could erupt in New York City, turning the skyscrapers, the streets, and the subways into killing fields. The cops, once again, would find themselves the last, hard-pressed guarantors of the city's peace and security in a world of terror.

Looking back on the last seven years, it strikes me that the greatest innovation in Kelly's police force may have been one of the first, and it was neither procedural nor legal nor technological, but cultural. He took what many in Washington and in other parts of the country might have seen as New York City's greatest weakness, the presence of millions of people born outside the United States—that foreign 40 percent of the population—and recognized that those immigrants would be the core of its defense. They provided the key linguistic skills and the invaluable human intelligence; they literally talked the talk and walked the walk of cultures everywhere on earth. They were what gave the NYPD "the reach that you potentially can have throughout the world," Kelly said. But more than that, they shared a notion of freedom and security, opportunity and prosperity. It sometimes seems a delicate thing, the American dream, but those who believe in it are amazingly resistant to those who would attack it, and when law enforcement understands that, then the city—and the nation—can remain secure.

A Note on Target Cities

Which cities in the United States are most at risk of terrorist attack?

A lot of lives ride on that question, as do billions of dollars in grants from the Department of Homeland Security and other federal funds. Partly because it is so clearly in terrorist sights, New York gets some $125 million a year from DHS. But it needs every penny and often has to fight for it.

The DHS says its roster of those cities sufficiently at risk to be eligible for grants is based on three variables: *threat*, the likelihood of an attack occurring; *vulnerability*, the relative exposure to attack; and *consequence*, the expected impact of an attack. Threat counts for about 20 percent of the evaluation, and consequences and vulnerability count for 80 percent.[1] But almost every element of the equation is open to question. A statistical study of "vulnerability" to terrorist attack funded by DHS in 2007, for instance, listed Boise, Idaho, a town of 200,000 people, among the top-ten riskiest places to live. It was not an unreasonable study by a University of South Carolina team working with University of Arizona statistician Walter W. Piegorsch. It simply made no effort to judge plausible terrorist intent.[2]

The DHS list of six "Tier I" cities does reflect unspecified input on terrorist intentions and appears more balanced, given the known record. There is no ranking among the six, which are: New York–Newark, the District of Columbia and environs, metropolitan Chicago, Los Angeles, the San Francisco Bay area, and Houston.

Once you get down to the dozens more urban areas listed as "Tier II," however, many terrorism experts suspect pork-barrel politics plays a major role in the final outcome. The number of cities starts to change from year to year, and during the tight congressional elections of 2006, especially, reliable red-state constituencies, or closely contested ones, seemed to be getting money taken from persistently blue ones. In one truly bizarre 2006 ruling, DHS decided New York City had no national monuments or icons—which might surprise some forty-one million tourists a year visiting the Statue of Liberty and the Empire State Building—and then tried to cut counterterrorism funding to New York City by 40 percent in order to give more money to Jacksonville, Florida; Louisville, Kentucky; and Omaha, Nebraska.[3]

Mayor Bloomberg was perfectly blunt. "When you catch a terrorist and look at the map in his or her pocket, it is always a map of New York; it's not a map of some other place," he said. President Bush and Homeland Security Secretary Michael Chertoff had said repeatedly that funds would be distributed based on risk assessments. "I think, unfortunately, that process has been compromised," said Bloomberg. "And by just defining forty-five cities instead of four or five cities as places where risk exists, it has degenerated back into the kind of distribution of funds that is something for everyone. The truth of the matter is that the risks are concentrated in New York, Washington, a handful of other cities. And even though there are potential targets every place, Homeland Security funds shouldn't be going to where there are risks, it's to where there are targets."

Terrorism analyst Mia Bloom agrees. "Local law enforcement in the U.S. tends to exaggerate the threat because there is so much money involved," she says. "They come up with these elaborate potential terrorist scenarios, which, God forbid, the terrorists should ever get their hands on."

It doesn't take clairvoyance to reach reasonable judgments about the kind of targets that Al Qaeda and its sympathizers prefer, in fact, and the redoubtable Alain Bauer cautions that small ones with high symbolic value—Mount Vernon, Virginia, for instance, or Gettysburg—have to be watched carefully. He also points to Al Qaeda's penchant for attacking what he calls "Sodom and Gomorrah or Babylon," which would elevate the importance of Las Vegas or Atlantic City as a potential target. But fundamentally, as New York's long experience attests, terrorists want to strike cities that are symbols of wealth. They favor targets that can get instant and massive media coverage, and some certainly have been inspired by the apocalyptic spectacles in disaster movies.

The following list takes basic Homeland Security data made public in 2007, including the Piegorsch report on relative vulnerabilities, then adds extra weight to a city's rank if it is listed as Tier I or Tier II, if it is known to have been a target of Al Qaeda plotters in the past, if it has experienced domestic or foreign terrorist attacks in the last forty years, and if it suffered any casualties from those attacks. For a professional statistician like Piegorsch, this is hardly satisfactory. "It would be good to include the number of casualties and these other variables, but it's very hard, which is why we didn't do it this time," he said. But the approach used here does give a rough indication of both terrorist intent and inherent risks.

Thus, New Orleans is in the top ten mainly because of the extreme vulnerability of its socioeconomic and physical infrastructure, but also because it is on the 2007 Tier II list at DHS and was the scene of minor domestic terrorist incidents in the 1990s. Los Angeles has been the target of repeated terrorist plots and attacks, but has strong physical infrastructure and a spread-out population that reduce some of the risks, so it is a bit farther down the list. Seattle and Las Vegas are both known to interest Al Qaeda planners, but they have relatively strong rankings when it comes to socioeconomic factors, risk of natural hazards, and the sturdiness of their big buildings. Farther down, questions of vulnerability and half-forgotten domestic terrorists incidents give some surprising results. Mission Viejo, California, made some lists of terrorist incidents in 1996 when teenagers set off bombs in a schoolyard after getting the designs off the Internet. Orlando would seem to be an ideal symbolic target, with all its theme parks, and it is a Tier II city, but it has good infrastructure and has never been the scene of a terrorist incident.

No effort has been made to factor in the 2,972 people killed and 12,000 injured on September 11, 2001, but that would not change the order of the list in any case.

1. New York City, NY, area
2. Washington, DC, area
3. Chicago, IL
4. New Orleans, LA
5. Los Angeles, CA
6. Houston, TX
7. Philadelphia, PA
8. Atlanta, GA
9. Miami/Fort Lauderdale, FL
10. Cleveland/Akron, OH
11. Tampa/Saint Petersburg, FL
12. San Francisco, CA
13. Baton Rouge, LA
14. Saint Louis, MO
15. Pittsburgh, PA
16. Boston, MA
17. Dallas/Fort Worth, TX
18. Norfolk, VA
19. Baltimore/Annapolis, MD
20. Detroit/Warren, MI
21. Denver, CO
22. Oklahoma City, OK
23. Richmond, VA
24. Greensboro/Winston-Salem, NC
25. Sacramento, CA
26. Boise, ID
27. Seattle, WA
28. Pensacola, FL
29. Las Vegas, NV
30. Charleston, SC

31. San Diego, CA
32. Albany, NY
33. Trenton, NJ
34. Minneapolis/Saint Paul, MN
35. Omaha, NE
36. Buffalo, NY
37. Kansas City, MO
38. Cincinnati, OH
39. Birmingham, AL
40. Mission Viejo, CA
41. New Haven, CT
42. Phoenix, AZ
43. Jacksonville, FL
44. Charlotte, NC
45. Salt Lake City/Ogden, UT
46. San Antonio, TX
47. Memphis, TN
48. Orlando, FL
49. Jackson, MS
50. Milwaukee, WI

NOTES

I have included extensive notes here for several reasons. Some chapters of this book drew heavily on court records and government documents concerning highly controversial cases, and I wanted to make sure that the interested reader is able to consult the originals. When they are openly available on the Internet, I have tried to supply those links. Others can be obtained through the subscription service Public Access to Court Electronic Records (PACER). There is also, of course, a great body of literature about the NYPD, its history, and the fight against terrorists from the 19th century to the present day. I wanted to be sure to credit those books I found most useful, as well as the fine reporting of my colleagues at *Newsweek,* the reporters at the major New York City dailies, and other journalists. But most of this book is based on interviews. Where they are on the record, I believe that is obvious in the text. When they were confidential, it would be superfluous to reiterate that fact in notes, so no such references to interviews are given.

THE COP

1 Jimmy Breslin, "It Happens Here, Too," *Newsday,* May 6, 2004, p. A06.

2 William Bratton with Peter Knobler, *Turnaround: How America's Top Cop Reversed the Crime Epidemic* (New York: Random House, 1998), p. x.

3 Simon Reeve, *The New Jackals: Ramzi Yousef, Osama bin Laden and the Future of Terrorism* (London: André Deutsch, 1999), pp. 108–111. Much of the book's reporting on Bin Laden has, of course, been superseded by events and the avalanche of intelligence in the nine years since it was published. But it offers a wonderfully detailed depiction of Yousef and his extraordinary activities based mainly on interviews with investigators and court documents. Reeve notes that the FBI agent adamantly stands by this story, while Yousef adamantly denied it.

THE SPY

1 Anthony Cave Brown, *The Last Hero: Wild Bill Donovan* (New York: Vintage Books, 1984) p. 324.

2 Arthur M. Schlesinger Jr., *Journals: 1952–2000* (New York: Penguin, 2007), p. 584.

3 There are many confusing transliterations of the Libyan leader's name because of the different ways some of the letters are pronounced in regional variations of Arabic. In 2007, I asked his British-educated son Seif al-Islam which spelling he preferred. He said Qadhafi, so it seems reasonable to stick with that.

4 Ted Gup, *The Book of Honor: The Secret Lives and Deaths of CIA Operatives* (New York: Anchor Books, 2001), p. 2.

5 Robert Baer, *See No Evil: The True Story of a Ground Soldier in the CIA's War on Terrorism* (New York: Three Rivers Press, 2002), p. 230.

6 Dan Stober and Ian Hoffman, *A Convenient Spy: Wen Ho Lee and the Politics of Nuclear Espionage* (New York: Simon & Schuster, 2002), p. 171.

7 Baer, pp. 230–231.

8 Louis J. Freeh, *My FBI: Bringing Down the Mafia, Investigating Bill Clinton, and Fighting the War on Terror* (New York: St. Martin's Press, 2005), p. 185.

9 Baer, p. 231.

10 Stan Crock, "Nora Slatkin's Impossible Mission," *BusinessWeek,* February 26, 1996.

11 Baer, p. 241.

THE DARK SIDE

1   Thomas H. Kean, Lee H. Hamilton, et al., *The 9/11 Commission Report: Fully Updated with Controversial Third Monograph and Never-Before-Published Progress Reports from the 9/11 Commission* (New York: Barnes & Noble, 2006), pp. 147–150.

2   Dan Stober and Ian Hoffman, *A Convenient Spy: Wen Ho Lee and the Politics of Nuclear Espionage* (New York: Simon & Schuster, 2002), p. 171.

3   "The Warrior Spies," Editorial, *The New York Times*, May 4, 1997.

4   Ronald Kessler, *The CIA at War: Inside the Secret Campaign Against Terror* (New York: St. Martin's Press, 2003), p. 204: "The New York station was at 7 World Trade Center, a forty-seven-story building in the shadow of the Twin Towers. Marked with a U.S. Army Logistics sign, the office consisted of forty employees, of whom half were case officers. Another contingent of roughly half that number was based at the United Nations."

THE CITY

1   Often, the "other stuff" was escorting VIPs around town.

2   http://www.fbi.gov/page2/dec04/jttf120114.htm.

3   James Lardner and Thomas Reppetto, *NYPD: A City and Its Police* (New York: Henry Holt, 2000), pp. 142–143.

4   Jules Witcover, *Sabotage at Black Tom: Imperial Germany's Secret War in America, 1914-1917* (Chapel Hill, NC: Algonquin Books, 1989), pp. 98–99; Lardner and Reppetto, pp. 179-180.

5   Witcover, p. 11.

6   Ibid., p. 12.

7   Ibid., p. 13.

8   John L. Heaton, *Cobb of the World* (New York: Dutton, 1924), p. 270.

9   Lardner and Reppetto, p. 131.

10 Jacob A. Riis, *How the Other Half Lives: Studies Among the Tenements of New York* (New York: Bartleby.com, 2000), http://www.bartleby.com/208/3.html.

11 Karen J. Greenberg, editor, *The Torture Debate in America* (New York: Cambridge University Press, 2006), p. 397. A massive companion volume produced by Greenberg's Center on Law and Security is Karen J. Greenberg and Joshua L. Dratel, editors, *The Torture Papers: The Road to Abu Ghraib* (New York: Cambridge University Press, 2005). Although this is a

collection of declassified U.S. government memoranda and court papers, the U.S. government apparently thinks it's dangerously incendiary when read by detainees at Guantánamo. In an August 25, 2006, affidavit from U.S. Navy Commander Patrick M. McCarthy, who was then serving as the staff judge advocate on the base, McCarthy addresses the problem of "legal" and "illegal" mail for the prisoners: "On or about January 24, 2006, a detainee was observed by guards and heard to be reading from 'The Torture Papers: The Road to Abu Ghraib,' which was labeled 'legal' by hand on the page edges. The book had not been submitted for a security review as non-legal mail. The book contained a number of documents related to investigations into the military operations of the United States in Iraq, to include information related to the investigations at Abu Ghraib. JTF-GTMO confiscated the book, as it was a serious threat to the security of the camp. Such materials could incite detainees to violence, leading to a destabilization of the camp." Submitted in the case of Haji Bismullah, et al, *Petitioners v. Donald Rumsfeld, Secretary of Defense, Respondent, No. 06–1197,* U.S. Court of Appeals for the District of Columbia Circuit.

12   "Red Plot Seen in Blast," *The New York Times,* September 17, 1920; "Thinks Bomb Held 100 Pounds of TNT," *The New York Times,* September 21, 1920; "Bayonne Prisoner Identified by 5 as Bomb Wagon Driver," *The New York Times,* May 20, 1921; "Arrest Russian Red as Wall St. Bomber," *The New York Times,* May 13, 1923; Daniel Gross, "Previous Terror on Wall Street—A Look at a 1920 Bombing," TheStreet.com, September 20, 2001. (Written in the immediate aftermath of the September 11, 2001 attacks, this is an especially vivid retelling of the 1920 story.)

13   Jane Pirone, publisher, et al., *Not for Tourists Guide to New York City: 2008* (2008: Not for Tourists), p. 38. (The location on the map is labeled "Site of Weathermen Explosion.")

14   Mel Gussow, "The House on West 11th Street," *The New York Times,* March 5, 2000.

15   James Merrill, "18 West 11th Street," June 29, 1972, *The New York Review of Books,* Volume 18, Number 12. One of the three members of Weatherman killed in the house was Diana Oughton, the girlfriend of William Ayers, a founder of the organization whose subsequent acquaintance with Barack Obama in Chicago in the 1990s became an issue in the 2008 U.S. presidential election campaign. See, among other articles, Christopher Dickey, "Stormy Weatherman," *Newsweek* online, October 16, 2003, http://www.newsweek.com/id/164223. Because the FBI had run a covert campaign known as COINTELPRO to infiltrate, divide, and

discredit the Weatherman organization and similar groups, federal prosecutors found it impossible to gain convictions in the courts when Ayers and others decided to turn themselves in. But the program was largely successful in destroying the organization.

16 http://www.latinamericanstudies.org/puertorico/FALN-1.pdf.

17 Rocco Parascandola, "A grim anniversary," *Newsday*, January 1, 2008, p. A7.

THE BATTLEGROUND

1 Samuel M. Katz, *Jihad in Brooklyn: The NYPD Raid That Stopped America's First Suicide Bombers* (New York: New American Library, 2005), p. 120.

2 Christopher Dickey, "Scolding the Dog, Beating the Chicken," *Newsweek* (U.S. edition), January 20, 2003, http://www.newsweek.com/id/62843.

3 Christopher Dickey, *Expats: Travels in Arabia from Tripoli to Tehran* (New York: Atlantic Monthly Press, 1990), pp. 3–17. I was in Tripoli during the air strikes. Forty-one Libyans were killed , including a child Qadhafi claimed was his fifteen-month-old adopted daughter.

4 Ronald Reagan, "Address to the Nation on the United States Air Strike Against Libya," April 14, 1986, Ronald Reagan Presidential Library, http://www.reagan.utexas.edu/archives/speeches/1986/41486g.htm.

5 L. Paul Bremer, "Countering Terrorism in the 1980s and 1990s," *U.S. Department of State Bulletin,* February 1989, http://findarticles.com/p/articles/mi_m1079/is_n2143_v89/ai_7465113.

6 The most notorious attack by the Japanese Red Army was against Israel's Lod airport in 1972, when twenty-six people were killed.

7 Robert Hanley, "Suspected Terrorist Convicted in Bomb Case," *The New York Times,* November 30, 1988.

8 John J. Goldman, "Suspected Terrorist Arrested in N.J.," *Los Angeles Times,* April 16, 1988, p. A2.

9 L. Paul Bremer, http://findarticles.com/p/articles/mi_m1079/is_n2143_v89/ai_7465113.

10 Barbara Victor, Army of Roses: *Inside the World of Palestinian Women Suicide Bombers* (Emmaus, Pa.: Rodale, 2003), p. 21 (foreword by Christopher Dickey).

11 "World Jewish Population." Data is from Judaism Online. According to this report, the only city in the world with a larger Jewish population than New York in 2001 was metropolitan Tel Aviv. The breakdown was

as follows: "Metropolitan Tel Aviv, with 2.5 million Jews, is the world's largest Jewish city. It is followed by New York, with 1.9 million, Haifa 655,000, Los Angeles 621,000, Jerusalem 570,000, and southeast Florida 514,000." The statistics are attributed to Hebrew University demographer Sergio Della Pergola and *The American Jewish Year Book,* http://www.simpletoremember.com/vitals/world-jewish-population.htm#_ftn1. However, other reports suggest that Tel Aviv's Jewish population did not exceed New York's until 2005. Questions of "who is a Jew?" and "what is a metropolitan area?" affect such debates. But there is no question that New York's Jewish population is much larger than Jerusalem's.

12 See http://www.adl.org/extremism/jdl_chron.asp.

13 *Kahane Chai, et al., Petitioners v. Department of State and Condoleezza Rice, Secretary of State, Respondents, No. 03–1392,* United States Court of Appeals for the District of Columbia Circuit, October 17, 2006.

14 See http://www.adl.org/extremism/jdl_chron.asp.

15 Bruce Hoffman, *Inside Terrorism,* revised and expanded edition (New York: Columbia University Press, 2005), p. 98 and p. 317, n. 65. Kahane was speaking at the University of California, Northridge, in March 1988. Hoffman attended the talk.

16 John T. McQuiston, "Kahane Is Killed After Giving Talk in New York," *The New York Times,* November 6, 1990.

17 Robert D. McFadden, "For Jurors, Evidence in Kahane Case Was Riddled with Gaps," *The New York Times,* December 23, 1991.

18 Michael Daly, "Terror Clues in '90 Killing," New York *Daily News,* May 29, 2002, p. 5. Norris went on to gain fame and infamy as the police commissioner of Baltimore, the head of the Maryland State Police, and as a police detective named Ed Norris appearing occasionally on the hit HBO series *The Wire.*

19 Chitra Ragavan, "Tracing Terror's Roots: How the First World Trade Center Plot Sowed the Seed for 9/11," *U.S. News & World Report,* February 16, 2003, http://www.usnews.com/usnews/news/articles/030224/24wtc.htm.

20 Hoffman, p. 100.

21 Ronald Sullivan, "F.B.I. Rebuff for Witness in Shooting," *The New York Times,* November 3, 1994. Also see Francis X. Clines, "Brooklyn Bridge Shooting; Complex Picture Is Emerging of Gunman in Van Shootings," *The New York Times,* March 4, 1994, and Francis X. Clines and Joe Sexton, " 'What Are You, Rashid?' " *The New York Times,* March 14, 1994.

22 Hoffman, p. 150.

23 Joseph P. Fried, "Agent Testifies on Content of Pipe Bomb," *The New York Times*, July 17, 1998.

24 Katz, p. 129.

25 Christopher Davis, "Fear on Fourth Avenue," *Reader's Digest*, October 2000, p. 117, cited in Katz, p. 129.

26 Katz, p. 135.

27 Katz, pp. 211–212.

28 Helen Peterson, "Bomb Diagram Found in Trash," *New York Daily News*, July 16, 1998, p. 38.

29 Ron Suskind, *The One Percent Doctrine: Deep Inside America's Pursuit of Its Enemies Since 9/11* (New York: Simon & Schuster, 2006), p. 89. Suskind reports Abu Zubaydah's safe house was stormed at 3:00 a.m. on March 28, 2002, which would have been less than five hours after the Netanya bombing in Israel.

30 "Substitution for the Testimony of Khalid Sheikh Mohammed," Defendant's Exhibit 941, *U.S. v. Moussaoui Cr. No. 01-455-A*, pp. 76–89, http://www .vaed.uscourts.gov/notablecases/moussaoui/exhibits/defense/941.pdf.

THE BLACK SITES

1 The FBI eventually concluded that the first scientist whom it suspected at Fort Detrick's Army Medical Research Institute of Infectious Diseases was in fact innocent, and it focused its attention on another one, Bruce E. Ivins. But that lead did not become widely known until July 2008, when Ivins committed suicide. Subsequently, the FBI took pains to present what it considered scientific proof of Ivins's culpability. See Eric Lichtblau and Nicholas Wade, "F.B.I. Presents Anthrax Details But Says It Can't Erase Doubts," *The New York Times*, August 19, 2008, p. A1.

2 Thomas H. Kean, Lee H. Hamilton, et al., *The 9/11 Commission Report: Fully Updated with Controversial Third Monograph and Never-Before-Published Progress Reports from the 9/11 Commissioners* (New York: Barnes & Noble, 2006). The original report was published in 2004. See especially "Late Leads—Mihdhar, Moussaoui, and KSM," pp. 266–277; also, "OIG Report on CIA Accountability with Respect to the 9/11 Attacks—Executive Summary," June 2005 (approved for release August 2007).

The CIA had picked up the trail of two future 9/11 hijackers, Khalid al-Mihdhar and Nawaf al-Hazmi, at an Al Qaeda "summit" in Malaysia in early January 2000, then lost track of them. In fact, they both flew to California and took up residence there, but were not put on any watch list to which U.S. immigration officials or the FBI had access until August 2001, and by then they had dropped out of sight once more. The report from the CIA's Office of the Inspector General is especially disturbing for anyone concerned with information sharing, as it shows the failure not only of formal but of informal networking possibilities: "In the period January through March 2000, some 50 to 60 individuals read one or more of six Agency cables containing travel information related to these terrorists. These cables originated in four field locations and Headquarters. They were read by overseas officers and Headquarters personnel, operations officers and analysts, managers and junior employees, and CIA staff personnel as well as officers on rotation from NSA and FBI. Over an 18-month period, some of these officers had opportunities to review the information on multiple occasions, when they might have recognized its significance and shared it appropriately with other components and agencies. Ultimately the two terrorists were watchlisted in late August 2001 as a result of questions raised in May 2001 by a CIA officer on assignment at the FBI." https://www.cia.gov/library/reports/Executive%20Summary_OIG%20Report.pdf

3   "Richardson Names Director for DOE's Office of Intelligence," Department of Energy—News Release, October 5, 1998, http://www.fas.org/irp/news/1998/10/pr98137.htm.

4   When U.S. Ambassador to the United Nations Bill Richardson became secretary of energy in 1998, he essentially took Sanchez with him. Eventually, Wen Ho Lee sued the United States government in 1999, winning a $1.6 million settlement from it and causing five news organizations to decide to pay up in order to avoid having their reporters be compelled to divulge the name or names of the sources who had named Lee as the likely spy. See Paul Farhi, "U.S. Media Settle with Wen Ho Lee," *Washington Post,* June 3, 2006, p. A01, http://www.washingtonpost.com/wp-dyn/content/article/2006/06/02/AR2006060201060.html.

5   Brian Ross and Richard Esposito, "CIA's Harsh Interrogation Techniques Described," ABC News, November 18, 2005, http://abcnews.go.com/WNT/Investigation/story?id=1322866.

6   Brian Ross, "CIA–Abu Zubaydah: Interview with John Kiriakou," ABC News. Full transcript; an edited version is available at http://abcnews.go.com/Blotter/story?id=3978231. This is just one of many articles published on this subject, but has the advantage of sourcing a former CIA operative directly.

On February 5, 2008, CIA Director Michael Hayden told the Senate Select Committee on Intelligence in a public hearing that three and only three detainees had been waterboarded by the CIA in 2002 and 2003: Abu Zubaydah, Khalid Sheikh Mohammed, and Abd al-Rahim al-Nashiri, whose specialty was sea-borne operations.

7 Christopher Dickey, "The Constitution in Peril," *Newsweek*, October 8, 2007, http://www.newsweek.com/id/41874. This long essay looks at several books that address the secretive process of executive lawmaking in the Bush administration, most notably Charlie Savage's *Takeover: The Return of the Imperial Presidency and the Subversion of American Democracy*, and Jack Goldsmith's *The Terror Presidency: Law and Judgment Inside the Bush Administration*. Goldsmith, in a brief tenure as Assistant Attorney General Jay S. Bybee's successor, reversed the August 1, 2002, "Torture Memo" (see below), but for reasons that were essentially legalistic and technical rather than moral or, for that matter, practical.

8 "Memorandum for Alberto R. Gonzales, Counsel to the President, Re: Standards of Conduct for Interrogation under 18 U.S.C. 2340-2340A," U.S. Department of Justice, Office of Legal Counsel, p. 46. Often called "the Bybee Memo," after Jay S. Bybee, who was then the assistant attorney general in charge of the OLC, it was in fact drafted by John Yoo:

Conclusion

For the foregoing reasons, we conclude that torture as defined in and proscribed by Sections 2340-2340A, covers only extreme acts. Severe pain is generally of the kind difficult for the victim to endure. Where the pain is physical, it must be of an intensity akin to that which accompanies serious physical injury such as death or organ failure. Severe mental pain requires suffering not just at the moment of infliction but it also requires lasting psychological harm, such as seen in mental disorders like posttraumatic stress disorder. Additionally, such severe mental pain can arise only from the predicate acts listed in Section 2340. Because the acts inflicting torture are extreme, there is significant range of acts that though they might constitute cruel, inhuman, or degrading treatment or punishment fail to rise to the level of torture.

Further, we conclude that under the circumstances of the current war against al Qaeda and its allies, application of Section 2340A to interrogations undertaken pursuant to the President's Commander-in-Chief powers may be unconstitutional. Finally, even if an interrogation method might violate Section 2340A, necessity or self-defense could provide justifications that would eliminate any criminal liability.

Please let us know if we can be of further assistance.

Jay S. Bybee
Assistant Attorney General

See http://www.humanrightsfirst.org/us_law/etn/gonzales/memos_dir/memo_20020801_JD_%20Gonz_.pdf#search=%22bybee%20memo%20pdf%22.

9   Brian Ross and Richard Esposito, "Exclusive: Sources Tell ABC News Top Al Qaeda Figures Held in Secret CIA Prisons," December 5, 2005, http://abcnews.go.com/WNT/Investigation/story?id=1375123.

10   Brian Ross, "CIA–Abu Zubaydah: Interview."

11   Algerian-Canadian businessman Fateh Kamel, who was convicted of facilitating various aspects of an Al Qaeda support network in 2001, served four years in a French prison and then returned to Canada. His case bore critical links to several that had come before and many, including that of Ahmed Ressam, that came after. I talked to him briefly while he was waiting in the dock. Kamel was very polished. Slight and handsome, he bore a surprising resemblance to Tom Cruise. For an analysis of his role and the Canadian connection he represented, see Hayder Mili, "Securing the Northern Front: Canada and the War on Terror" in *Terrorism Monitor*, newsletter from the Jamestown Foundation, July 15, 2005, pp. 4–6, http://www.jamestown.org/terrorism/news/uploads/ter_003_014.pdf.

12   Christopher Dickey, "Training for Terror," *Newsweek*, September 24, 2001 (appeared on the stands September 17, 2001).

13   This sounds more eccentric in Western culture than it does to Arabs, especially those who romanticize the greatness of Islamic culture in the eighth and ninth centuries. "Islamic civilization was no mere mechanical juxtaposition of previous cultures, but rather a new creation in which all these elements were fused into a new and original civilization by the transposition into Arabic and Islamic forms, recognizable and characteristic in every phase of its achievement," the influential American scholar Bernard Lewis wrote in 1950. "The highest achievement of the Arabs in their own reckoning and the first in order of time was poetry, with the allied art of rhetoric." See Bernard Lewis, *The Arabs in History* (New York: Oxford University Press, 2002), p. 146.

14   Suskind's account of the capture is especially vivid; see Ron Suskind, *The One Percent Doctrine: Deep Inside America's Pursuit of Its Enemies Since 9/11* (New York: Simon & Schuster, 2006), pp. 87–89.

15   "Verbatim Transcript of Combatant Status Review Tribunal Hearing for ISN 10016," March 27, 2007, pp. 25–26, http://www.defenselink.mil/news/transcript_ISN10016.pdf.

16   The part of Abu Zubaydah's statement in which he describes his torture has been redacted out of the transcript.

17 The High Value Detainee Biographies, issued in 2006 by then-director of National Intelligence John D. Negroponte, can be found at http://www .fas.org/irp/news/2006/09/detaineebios.pdf. The Combatant Status Review hearing is also illuminating on this subject.

Anyone who has studied the history of Communist and other revolutionary movements will be familiar with their kaleidoscopic schisms. So, too, with Islamic revolutionaries, as Abu Zubaydah's Guantánamo testimony makes clear. One of the great divisions between the Palestinians who fought in Afghanistan and other Arabs close to Bin Laden was their desire to focus attacks on Israel. Bin Laden paid lip service to the fight against Israel, but focused all his resources elsewhere. His former mentor, the Palestinian Abdullah Azzam, meanwhile, was blown up by unknown assassins in 1989 while trying to enlist Arab Afghan veterans in a new anti-Israel jihad, according to his son, Huthaifa Azzam. One of the clearest passages in Abu Zubaydah's Guantánamo statement is on page 22, about Israel: "I am not here to lie to you, or cheat you, or to lie to myself by saying that I am not an enemy of your injustice. I have been an enemy of yours since I was a child because of your unjust acts against my people, the Palestinians, through your help and partnership with Israel in occupying our land and by killing our men and raping our women and kicking out our people and turning them into refugees for more than sixty years. Until now, half of my people are refugees in refugee camps."

18 Brian Ross, "CIA–Abu Zubaydah: Interview."

19 Suskind, p. 100.

20 Murray Weiss, Kate Sheehy, Kenneth Lovett, "Lady Liberty in the Cross Hairs—B'klyn Bridge Also a Target: Terror Stoolie," *New York Post,* May 22, 2002, p. 5.

21 Greg Smith, Michele McPhee, Richard Sisk, "Bin Laden Henchman Pulled the Strings for Global Terror," *New York Daily News,* May 27, 2002.

22 Ibid.

23 Mark Hosenball and Michael Isikoff, et al., "Are the Feds at Sea?" *Newsweek,* June 3, 2002 (published May 27, 2002), p. 20.

24 Suskind, p. 122.

25 Thomas H. Kean, Lee H. Hamilton, et al., *The 9/11 Commission Report: Fully Updated with Controversial Third Monograph and Never-Before-Published Progress Reports from the 9/11 Commissioners* (New York: Barnes & Noble, 2006), p. 272. The commission concluded that this report alone, if it had been addressed, would not have prevented the 9/11 attacks. But it could have led to other information that might have.

26 See http://news.bbc.co.uk/2/low/americas/1999514.stm.

27 Weiss, et al., *New York Post*, May 22, 2002.

THE SECOND WAVE

1 In those days before suicide bombings became commonplace, Yousef and KSM developed an incredibly intricate choreography of flight connections and transfers that would have allowed them and their people to place the explosives and get off the planes before they blew. Theoretically, at least.

2 Simon Reeve, *The New Jackals: Ramzi Yousef, Osama bin Laden, and the Future of Terrorism* (London: André Deutsch, 1999), pp. 91 and 100. In Reeve's book, he says the informant, whom he names as Ishtiaque Parker, had learned details of the reward from an article that appeared in *Newsweek* in January 1995 (Reeve, pp. 98 and 101). More likely Parker, or Yousef, had been carrying that around with him for a while. I had written a long piece about Yousef, "America's Most Wanted: How the World Trade Center Fugitives Got Away," in the July 4, 1994, issue of *Newsweek*. Federal investigators told one of *Newsweek*'s Washington reporters after the arrest that a copy of that article was with the supremely egotistical Yousef when he was caught.

3 Thomas H. Kean, Lee H. Hamilton, et al., *The 9/11 Commission Report: Fully Updated with Controversial Third Monograph and Never-Before-Published Progress Reports from the 9/11 Commissioners* (New York: Barnes & Noble, 2006), p. 147. The commission says KSM originally was persuaded to move to Qatar in 1992 by a former minister of Islamic affairs, Sheikh Abdallah bin Khalid bin Hamad al Thani.

4 *The 9/11 Commission Report,* p. 146.

5 Rohan Gunaratna, "Khalid Sheikh Mohammed: A look into the amazingly worldly life of a fanatic," *Playboy,* June 1, 2005, p. 79. Gunaratna is also the author of *Inside Al-Qaeda: Global Network of Terror* (London: Hurst & Co., 2002), which he wrote while at the Centre for the Study of Terrorism and Political Violence at St. Andrews University, Scotland.

6 *The 9/11 Commission Report,* p. 147.

7 "Substitution for the Testimony of Khalid Sheikh Mohammed," Defendant's Exhibit 941, *U.S. v. Cr. No. 01-455-A Moussaoui,* pp. 37–39, http://www.vaed.uscourts.gov/notablecases/moussaoui/exhibits/defense/941.pdf.

8 Ibid., p. 41.

9 Al-Tunisi, real name Abderraouf Ben Habib Jdey, left Canada shortly thereafter and remains a fugitive. The United States government has put a $5 million price on his head; http://www.rewardsforjustice.net/index.cfm ?page=abderraouf&language=english.

10 "Substitution for the Testimony of Khalid Sheikh Mohammed," Moussaoui trial, p. 42.

11 "Verbatim Transcript of Combatant Status Review Tribunal Hearing for ISN 10024," p. 18, item 7, March 10, 2007.

12 Vikram Dodd, "Former Grammar School Boy [Saajid Badat] Gets 13 Years for Shoe Bomb Plot," *The Guardian,* April 23, 2005, http://www .guardian.co.uk/uk_news/story/0,1468522,00.html.

13 Andrew Welsh-Huggins, " 'A secret double-life' alleged in case of Ohioan who admitted aiding terrorists," The Associated Press, September 23, 2003.

14 *United States of America v. Iyman Faris a/k/a Mohammad Rauf,* U.S. District Court for the Eastern District of Virginia, "Statement of Facts."

15 Katherine Shrader, "An Immigrant's Journey from Md. To Gitmo," The Associated Press, March 22, 2007.

16 "Verbatim Transcript of Combatant Status Review Tribunal Hearing for ISN 10020," April 15, 2007, p. 4. This account is largely based on the testimony of Faris in 2003 when he was cooperating with federal authorities. After Faris was sentenced to twenty years in prison anyway, he recanted, and in written response to questions about those meetings at the Khan house in Baltimore called the account of Majid Khan saying he wanted to martyr himself in a suicide attack against Musharraf "an absolute lie."

17 The High Value Detainee Biographies: Ali 'Abd al-'Aziz 'Ali, alias 'Ammar al-Baluchi.' See http://www.fas.org/irp/news/2006/09/detainee/os.pdf.

18 According to the High Value Detainee Biographies, ibid., Zubair and another operative known as Lillie worked closely with the infamous Hambali, a longtime KSM associate who was the key intermediary between Al Qaeda and the Southeast Asian organization known as Jamaa Islamiya. Zubair and Lillie were supposed to have been involved in a second-wave attack on Los Angeles, if that had materialized.

19 The High Value Detainee Biography: Majid Khan. See http://www.fas.org/ irp/news/2006/09/detaineebios.pdf.

20 *Saifullah Paracha v. George W. Bush, et al,* U.S. District Court for the District of Columbia, Civic Action No. 04-CV-2022 (PLF), Enclosure 1 to Combatant Status Review Tribunal Decision Report.

21 Daniel Klaidman, Evan Thomas, et al., "Al Qaeda's 'Pre-Election' Plot," *Newsweek,* August 16, 2004, p. 22.

22 Dominic Kennedy, "Slip of Tongue in Interview Betrays Secret that Bin Laden is Dead," *The Times* (London), September 9, 2002, p. 11.

23 According to Ron Suskind's account of the Fouda interview in his 2006 book, *The One Percent Doctrine,* the Al Jazeera reporter told his betters in Qatar that he'd seen KSM and Bin al-Shibh in Karachi, and even though Fouda had been blindfolded he was able to guess more or less where their conversation took place. That information was passed on directly to George Tenet, the director of Central Intelligence, without the reporter knowing. (The Qatari royals, having given both Ramzi Yousef and KSM refuge in the years before the 9/11 attacks, might well have been anxious in the aftermath to show just how helpful they could be to the enraged Americans.)

24 "Verbatim Transcript of Combatant Status Review Tribunal Hearing for ISN 10020," April 15, 2007, p. 13.

25 Ron Suskind, *The One Percent Doctrine: Deep Inside America's Pursuit of Its Enemies Since 9/11* (New York: Simon & Schuster, 2006), pp. 218–220.

26 Jane Mayer, "The Black Sites," *The New Yorker,* August 13, 2007.

27 CQ Transcriptions, "Sen. John D. Rockefeller IV Holds a Hearing On the Annual Threat Assessment," February 5, 2008.

28 Jack Maple and Chris Mitchell, *The Crime Fighter: How You Can Make Your Community Crime Free* (New York: Broadway, 2000), p. 76.

29 Rockefeller hearing.

30 Maple, p. 72.

31 Maple, p. 74.

32 See http://freedetainees.org/aafia-siddiqui-children and http://www.fbi .gov/terrorinfo/siddiqui.htm. Siddiqui was detained in Ghazni, Afghanistan, on July 17, 2008, allegedly loitering outside the local governor's compound. When two FBI agents, two American soldiers, and an interpreter went to question her, they were unaware that she was in the same room with them behind a curtain. One of the soldiers put down his M-4 rifle. She picked it up and trained it on her interrogators, firing at least two shots without hitting anyone. She was subdued and reportedly "lost consciousness." She was brought to the United States and arraigned in New York City on August 5, 2008. See Eric Schmitt, "Pakistani Suspected of Qaeda Ties Is Held," *The New York Times,* August 5, 2008, p. A6.

33 Briefing at National Press Club, Washington, D.C., July 17, 2007.

SAFE STREETS

1 Joyce Purnick, "Recalling the 70's, Warily," *The New York Times*, November 11, 2001.

2 Jack Maple and Chris Mitchell, *The Crime Fighter: How You Can Make Your Community Crime Free* (New York: Broadway, 2000), p. 19.

3 Ibid., pp. 154–155.

4 Ibid., p. 30.

5 Ibid., p. 32.

6 Ibid., p. 103.

7 Ibid., p. 23.

8 Ibid., p. 101.

9 Ibid., p. 93.

10 Bratton, p. 294.

11 John Marzulli, Alice McQuillan, and Mike McAlary, "No. 2 Cop Blasts Choice, 'Won't Prop Up Howard Safir,' " *The Daily News*, March 29, 1996, p. 6.

12 Howard Safir with Ellis Whitman, *Security: Policing Your Homeland, Your State, Your City* (New York: Thomas Dunne Books, 2003), pp. 210–213.

13 Maple, p. 34.

14 Bratton, p. 238.

15 The CompStat system is now so integral to law enforcement in the United States and so widely known, at least as a catchphrase, that when Giuliani tried to run for president in 2008, he worked it into his campaign. Doing all he could to capitalize on the reputation for effective intelligence-led policing that Maple and Bratton had pioneered, Giuliani proposed "Borderstat" for organizing data to protect America's frontiers, and "Readystat" for information vital to preparedness in the face of disasters like Hurricane Katrina. And, yes, of course, "Terrorstat," an idea he actually attributed this time to William Bratton, now running the Los Angeles Police Department, and the venerable "broken windows" theorist William Kelling.

"Terrorists prepare for their activities with preattack surveillance and finance them with ordinary criminal actions," said Giuliani. He was right about that. They take pictures, and they sometimes rob gas stations or, more often, commit credit card fraud. But Giuliani did not explain how any variation of CompStat would spot individual terrorists, even cells of eight or ten, among millions of other petty criminals in the country—or for that matter among hundreds of millions of ordinary people who take snapshots of monuments, businesses, and other potential terrorist targets. In a national program, there simply are not enough terrorists to set off a blip on the statistical screen. But at a local level, if cops know their neighborhoods and have the training and background to understand the way "groups of guys" or "clusters" can organize around the notion of jihad, there's much to be learned.

16 See   http://home2.nyc.gov/html/nypd/html/crime_prevention/crime_statistics.shtml.

17 Jacob A. Riis, *How the Other Half Lives: Studies Among the Tenements of New York* (New York: Bartleby.com, 2000), www.bartleby.com/207/9.html.

SHOWTIME

1 People in Brooklyn's Seventy-seventh Precinct or Staten Island's 123rd (the "seven-seven" and the "one-two-three" in cop speak) may be surprised to learn there are only seventy-six precincts in the city. The others have been lost to reorganizations and consolidations over the years but were never renumbered. In practice, there certainly are days when not all seventy-six precincts contribute a car to the surge. I have seen half that number on some CRV exercises. But seventy-six remains the goal.

Another anomaly: There are five boroughs in New York, but for the police there are eight "patrol boroughs": Manhattan North, Manhattan South, Queens North, Queens South, Brooklyn North, Brooklyn South, the Bronx, and Staten Island.

2 Federal Bureau of Investigation, PENTTBOM, Major Case 182, AOT-IT, November 5, 2001, pp. 4–5.

3 Department of Defense, Office for the Administrative Review of the Detention of Enemy Combatats at U.S. Naval Base Guantánamo Bay, Cuba, "Summary of Evidence for Combatant Status Review Tribunal—Al Nashiri, Abd Al Rahim Hussein Mohammed," February 8, 2007.

4 That was Bilal's second try. A few months earlier, at the time of the millennium, his minions had taken a run at the USS *The Sullivans* in the same harbor, but they overloaded their boat and foundered.

While KSM and Mohammed Atta's hijackers plotted the September 11 attacks against the United States, Bilal worked on a grand plan of his own. He wanted to sink a U.S. warship in the Strait of Hormuz with everyone aboard, and his scenario was as elaborate and spectacular as something out of an old James Bond movie. Through a front company, Bilal bought a 400,000-ton freighter equipped with a heavy-duty crane. He also bought several small speedboats from a manufacturer in the United Arab Emirates. The plan was to carry the smaller craft on the mother ship, fill them with explosives, lower them into the water, and send them on their way toward the warship as, in effect, suicide torpedoes. If those failed—and they would have been vulnerable to defensive fire if the ship's crew was alert—the freighter itself was to be filled with explosives, making it the biggest conventional bomb ever built. It wouldn't have to ram the warship to sink it, just explode nearby. Most of the crew on the Al Qaeda freighter didn't even know what was going on. Some were from Pakistan, others from India. A few were Christians.

By one account, Nashiri had trouble getting the enormous quantity of explosives needed for the Hormuz plot. But the same Arab intelligence officer familiar with the case told me no, "It was all to do with the timing and the moving of the elements. The problem was security procedures." The more grandiose a plan, the more people who are involved, the greater the chance it will be compromised and some or all of the plotters caught. Even in 2001, Mullah Bilal knew he was being hunted by the CIA. Jordan's intelligence service had been tracking him since 1997. Rather than risk giving away the whole game—possibly the whole 9/11 plot—the operation was called off.

5 Jason Burke, Martin Bright, and Ed Vulliamy, "The Return of Al Qaeda: Special Report," *The Observer,* June 16, 2002, p. 14.

6 Al-Nashiri (Bilal) is one of the three people that CIA Director Michael Hayden acknowledges were submitted to this torture, along with Abu Zubaydah and KSM. Al-Nashiri later retracted his confession at his enemy combatant hearing in February 2007.

7 Christopher Dickey, "Al Qaeda at Sea," *Newsweek,* January 27, 2003, http://www.newsweek.com/id/62899.

8 Leonard Levitt, "Overeager Division," NYPD Confidential website, November 3, 2003, http://nypdconfidential.com/columns/2003/031103 .html.

9 The Associated Press, "Part II of Powell's Remarks at the U.N." February 5, 2003.

10 For an exhaustive account of the Bourgass case, see William Langewiesche, "A Face in the Crowd," *Vanity Fair,* February 2008, p. 124.

RED CELLS

1 Michael A. Sheehan, *Crush the Cell: How to Defeat Terrorism Without Terrorizing Ourselves* (New York: Crown, 2008), p. 14.

2 The basic story has been recounted in many places and I reported it first-hand in 1993, but some of the details here and the name of Don Sadowy are from Robert S. Mueller, Remarks to Citizens Crime Commission, James Fox Memorial Lecture, New York, New York, April 26, 2006, http://www.fbi.gov/pressrel/speeches/mueller042606.htm.

3 Even though there had been an IRA warning call beforehand and police had tried to evacuate the shopping area in the center of the city, more than two hundred people were injured.

4 Sheehan, pp. 207–208. In his book *Crush the Cell*, the former deputy commissioner described Operation Kaboom a little differently and with perhaps a bit of police, if not poetic, license. He wrote that "the purchases were to be made by ethnic cops, not burly white guys (although a terrorist can certainly fit any physical profile). In fact, I wanted one of our Pakistani detectives to purchase the explosive materials. . . ." Chris is in fact a burly white guy. Sheehan also wrote that "in ten weeks, ten guys with about $10,000 were able to construct a ten-thousand-pound bomb." It was big, but not that big.

5 Jane Glenn Cannon, "Wednesday OU bombing accidental, experts say," *Daily Oklahoman*, distributed by Knight/Ridder Tribune News Service, March 1, 2006.

6 Nolan Clay, "OU bomber left a final message: 'None of you are worth living with,' " *The Oklahoman*, Saturday city edition, November 19, 2005, Section: News; pg. 1A.

GREEN CLOUDS

1 Christine Hauser and Sewell Chan, "Gas-Like Odor Permeates Parts of New York City," *The New York Times*, January 8, 2007; Tom Liddy, Dan Kadison, and Andy Geller, "N.J.'s P.U. Ripens Apple—Belching Bog Blamed for Citywide Gas Stink," *New York Post*, January 8, 2007.

2 Chlorine figures in my 2004 novel *The Sleeper* as a terrorist weapon of choice.

3 Borzou Daragahi, "Another chlorine gas bomb attack in Iraq; For the second day in a row, a crude chemical weapon is used to target civilians,

killing two; 40 die in other violence," *Los Angeles Times,* February 22, 2007, Part A; p. 8.

4   Police commissioner remarks and transcript of video, NYPD Shield Conference, February 13, 2008.

5   EDCH Political Transcripts, "George W. Bush Delivers Remarks on Iraq," October 7, 2002.

6   John McPhee, *The Curve of Binding Energy: A Journey into the Awesome and Alarming World of Theodore B. Taylor* (New York: Farrar, Straus & Giroux, 1994), p. 3.

7   See Bruce Hoffman, *Inside Terrorism,* revised and expanded edition (New York: Columbia University Press, 2005), pp. 119–127.

8   See http://www.debka.com/headline.php?hid=4482.

NARRATIVE: IRANIAN PROBES—2003

1   A good summary of the evidence in Spanish can be found in Carlos S. Fayt, *Criminalidad del Terrorismo Sagrado: El Atentado a la Embajada de Israel en Argentina* (LaPlata, Argentina: Editorial Universitaria de La Plata, 2001).

2   Louis J. Freeh, who was the FBI director at the time, was embittered by what he saw not only as intelligence failures before the attack, but the reluctance of the Clinton administration to pursue the killers—and the Iranian government—after it. See Louis J. Freeh and Howard Means, *My FBI: Bringing Down the Mafia, Investigating Bill Clinton, and Fighting the War on Terror* (New York: St. Martin's Press, 2005), pp. 10–11 specifically and 1–34 passim.

3   *United States of America v. Ahmed Al-Mughassil, et al.,* U.S. District Court Eastern District of Virginia (Alexandria) 1:01-cr-00228-CMH-1, filed June 21, 2001.

THE WAREHOUSE

1   Janice G. Raymond and Donna M. Hughes, "Sex Trafficking of Women in the United States: International and Domestic Trends," Coalition Against Trafficking Women, March 2001.

2   Thomas H. Kean, Lee H. Hamilton, et al., *The 9/11 Commission Report: Fully Updated with Controversial Third Monograph and Never-Before-*

Published Progress Reports from the 9/11 Commission (New York: Barnes & Noble, 2006), p. 92.

3 James A. Baker, Lee H. Hamilton, et al., *The Iraq Study Group Report: The Way Forward—A New Approach* (New York: Vintage Books, 2006), p. 92.

4 Louis J. Freeh and Howard Means, *My FBI: Bringing Down the Mafia, Investigating Bill Clinton, and Fighting the War on Terror* (New York: St. Martin's Press, 2005), p. 185.

THE FEDS

1 Dafna Linzer, "In New York, a Turf War in the Battle Against Terrorism," *Washington Post,* March 22, 2008, p. A01.

2 Ibid. Still, Kelly and Cohen kept pushing for one at headquarters. Finally, five years later, the FBI gave in. The *Washington Post* had gotten wind of the problem and called Mark Mershon, who was by then the special agent-in-charge of the FBI's New York office. The resistance had come from senior FBI officials, he said, who worried that the NYPD would "bypass the FBI and establish its own links with the intelligence community," but "clearly that has happened anyway, so I have called David Cohen and told him that we will be pleased to certify the SCIF."

3 Summarized Sworn Detainee Statement, included as document in filings for *Saifullah Paracha v. George W. Bush, et al.* Civil Action No. 04-CV-2022 (PLF), p. 20.

4 Ibid. Also see *United States of America v. Iyman Faris a/k/a Mohammad Rauf,* U.S. District Court for the Eastern District of Virginia, "Statement of Facts." The correlation between "Mir's" actions and those of C-1 are clear.

5 *Saifullah Paracha v. George W. Bush, et al.* documents, Civil Action No. 04-CV-2022 (PLF), documents, p. 9.

6 Ibid., p. 20.

7 The case would come back to haunt the CIA when the Egyptians briefly released Abu Omar the following year and he started telling his story. The CIA's tradecraft was so sloppy that Italian investigators were able to trace the identities of more than thirty operatives involved with the case, all of whom were indicted in absentia for kidnapping and related offenses.

8 Much has since been written about these cases, including the script for a remarkable documentary called *Taxi to the Dark Side* that came out in early 2008. See especially Tim Golden, "In U.S. Report, Brutal Details of

2 Afghan Inmates' Deaths," *The New York Times,* May 20, 2005, and the original reports published in Jameel Jaffer and Amrit Singh, *Administration of Torture: A Documentary Record from Washington to Abu Ghraib and Beyond* (New York: Columbia University Press, 2007), pp. A-185 to A-188.

9 "NYPD detectives interrogate people by just talking to them, that's what they do, and they do it very, very well," Sheehan said. The cops' history of violent incidents notwithstanding (Abner Louima among many), physical abuse was not part of the picture as Sheehan saw it, and television programs that dramatized punch-ups in the interrogation rooms missed their mark: "The stuff on TV is bullshit."

10 See Linzer, op cit.; also see Jack Maple quoted in chapter 8.

11 United States District Court for the District of Columbia, Bassem Youssef, Plaintiff, v. Civil Action No. 1:03CV01551(CKK) Federal Bureau of Investigation, et al., Defendants, Tuesday, November 30, 2004, Oral Deposition of: Pasquale J. D'Amuro.

12 Murray Weiss, "Fed Up," *The New York Post,* April 29, 2006.

NARRATIVE: THE MADRID BOMBINGS—2004

1 A very detailed narrative of the case can be found in the Madrid court document Sección 2a Salade lo Penal, Audiencia Nacional, Rollo 5/2005, JCI 6, Sumario 20/04, November 15, 2006.

2 Mitchell D. Silber and Arvin Bhatt, *Radicalization in the West: The Homegrown Threat,* August 2007, p. 46. See http://www.nyc.gov/html/nypd/pdf/dcpi/NYPD_Report-Radicalization_in_the_West.pdf.

NEIGHBORS

1 Jonathan Schuppe, "Two Intelligence Aces Scan the Shadows in Jersey for Terrorists," *Newark Star-Ledger,* March 28, 2003, p. 1.

2 Ibid.

3 George L. Kelling and William J. Bratton, "Policing Terrorism," *Civic Bulletin,* Manhattan Institute for Policy Research, No. 43, September 2006. http://www.manhattan-institute.org/html/cb_43.htm.

4 Ibid.

APATHY

1   See http://www.usatoday.com/news/washington/2003-07-02-bush-speech-text_x.htm.

2   Ron Suskind, *The One Percent Doctrine: Deep Inside America's Pursuit of Its Enemies Since 9/11,* (New York: Simon & Schuster, 2006), pp. 194–198.

3   RNC Documents Overview, New York City Police Department, 2007. (No longer available on NYPD website.)

4   Michael Isikoff, Mark Hosenball, et al., "Al Qaeda's 'Pre-election Plot,' *Newsweek,* August 16, 2004.

5   Ibid.

6   Todd Gitlin, "Having a Riot," *Newsweek,* July 23, 2001.

7   Christopher Dickey and Rod Nordland, "First Blood: Death and Violence in Genoa Mark a Permanent Split in the Ranks of the Anti-Globalization Movement. Radical Hooligans, Says One Moderate, 'Have Hijacked the Whole Thing,' " *Newsweek* international edition, July 30, 2001.

8   See http://news.bbc.co.uk/2/hi/europe/2636647.stm.

9   Key Findings, December 30, 2003, RNC documents, Bates Stamp No. 102598, http://www.nyclu.org/rncdocs.

10 See http://www.altlaw.org/v1/cases/548026.

11 Cohen affidavit from *The New York Times* website; see http://www.nytimes.com/2007/03/25/nyregion/25infiltrate.html?pagewanted=1&_r=1&sq=handschu&st=nyt&scp=4. Judge Haight subsequently went back on his decision, and then reversed himself yet again, leaving the police with the freedom to operate that they wanted.

12 Activists Network Expands Scope of Influence Outside the United States Encompassing International Issues, undated, RNC documents, Bates Stamp No. 102617-618, http://www.nyclu.org/rncdocs.

13 See http://www.nytimes.com/2006/05/19/nyregion/19herald.html?_r=1&oref=slogin&pagewanted=print. (Details from the testimony are from a *New York Times* article on May 19, 2006—"Detective Was 'Walking Camera' Among City Muslims, He Testifies," William K. Rashbaum—but primary information should come from transcript above.)

14 Interview with Siraj's attorney Martin Stolar, June 2007. At the time of the Crusades, the Ismailis were known as the cult of the assassins, but those days are long past. See Bernard Lewis, *The Assassins: A Radical Sect in Islam* (Oxford, UK: Oxford University Press, 1967).

15 William Rashbaum of *The New York Times* covered the Siraj case in great and perceptive detail. See in particular William Rashbaum, "Police Informer in Terror Trial Takes Stand," *The New York Times,* April 25, 2006. Also Robin Shulman, "The Informer: Behind the Scenes, or Setting the Scene?" *The Washington Post,* May 29, 2007. Craig Horowitz's account of the case for *New York* magazine, "Anatomy of a Foiled Plot," was anthologized subsequently as one of the best-written crime stories of the year. See Otto Penzler and Thomas H. Cook, editors, *The Best Crime Writing 2005,* with an introduction by James Ellroy (New York: Harper, 2005), pp. 177–189.

ANGER

1 Daniel Klaidman, Evan Thomas, et al., "Al Qaeda's 'Pre-Election' Plot," *Newsweek,* August 16, 2004.

2 Douglas Jehl and David Rohde, Threats and Responses: Intelligence; "Captured Qaeda Figure Led Way To Information Behind Warning," *The New York Times,* August 2, 2004.

3 http://www.senate.gov/~schumer/SchumerWebsite/pressroom/press_releases/2004/PR02808.alqaeda080904.html.

4 http://www.harpers.org/archive/2006/10/0081216.

5 RNC Documents, Bates Stamp No. 014002.

6 See http://www.democracynow.org/2004/9/2/making_protest_painful_detained_rnc_protesters.

7 The New York Civil Liberties Union has waged a relentless campaign in the courts on behalf of several of the detainees, with most of the legal maneuvering centered on efforts to force the release of documents that would reveal precisely who was spied on by the intelligence division and how. See especially: Christopher Dunn, Donna Liebermann, et al., *Rights and Wrongs at the RNC: A Special Report About Police and Protest at the Republican National Convention* (New York: New York Civil Liberties Union, 2005), available in portable document format at http://www.nyclu.org/node/1039, as well as press releases dealing with recent rulings in the case of *Schiller v. NYC:* http://www.nyclu.org/node/1137, http://www.nyclu.org/node/963, and http://www.nyclu.org/node/1929. A related group of cases are *Gutman v. NYC, Stauber v. NYC,* and *Conrad v. NYC,* which concern New York City police tactics breaking up a protest in February 2003. See http://www.nyclu.org/node/1094. In a separate case in August 2008 the city agreed to a $2 million settlement with

fifty-two Iraq War activists who claimed they were unjustly arrested while demonstrating in front of the offices of The Carlyle Group, affiliated with the Bush family, in April 2003. One was Sarah Kunstler, daughter of the famous defense attorney William Kunstler. See Larry Neumeister, "NYC to pay $2 million to arrested war protesters," The Associated Press, August 20, 2008.

8   Michael Slackman, et al, "The Republicans: The Convention in New York—The Demonstrations; Police Tactics Mute Protesters and Messages," The New York Times, September 2, 2004.

9   Michael Isikoff and Mark Hosenball, "Terror Watch: The Real Target?" Newsweek Web exclusive, November 17, 2004. See http://www.newsweek.com/id/55440/page/3.

NARRATIVE: THE LONDON BOMBINGS—2005

1   http://www.guardian.co.uk/world/2003/may/04/terrorism.religion.

2   Israeli Ministry of Foreign Affairs, "Details of April 30, 2003, Tel Aviv Suicide Bombing," June 3, 2003, http://www.mfa.gov.il/MFA/Government/Communiques/2003/Details+of+April+30-+2003+Tel+Aviv+suicide+bombing.

3   "DAC Peter Clarke's speech on counter terrorism." Metropolitan Police, April 24, 2007, http://cms.met.police.uk/news/major_operational_announcements/terrorism/dac_peter_clark_s_speech_on_counter_terrorism.

4   Jon Gilbert, "The supergrass I helped to create," TimesOnLine, May 3, 2007, http://www.timesonline.co.uk/tol/news/uk/crime/article1737411.ece; Diane Cardwell and William K. Rashbaum, "Plea Accord for American Linked to Plot in Britain," The New York Times, June 18, 2004.

5   Gilbert, ibid.

6   "Waiting for al-Qaeda's next bomb—MI5 and al-Qaeda," The Economist, May 5, 2007.

7   Bruce Hoffman, "Terrorism, Radicalization and Subversion: The 7/7/05 London Attacks, 2006 Airline Plots and Al Qaeda Resurgence," PowerPoint presentation at Georgetown University, October 2007.

8   "Report of the Official Account of the Bombings in London on 7th July 2005," HC 1087, May 11, 2006.

9   Brendan MacWade, Andrew Schonebaum, Joseph Gehring Jr., Partha Banerjee, and Norman Murphy, Plaintiffs v. Raymond Kelly, Commissioner of the New York City Police Department, and the City of New York,

05CV6291, United States District Court, Southern District of New York, August 4, 2005.

10 "NYPD clarifies bomb disclosures," BBC News, August 4, 2005, http://news.bbc.co.uk/2/hi/uk_news/4746835.stm.

11 Sam Knight, "July 7 bombs used hair dye, say NYPD," Times Online, August 4, 2005, http://www.timesonline.co.uk/tol/news/uk/article55 1443.ece.

12 Bruce Hoffman, "The Global Terrorist Threat: Is Al-Qaeda on the Run or on the March?" *Middle East Policy*, Summer 2007. Also see, BBC News Media Exchange, "Britain's First Suicide Bombers," broadcast on BBC2 on July 11, 2006.

BAD NUMBERS

1 See http://www.nycpolicefoundation.org/global.asp.

2 In May 2008, police recruits finally got a raise from $25,100 to $35,881, but Commissioner Kelly still was not satisfied. Three months later, Kelly told me the department he wanted to leave behind would have to continue to attract world-class people. But it had to do that at all levels, not just among the young brains in Cohen's shop, or the retired veterans of the CIA, FBI, and the National Security Agency who held senior positions at both the intel and counterterror divisions. "I look down the road," said Kelly, "and we need educated officers, we need trained officers," that is, the cops out on the beat. The raise for recruits in May was still four thousand dollars less than they were earning in 2005, Kelly said, and his force had five thousand fewer cops than it did at the beginning of the decade. "You've got to have the boots on the ground," said Kelly. And the brains. But to get those, you had to have money. At the end of August 2008, a tentative contract brought the pay range up to $41,975 for rookies and $76,488 for veterans. (See Kathleen Lucadamo, "It's NYPD Green as Cops Get Nice Raise," *Daily News*, August 22, 2008, p. 3.)

Kelly also was concerned, however, that funds for the department would be drying up as the global financial crisis cut into the city's tax revenues. Several weeks later, in late September 2008, Mayor Michael R. Bloomberg ordered city agencies to cut spending by $500 million over the remainder of the year, and by $1 billion in 2009. The cuts were across the board, including for the Police Department, which was to reduce expenditures by $95 million by the end of 2008. See Michael Barbaro and

Fernanda Santos, "Mayor Asks All Agencies For Cutback Over 2 Years," *The New York Times*, September 24, 2008.

3 Jack Maple and Chris Mitchell, *The Crime Fighter: How You Can Make Your Community Crime Free* (New York: Broadway, 2000), p. 235.

4 Murray Weiss, "Crooked-Cop Cases Surge," *New York Post*, October 22, 2007, https://www.nypost.com/seven/10222007/news/columnists/crooked_cop_cases_surge.htm.

5 Most of this account is from the statement read to the court by Judge Arthur Cooperman, explaining his determination that the three officers were not guilty. It was made available on the Web by National Public Radio: www.npr.org/documents/2008/apr/bell_verdict_statement.pdf; the account of Coicou's testimony is from Nicole Bode and Corkey Siemaszko, "Man who argued with Bell said no one threatened him with a gun," *New York Daily News*, March 20, 2008.

6 Oliver testimony as reported by Nicole Bode and Corky Siemasko, "Detective Michael Oliver said he feared for his life," *New York Daily News*, March 25, 2008.

7 Jim Dwyer, "Fatally Flawed Police Work, but Not Criminal," *The New York Times*, April 26, 2008.

LONERS AND COPYCATS

1 Jeffrey D. Simon, "The Alphabet Bomber (1974)," in *Toxic Terror: Assessing Terrorist Use of Chemical and Biological Weapons*, Jonathan B. Tucker, editor (Monterey, CA: Monterey Institute of International Studies, 1999), p. 71.

2 Kurbegovich included a copy of the order in one of his letters to me.

3 David Johnston and James Risen, "Threats and Responses: Domestic Security; Lone Terrorists May Strike In the U.S., Agencies Warn," *The New York Times*, February 23, 2003.

CLUSTERS

1 Mitchell D. Silber and Arvin Bhatt, *Radicalization in the West: The Homegrown Threat*, August 2007; see http://www.nyc.gov/html/nypd/pdf/dcpi/NYPD_Report-Radicalization_in_the_West.pdf.

2 The eleven case studies: Madrid's March 2004 attack; Amsterdam's Hofstad Group (linked to the murderer of filmmaker Theo Van Gogh); London's July 2005 attack; Australia's Operation Pendennis, which

thwarted attacks in November 2005; the Toronto 18 case, which stopped an attack in June 2006; Lackawanna, New York (training in Afghanistan before 9/11, but no plot); Portland, Oregon (organized to fight the Americans in Afghanistan post 9/11, but failed to get there); Northern Virginia (ex-U.S. military trained with paintballs and hooked up with a Kashmiri terrorist organization in Pakistan); the Herald Square duo; "the Al-Muhajiroun two" in New York City; and the 9/11 plotters themselves.

3   The Lackawanna Six had been largely disillusioned by their training in Afghanistan. Four of the six dropped out of the program. One went to live in Yemen. They were trying to lie low after 9/11, but one of them went to Bahrain in September 2002 to get married. His e-mails back to the U.S. discussing the event were intercepted and the talk about an "upcoming wedding" and the "big meal" were deemed to be terrorist code—giving the Feds reason to arrest the whole bunch. See Silber and Bhatt, pp. 62–63.

4   Silber and Bhatt, p. 85.

5   An audio recording of the interview with Falkenrath is available on the WNYC website at http://www.wnyc.org/shows/bl/episodes/2007/08/16/segments/83998.

6   Stephen Schwartz, "CAIR vs. the NYPD: The Wahhabi lobby attacks," *The Weekly Standard,* April 11, 2008.

7   *United States of America v. Dritan Duka,* Criminal Complaint Magistrate No. 07–M–2046 (JS), United States District Court, District of New Jersey.

8   *United States of America v. Youssef Samir Megahed,* Case No. 8:07-CR-342-T-23MAP, United States District Court, Middle District of Florida, Tampa Division, "Government's Response and Memorandum of Law in Opposition to Defendant's Motion to Sever," p. 2.

9   Ibid., p. 3.

10   *United States of America v. Russell Defreitas, Kareem Ibrahim, Abdul Kadr and Abdel Nuf,* United States District Court, Eastern District of New York, complaint, June 1, 2007.

11   Mark Mazzetti and David E. Sanger, "Al Qaeda Threatens; US Frets," *The New York Times,* July 22, 2007.

12   Panel I of the Hearing of the Senate Committee on Homeland Security and Governmental Affairs; Subect: The Role of Local Law Enforcement in Countering Violent Islamist Extremism; chaired by: Senator Joseph Lieberman (I-CT); Witnesses: Lawrence Sanchez, assistant commissioner, New York City Police Department and Mitchell Silber, senior intelligence

analyst, New York City Police Department. Federal News Service, October 30, 2007. This and all quotes from Sanchez that follow are from this testimony.

THE FRENCH CONNECTION

1   Mitchell D. Silber and Arvin Bhatt, *Radicalization in the West: The Homegrown Threat,* http://www.nyc.gov/html/nypd/pdf/dcpi/NYPD_Report=Radicalization_in_the_West.pdf, p. 13.
2   Alain Bauer and Xavier Raufer, *World Chaos: Early Detection and Proactive Security: Principles and Practices* (Paris: Département de recherche sur les Menaces Criminelles Contemporaines, Université Pantheon-Assasm, 2007).

RINGS OF STEEL

1   Jeremy Olshan and Kevin Fasick, "Trashy WTC Security," *New York Post,* April 18, 2008.
2   Michael A. Sheehan, *Crush the Cell: How to Defeat Terrorism Without Terrorizing Ourselves* (New York: Crown, 2008), p. 244.
3   Ibid., pp. 244–253.
4   Owen Bowcott, "CCTV boom has failed to slash crime, say police," *The Guardian,* May 6, 2008.
5   http://www.nyclu.org/node/1968.

URBAN LEGENDS

1   Kathleen O'Leary Morgan and Scott Morgan, editors, *City Crime Rankings: 14th Edition* (Washington, D.C.: CQ Press, 2008), p. 6. Also available at http://www.cqpress.com/pages/citycrime2007.
2   David Brooks, "The Real Rudy," *The New York Times,* November 23, 2007.
3   "General Social Surveys, 1972–2006," Survey Documentation & Analysis, Computer-assisted Survey Methods Program (CSM), University of California, Berkeley. http://sda.berkeley.edu/D3/GSS/Doc/gs06v017.htm.
4   Rubén G. Rumbaut and Walter A. Ewing, "The Myth of Immigrant Criminality and the Paradox of Assimilation: Incarceration Rates Among Native And Foreign-born Men," (Special Report: Immigration Policy Center, Spring 2007), p. 1.

A NOTE ON TARGET CITIES

1 FY 2007 Homeland Security Grant Program, p. 8. The top six areas are alphabetically under the category "Tier 1:" the San Francisco Bay area in California, the Chicagoland area, the Houston area, the Los Angeles/ Long Beach area, the National Capital region, and the New York City/ Northern New Jersey area.

2 Walter W. Piegorsch, Susan L. Cutter, and Frank Hardisty, "Benchmark Analysis for Quantifying Urban Vulnerability to Terrorist Incidents," *Risk Analysis,* 2007, Vol. 27, No. 6, pp. 1411–1425.

3 Larry McShane, "N.Y. Steamed Over Terror Fund Cutbacks," The Associated Press, June 1, 2006.

ACKNOWLEDGMENTS

This is not an authorized account of the New York City Police Department's fight against terrorism. Its content has not been vetted by the NYPD in any form. But it could not have been reported without the cooperation of the top officials in the department. Commissioner Raymond Kelly, Deputy Commissioner David Cohen, Deputy Commissioner Richard Falkenrath, former Deputy Commissioner Michael Sheehan, and Deputy Commissioner for Public Information Paul Browne all sat down with me for extended interviews. They also opened the door to administrators, detectives, and analysts whose names are cited in the body of the book.

And then there were the others. I would like to thank those many members of the NYPD, agents of the Federal Bureau of Investigation, and operatives of the Central Intelligence Agency who were not authorized to speak and therefore are not named at all.

Much of this book draws on my own reporting about terrorist groups, trends, and specific cases over the last quarter century, but I also am indebted to the remarkable work of several other writers in the field, notably Bruce Hoffman at Georgetown University, who was kind enough to read and comment on my account of "the second wave;" Marc Sageman, now the "scholar in residence" at the NYPD; Alain Bauer of Alain Bauer Associates in Paris; and Samuel Katz, who has written extensively about the NYPD Emergency Service Unit as well as Middle East terrorism.

My editor at Simon & Schuster, the indefatigable and inspiring Alice Mayhew, and her colleague Roger Labrie have worked with me now on five books, the first of which appeared more than twenty years ago. It has been, for me, a wonderful partnership and one I hope will continue for years to come. My agent, Kathy Robbins, is always a great source of encouragement and support, but she worked especially closely with me when I was developing the idea for *Securing the City,* offering detailed and extremely useful advice during the reporting and writing. Her husband, the very talented editor and author (and fencer), Richard Cohen, offered some very sound advice.

I would also like to thank the editors of *Newsweek* magazine, who were enthusiastic about this project from the beginning, even though it meant my taking frequent breaks from my other duties covering Europe and the Middle East. Executive Editor Jon Meacham, Managing Editor Dan Klaidman, Chief of Correspondents Mark Miller, Foreign Editor Nisid Hajari, and Newsweek Online editor Arlene Getz all were tremendously supportive.

My wife Carol's love, encouragement, organizational skills, and good sense are what hold my life together and make my work possible. I am thankful for what she does and who she is every hour of every day.

INDEX